THE
CORONER'S
SILENCE

THE CORONER'S SILENCE

DEATH RECORDS AND THE HIDDEN VICTIMS OF POLICE VIOLENCE

TERENCE KEEL

BEACON PRESS
BOSTON

Beacon Press
24 Farnsworth Street
Boston, Massachusetts
www.beacon.org

Beacon Press books
are published under the auspices of
the Unitarian Universalist Association of Congregations.

28 27 26 25   8 7 6 5 4 3 2 1

This book is printed on acid-free paper that meets the uncoated paper
ANSI/NISO specifications for permanence as revised in 1992.

Text design and composition by Kim Arney

Library of Congress Cataloging-in-Publication
Data is available for this title.
ISBN: 978-0-8070-1751-7; e-book: 978-0-8070-1752-4;
audiobook: 978-0-8070-2230-6

The authorized representative in the EU for product safety and
compliance is Easy Access System Europe 16879218, Mustamäe tee 50,
10621 Tallinn, Estonia: http://beacon.org/eu-contact.

*For all of the
misremembered victims
of police violence.*

CONTENTS

PREFACE

I wrote *The Coroner's Silence* with several audiences in mind. First, there are the family and friends of people lost to police violence. Most have carried their stories alone. Some have struggled to put into words what has been taken from them. And more than a few have turned their tragedy into change. Linda Franks, a justice reform advocate who lost her son Lamar Johnson inside a Baton Rouge Parish prison, told me and a group of colleagues over dinner that she felt like she had been screaming without sound before finding allies committed to stopping in-custody death. It has been an honor to learn from the people closest to this issue. They have changed me and how I see what justice looks like in America. I've done my best to understand and name in plain language the legal, political, and moral systems that make dying in custody possible.

The Coroner's Silence is also for people concerned about police violence and looking for guidance on how to think about this issue. If you are one of these readers you will find plenty of data, history, facts about deaths in custody, and details about the laws determining if and how the reports of coroners and medical examiners are made public. In this book I focus on deaths that occur on American streets during arrest and within county jails; most Americans encounter law enforcement within these settings, and prison data is notoriously difficult to acquire. But this is not a book simply about data or facts; I am also making a moral argument about the flaws of our criminal justice system, our indifference to the people on the wrong side of the law, and perhaps most importantly the violence we are willing tolerate for the illusion of safety in a nation with staggering inequalities. For this reason, you will find stories, art, philosophy, my own personal experience, and reactions to what I learned while researching, writing, and working with families and organizations to stop in-custody deaths. It is an unusual book. But so are the autopsy records written for people killed by law enforcement.

Some of you might already know a few things about in-custody death. If you are one of these readers then you are likely aware that Black and Latino people shoulder an unequal burden of police violence. However, dying in custody is not simply a "minority" issue or a matter of identity politics, despite how things might be portrayed in media and popular culture. In this book you will find that every segment of America is affected by law enforcement violence and the efforts of death investigators to cover for the state. This means white people, Republicans, working-class folk, Christians, Asians, the elderly, single mothers, the disabled, and even children are dying in police custody. The first individual I knew personally that was killed by police was an Irish American teenager named Andrew Hesser. We attended the same high school in Elk Grove, California. The incident taught me then that Black men were not the only victims of lethal police violence. It also taught me that the degree of separation between ourselves and victims of police violence—lethal or not—is much smaller than we have been willing to talk about collectively. While people of color are dispropor-tionately impacted, their bodies end up on the same medical examiner tables as the rest of America. Despite how we may have lived, we are not divided in death.

There are readers who might come to this book skeptical of gov-ernment and the place of the state over our lives. While I critique state institutions, and remain skeptical of them, I am still committed to the idea that they ought to represent the will of the people and should be held accountable when they fail. When I first started conducting research for this book, I had very low expectations of government to take care of Black Americans and other marginalized communities. I knew many systems were not working, and some were even hostile to people that were unemployed, suffering from chronic health conditions, unhoused, disabled, or struggling with substance abuse. But I had no idea that law enforcement had become the preferred agency of local government to manage people in crisis because of diminishing social services and the evaporation of fair wages, affordable shelter, accessible medical care, and competent mental health services. It had not occurred to me that the state's inability to support everyday Americans was linked to the expanding power of law enforcement and the growing reliance on police to resolve problems set into motion by elected officials who put other matters ahead of the public's interest.

I believe there are people on both the Right and Left who distrust law enforcement and death investigators, who have encountered the cruelty of the state, and who know in their bones that American institutions are a shell of what they should be. But there is hardly any space in our current political culture to express collective grievances against the failures of government—especially when working-class folk are divided by officials who stoke the flames of racial resentment against their own interests. Learning about the many different victims of police violence has taught me that the law does not care about the political or ideological beliefs you might have; the same is true for the death investigators who write postmortem reports following lethal encounters with police. Chokeholds, fists, projectile ammunition, restraints, Tasers, and pepper spray are indifferent to who you believe the country belongs to. We are all vulnerable to police violence and the decisions of coroners, medical examiners, jail staff, and elected officials that diminish the public good.

Things can be different if "the people" withdraw their consent from this state of affairs and assert their power over the systems that police us and investigate our deaths while in the custody of the law. Until then, government will continue to fail us.

We should not fail—should not betray—ourselves.

CHAPTER 1

LOSING OURSELVES

This book was written after spending countless hours with the dead, their loved ones, and nearly a thousand autopsy records describing the deaths of people killed by police. It is a book that shows how our legal, medical, and scientific institutions produce these tragedies, questions our strange comfort with these losses, and introduces you to the people trying to stop a crisis hiding in plain sight.

To tell this story I had to become a reliable narrator. I could not allow my beliefs about democracy, truth, or even death to prevent me from seeing the violence and brutality we are willing to tolerate for the illusion of safety in America. Bearing witness to the many lives lost to police violence allowed me to realize that our shared experience of life's end does not inspire compassion among law enforcement or jail staff. Dying at the hands of police does not engender empathy from the investigators who write death records and official autopsies. In-custody deaths hardly seem to matter to lawmakers that enable these tragedies to thrive beyond the public's awareness. People in state custody become less than human, and those that perish are denied dignity, respect, and forgiveness. I did not fully understand this myself until I sat with the dead and saw how local governments misremember them. I wish I could tell you Americans are certain to solve this problem, but I can't. The future of our lives in state custody is far more precarious than we realize.

And so, a part of me had to perish to write these pages. That part wanted to believe America was growing into our best values and evolving beyond the darkness of our past. I am grateful for this loss. Forfeiting these beliefs freed me from the fear and indifference we often carry for people who find themselves on the wrong side of the law. Whether we admit it or not, the people who cross the law test our patience, activate our fear and need for security. It is a strange thing to see how the dissemination of crime statistics without context or history can turn even libertarians and progressives into champions of law and order—if only these criminals were to become law-abiding and virtuous, American freedom would be secure, our society made whole. But this line of thinking has causality moving in the wrong direction. Surely no one is born a criminal. Political, economic, and legal systems that lack virtue and sow inequality create the desperate conditions for crime and in turn violent policing.

Rarely do we ask if the rules police enforce on our behalf are just and fair. Do they make us safe and healthy? Do law enforcement and jail solve the root causes of crime and threats to the common good? Unfortunately, the space between law and order has become so thin in the minds of lawmakers that there is hardly any room for collective discussion about which rules are failing us, which work, and what new solutions we might create to establish safety and accountability within our communities.

The problem is not merely about the failure of state institutions. We are also to blame.

Before writing this book, I had not fully grasped the fatigue and contempt many Americans carry for the people who remind us where society is broken. While I understood deaths in custody were symptoms of an unjust criminal justice system, I could not imagine how often these deaths occurred, how they were hidden from the public, or the sheer magnitude of lethal police violence. Emotional and political distance from the issue offers us an escape and maintains the illusion that "things would improve" or "surely someone was working on the problem." Without realizing it, I had fallen victim to this retreat into empty optimism; I carried distance between myself and the work required to change what safety and accountability look like in the places I called home, even though I had been racially profiled countless times by police and had family and friends impacted by law enforcement violence.

Over the course of writing this book I would learn about families and communities living in the wake of police violence and leading reform efforts by themselves—often with local government actively opposing them. I also learned that many Americans believe that people who die during arrest and in jail lose their lives because of the choices they made, or because they were already in poor health; for many, in-custody deaths do not register as a crisis or miscarriage of justice.

A nation that takes the lives of unarmed civilians for minor offenses during arrest, in jail, and too often before trial is not a democracy but a dying republic filled with people condemned by our irrational expectations for safety in a perilous society.

The security most Americans want will not come from more police or conservative lawmaking. It will come from wages stronger than inflation, food security, free and competent healthcare, treatment for mental illness, fewer prescription drugs, more affordable shelter, the elimination of heat islands in a world with rising global temperatures, clean air, and safe water. Law enforcement is not a solution for these material threats to our lives. And yet so many victims of police violence were first victims of our nation's inability to provide the most basic and essential human needs. In this sense they died twice.

In reading this book, I hope you lose a part of yourself and gain in return the ability to see the humanity of the people we are socialized to forget.

LOSING JOHN HORTON III

More Americans will die this year while in the custody of law enforcement than in Canada, Germany, Australia, New Zealand, and the United Kingdom combined.

When a death is violent, unexpected, mysterious, or outside a hospital setting, US state law requires an investigation. These investigations are conducted by medical examiners (who are licensed physicians) or by coroners (who usually are not). Each death is assigned one of the following classifications: homicide, natural, suicide, accident, undetermined. While Black and Latino men between the ages of eighteen and forty-five will die more often than any other group during arrest or while in jail, every segment of American society can be found in our nation's death ledger.

You can find in-custody deaths involving single mothers in New York managing opioid addiction, eighty-seven-year-old white women in Oregon grappling with mental illness, elderly Asian men in Minnesota, middle-aged Arab women in Texas, transgender people, mixed-race folk, college students, retirees, white Republicans, and Indigenous people. In many of these cases, the medical examiner or coroner will say that a preexisting health condition or the behavior of the victim was the cause of death—that the victim was responsible for their own perishing. And with this judgment they will use science and medicine to provide cover for the mistakes of police and local government.

I was inspired to write this book after learning about the death of a young Black man whose autopsy gave the impression he took his own life. His name was John Horton III and he died on March 30, 2009, shortly after his twenty-second birthday, inside Men's Central Jail in downtown Los Angeles.

John was the son of Helen Jones, herself a native of Watts by way of Black migrants that came to Los Angeles from Oklahoma for the job opportunities available during the Second World War. John was raised with his seven siblings in a family full of Baptists and artists. Like his mother, John was tall and dark, with soft, bright eyes and high cheek-bones. He was a writer, a musician, and an executive producer at a music label named HeadHigh Entertainment and dreamed of opening a youth center in South Central Los Angeles. His death was sudden, unexpected, and devastating for everyone who knew him.

I met John's mother in late 2020, as global protests for George Floyd and Breonna Taylor were starting to wane. At the time, Helen was a community organizer with Dignity and Power Now, a grassroots organization based in Los Angeles committed to transforming what justice looks like throughout the county and developing alternatives to incarceration. It is one of the few social justice organizations in the country staffed and led by people directly impacted by police violence and discrimination. Helen was gathering stories from families in Los Angeles whose loved ones and friends died while incarcerated for mental health concerns or the inability to pay bail for minor offenses. Helen and the families she worked with were focused on deaths that occurred in jails, detention centers, and other places of incarceration, places that rarely receive media attention.

Like millions of Americans, I witnessed the video of George Floyd's death. As unbearable as it was, I watched police officer Derek Chauvin carefully. Why was he indifferent to Floyd's pleas? Had Chauvin done this before? Had it resulted in death not witnessed? I looked for the answer in autopsies of other victims of state violence, like Sandra Bland, Freddie Gray, and Eric Garner. How did the medical examiner explain who and what broke Freddie Gray's spine while he was handcuffed in the back of a police wagon? Did Sandra Bland have other injuries apart from those associated with allegedly hanging herself? Was Eric Garner's medical history relevant for explaining why he died while being detained by an officer using a lethal chokehold?

Helen had been asking similar questions for nearly a decade after losing John. His death had been set in motion by a health crisis that began on the night of February 23, 2009. During a visit with his cousin, John had begun vomiting. He couldn't stop. As his health worsened, the family called 911 and requested paramedics. When they arrived, John was rushed to St. Francis Medical Center in Lynnwood, a small, predominantly Black and Latino community of Los Angeles less than five miles from Men's Central Jail (MCJ). The nursing staff said he might have had a PCP overdose. But the blood screen they gave John for controlled substances only showed evidence of THC in his system. After a few hours of monitoring, the medical staff released John to his mother and sister. The next morning his symptoms returned. Again, the family called 911, requesting paramedics. This time they were accompanied by officers from the Los Angeles County Sheriff's Department who were there to arrest John for failing to participate in a court-ordered drug program. Having lived in Watts for most of her adult life, Helen recognized one of the deputies; he was an officer with a reputation for sending Black men to the county jail. While John was still violently ill, the officers ordered Helen to place him in handcuffs. When she refused, the deputies began arguing with her, telling her that John's erratic behavior was evidence of a PCP overdose—the same misperception made by the medical staff at St. Francis. Helen responded by demanding that they take him back to the hospital for treatment and reevaluation. Eventually, the officers relented and the family helped paramedics get John into the ambulance—without restraints. Officers told Helen they would follow John to St. Francis and then take him to jail at Twin Towers, where medical staff would determine if he was healthy enough to be placed into the general population. John never made it to Twin Towers. He was briefly seen at St. Francis and then escorted by deputies to MCJ and placed in solitary confinement.

The next time Helen saw John, it was three days later during visiting hours at the jail. He was no longer vomiting, but he seemed heavily sedated and barely coherent. Deputies surrounded him and tried to cut Helen's time short, but she was determined to have her full fifteen minutes and ask all the questions she could, even as John was unable to answer them. Early the next morning she returned to MCJ to file for a visiting pass. The pass was denied without an explanation. She returned five days later, on February 28, and was denied again without explanation. This continued for the next two weeks.

Finally, after talking with MCJ staff on the phone, Helen learned that John had been given a March 15 court date. This would be Helen's first time seeing John in nineteen days.

Inmates are brought to the county courthouse from the jail by the Sheriff's Department (LASD), which oversees all of the facilities that make up the Los Angeles County jail system. Helen sat on the shiny wooden benches of the courtroom the entire day waiting for them to bring out John, but he never appeared. Another date was set for March 17, and again John was not brought to the courtroom. This time the judge demanded an explanation. Deputies from LASD claimed that John refused to leave solitary confinement. Furious, the judge insisted that he appear in court on March 18 even if deputies had to use force. The exchange was heard by everyone in the courtroom and left Helen deeply worried. On her way out of the courthouse, she spoke with a bailiff, asking if he had any idea about what might be happening. With lawyers and families bustling by, the bailiff quietly shared that there was talk inside MCJ about John having a fight with deputies several weeks ago.

When John finally appeared in court on March 18, 2009, he didn't look at his mother once during the deliberations. This was unusual. He and Helen had a way of communicating without words, using their eyes and face to convey a great number of things. The only time John looked to Helen that day was for a brief moment as he was returning to MCJ in handcuffs. He flashed a quick head nod beyond the vision of the deputies flanking him, as if to say, "Things aren't good." Helen's heart sank. She asked to speak privately with the judge to explain that John needed help, not jail. Miraculously, the judge ordered John to be placed under medical supervision. He also agreed to transfer John into the county's firefighting camp program, where inmates are given training and offer their labor to fight county fires while serving time. Helen left the court with a small measure of hope.

Twelve days later, on the evening of March 30, Helen's husband was playing basketball in their driveway when two detectives from the county jail pulled up to their home. Helen was inside designing a dress for John's sister. When the detectives asked to speak to her, she refused to see them. She knew John was gone. The detectives told her husband and daughter that John had killed himself inside his cell earlier that morning.

The Los Angeles County medical examiner would not allow Helen to see John's body during their investigation. At this time, she did not know that most medical examiners and coroners do not run for public office, meaning they are not directly accountable to victim's families or to "the people" more generally. Instead, they are beholden to the local officials who appoint them. These same officials are often responsible for paying financial settlements when families sue the county in the wake of police violence. In Los Angeles, the power to appoint or fire the chief medical examiner resides with the Board of Supervisors, a five-member governing body with executive, legislative, and judicial responsibilities for the eleven million residents within Los Angeles County. We will learn throughout this book how death investigations involving someone who has died in police custody often protect the government from the public, not the other way around. This is why Helen was left in dark while the county examined John's body.

In many cases, when an inmate dies inside a Los Angeles County jail, the next of kin are summoned to the jail or the coroner's office to confirm the identity of the deceased. This didn't happen with John. According to the report written by the forensic investigator who witnessed the scene of his death, John's identity was verified by a fingerprinting database under the Department of Justice just before 1 p.m. on the day of his death. The county knew John's identity yet still waited hours before telling his family.

Helen did not see John until three days later at a Black-owned mortuary near 111th Street in South Central Los Angeles. Helen's cousin Moe worked there and brought John from the county coroner—a part of himself did not complete the journey. When Moe arrived at the mortuary to begin the careful process of preparing his cousin's body, he found a twenty-six-inch braided white cloth along with John's belongings. It was the noose that the medical examiner claimed John used to hang himself. This ligature, made of frayed bedsheets cut by a sharp object, was evidence that should have remained with Los Angeles County. Yet here it was, a key piece of information left with John as he traveled back to his grieving family.

Helen found John's body itself a testimony to violence: the bridge of his nose appeared broken, there were open wounds and bruising on his forehead and near his right temple, as well as abrasions on his right shoulder, and the skin around his left wrist was ripped open, creating a small ring just below the hand. The embalmer, a Mexican American woman, told Helen that she had seen this type of wrist injury before on bodies that had struggled while being handcuffed by law enforcement. Helen could also see lacerations around John's neck. She took pictures of everything. Then, standing in the darkness of the mortuary with John's disfigured body and a rope of bedsheets, Helen realized, "Deputies beat my son to death and made it look like he hung himself."

John's official autopsy took three months to complete because the medical examiner ordered a microscopic analysis of tissue samples from his body. When the lab results returned, they revealed that John had sustained recent injuries to his abdomen, adrenal glands, skeletal muscles in his lower back, and kidneys. The medical examiner wrote in his assessment, "The presence of intra-abdominal/perinephric hematoma and right back muscle hematoma indicates recent blunt force torso injury. Circumstances on how the recent trauma was sustained are not clear." This was enough to change John's death from suicide to "undetermined." According to the National Association of Medical Examiners (NAME)—a professional organization of forensic pathologists and death investigators founded in 1966 with the purpose of developing national standards for death investigation—"undetermined" should only be used when there are at least two equally compelling explanations for why a person died. It can also be used in the very rare circumstance when there is not enough information to establish even the most basic idea of how a death occurred.[1] John's body was thought to have evidence for both homicide and suicide, which Helen believed was a clear contradiction—either John killed himself or he didn't.

The medical examiner still believed suicide was the most plausible explanation, interpreting the flesh wounds around John's wrist—which the embalmer believed were caused by handcuffs—as suicide "hesitation marks" and evidence of "suicidal ideation." A final letter or a suicide note are often considered a key source of information to declare a jail death a suicide. Communication between John and his family had been very limited since February 23, 2009. Yet Helen believed that if, by some tragedy, John had taken his own life, he would have left her a note—they were too close for him to leave the earth without saying goodbye. According to the forensic investigator who entered John's cell after his death, the county did not find any messages left for Helen or anyone else. Still, John's autopsy declared he died from "hanging and other undetermined factors" (figure 1.1).[2]

John had no record of mental illness and was not under suicide watch while in prison. According to the autopsy report that Helen received in July 2009, there was no official record of the last time John was seen alive (figure 1.2)—a troubling omission given that deputies are required by California state law to provide routine safety checks of the incarcerated.[3] Also missing from the report was a clear explanation for the injuries to John's nose, the hematoma on the right side of his forehead, the abrasions on his right shoulder, the one-inch hemorrhage on the

FIGURE 1.1 Summary of John Horton autopsy

COUNTY OF LOS ANGELES   DEPARTMENT OF CORONER

12 AUTOPSY REPORT

I performed an autopsy on the body of ➡

No.
2009–02315

HORTON, JOHN

at _____ the DEPARTMENT OF CORONER

Los Angeles, California _____ on APRIL 1, 2009 @ 1100 HOURS
                                   (Date)   (Time)

From the anatomic findings and pertinent history I ascribe the death to:

(A)   HANGING AND OTHER UNDETERMINED FACTORS
DUE TO OR AS A CONSEQUENCE OF

(B)
DUE TO OR AS A CONSEQUENCE OF

(C)
DUE TO OR AS A CONSEQUENCE OF

(D)
OTHER CONDITIONS CONTRIBUTING BUT NOT RELATED TO THE IMMEDIATE CAUSE OF DEATH:

Anatomical Summary:

The decedent was a 22-year-old Black male who was found hanging in a single jail cell. He was pronounced at the scene.

Autopsy findings:

1. Well-developed male (74 inches, 182 pounds).

2. Ligature mark around the neck 1/2 inch to 1 inch wide. Neck dissection reveals small hemorrhage of right sternocleidomastoid muscle. No petechia found.

3. Abrasions with minimal vital reaction:

    a. Forehead, 1 x 1/2 inch.

    b. Bridge of nose, 1/4 inch.

    c. Right temple, 1/4 inch.

    d. Right shoulder, 1-1/2 inches x 1/2 inch.

4. Parallel linear abrasions (four) of left wrist 1 inch to 2-1/2 inches with vital reaction.

78A798P—Rev. 2/09

Source: Los Angeles County Department of Medical Examiner-Coroner, "Autopsy Report of John Horton," Case #2009–02315, Los Angeles, CA, 2009.

lower right side of his back, and the soft tissue hemorrhages within his liver and kidneys (figures 1.3 and 1.4). How could these recent wounds have happened if he was alone in a cell? While these details were left on his record without an explanation, the coroner, who arrived on the scene, went out of her way to describe John's cell as "filthy and covered with food, papers, and toiletries that are strewn about the area."[4]

FIGURE 1.2 Preliminary examination report from John Horton's death, completed by a forensic investigator from the location of his death inside Men's Central Jail

COUNTY OF LOS ANGELES   **PRELIMINARY EXAMINATION REPORT - FIELD**   DEPARTMENT OF CORONER

6

WAS ORIGINAL SCENE DISTURBED BY OTHERS?   Y [X]   N [ ]
IF YES, NOTE CHANGES IN NARRATIVE FORM #3.
DATE _____03/30/2009_____
AMBIENT #1 ___70.3___ F   TIME ___8:57___
AMBIENT #2 _____ F   TIME _____
WATER _____ F   TIME _____

2009-02315
HORTON, John
Sui - Hana
DOD- 3/30/2009

LIVER TEMPERATURE #1 ___87.4___ F   TIME ___8:58___   THERMOMETER # ___07-12___
LIVER TEMPERATURE #2 _____ F   TIME _____

DATE & TIME FOUND ___03/30/2009 @ 3:45___   LAST KNOWN ALIVE _____ @ _____
APPROX. AGE _22_ SEX _Male_ EST. HEIGHT _74_ EST. WEIGHT _182_ CLOTHED? YES[X] NO[] IF YES, DESCRIBE:
Pants, Underwear, Socks

DESCRIPTION AS TO WHERE REMAINS FOUND AND CONTACT MATERIAL TO BODY:
Supine on cement jail floor

SCENE TEMPERATURE REGULATED? YES [] NO[X] IF YES, THERMOSTAT SET AT _____ DEGREES F.
LIVOR MORTIS: TIME OBSERVED _8:30_   RIGOR MORTIS: TIME OBSERVED __8:20__

NECK FLEXION:
ANTERIOR _____3_____
POSTERIOR _____3_____
RT. LATERAL_____3_____
LT. LATERAL_____3_____
JAW _____4_____   HIP ___3___
SHOULDER ___3___   KNEE ___3___
ELBOW ___3___   ANKLE ___3___
WRIST ___3___

SCALE
0 = ABSENT / NEGATIVE
1 +
2 +
3 +
4 = EXTREME DEGREE

USE SCALE TO DESCRIBE INTENSITY OF RIGOR

SHADE DIAGRAMS TO ILLUSTRATE THE LOCATION OF LIVOR MORTIS.

DESCRIBE INTENSITY OF COLORATION AND WHETHER LIVOR MORTIS IS PERMANENT OR BLANCHES UNDER PRESSURE

Not discernible

B. Magdaleno # 469800
Investigator   REVIEWED BY:

NOTE: ALL DATA COLLECTED FOR THIS FORM MUST BE COLLECTED AT SCENE.

Source: Los Angeles County Department of Medical Examiner-Coroner, "Autopsy Report of John Horton," Case #2009–02315, Los Angeles, CA, 2009.

The year John died inside MCJ, there were thirty-eight reported deaths across Los Angeles County's five prisons, by far the most of any county in California that year.[5] It was a record that would stand for the next decade and be surpassed only in 2021, when fifty-five deaths were reported inside Los Angeles County jails.[6] In November 2016, the Los

FIGURE 1.3 Microscopic report, which provides an analysis of tissue samples and subsequent findings of recent injuries to John Horton's internal organs and soft tissue

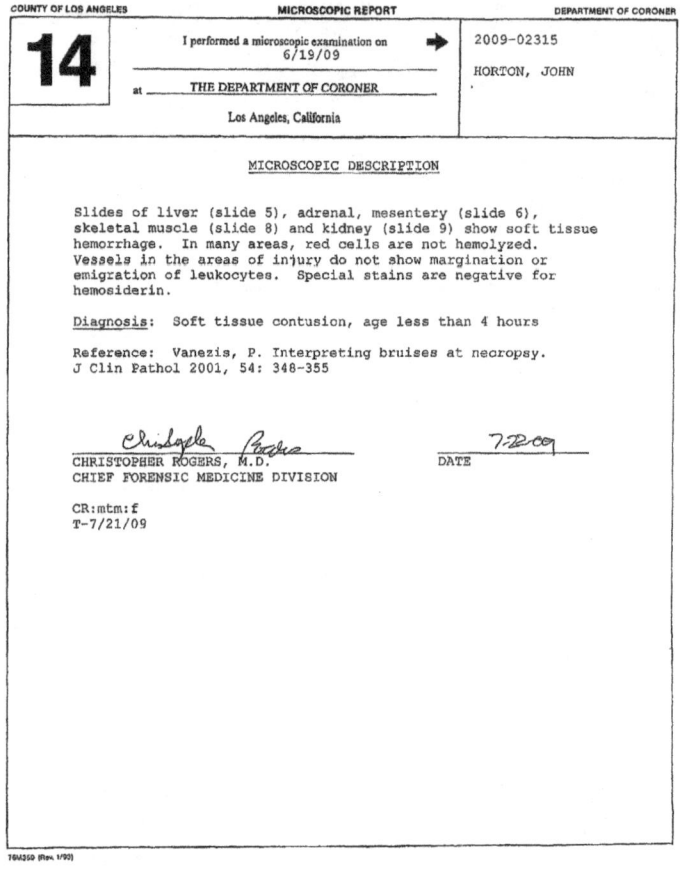

Source: Los Angeles County Department of Medical Examiner-Coroner, "Autopsy Report of John Horton," Case #2009–02315, Los Angeles, CA, 2009.

Angeles County Board of Supervisors agreed to a $2 million settlement with John's family.[7] Although the county conceded that deputies had not properly monitored John while he was in solitary confinement, the settlement did not admit that he was murdered, nor did it identify the actors responsible for the violence against John's body and his death.

Helen continues searching for answers and for the people who killed her son.

FIGURE 1.4 Medical opinion provided by the deputy medical examiner concerning the cause of John Horton's death, noting recent intra-abdominal injuries that could have been contributing factors in his death

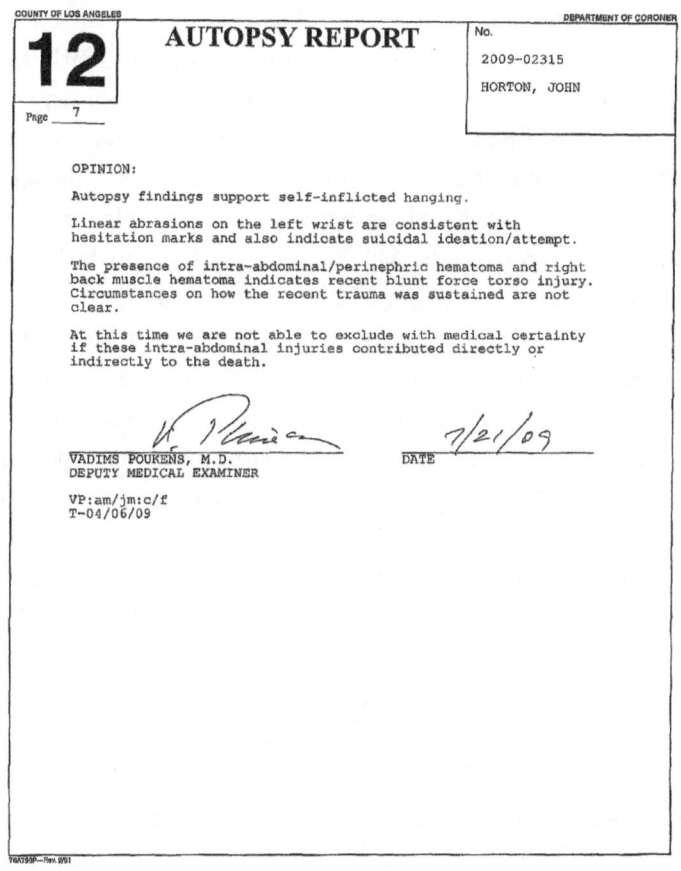

COUNTY OF LOS ANGELES   DEPARTMENT OF CORONER

12   **AUTOPSY REPORT**

No.

2009-02315

HORTON, JOHN

Page 7

OPINION:

Autopsy findings support self-inflicted hanging.

Linear abrasions on the left wrist are consistent with hesitation marks and also indicate suicidal ideation/attempt.

The presence of intra-abdominal/perinephric hematoma and right back muscle hematoma indicates recent blunt force torso injury. Circumstances on how the recent trauma was sustained are not clear.

At this time we are not able to exclude with medical certainty if these intra-abdominal injuries contributed directly or indirectly to the death.

VADIMS POUKENS, M.D.   DATE   7/21/09
DEPUTY MEDICAL EXAMINER

VP:am/jm:c/f
T-04/06/09

Source: Los Angeles County Department of Medical Examiner-Coroner, "Autopsy Report of John Horton," Case #2009–02315, Los Angeles, CA, 2009.

SEEING DOUBLE

I used to wonder what medical examiners and coroners saw in the bodies they examined. Did they see the life story of a person? What they endured and shouldered? Did they see a son, father, or mother? Someone who reflected the society that shapes us all? Or did they see only a natural body—a corpse needing a medical explanation? Autopsy after autopsy

I searched for some indication that death investigators saw a complete person. But the more records I reviewed the more convinced I became that something was profoundly wrong with their vision.

I carried this feeling for months. Then I had a realization while in New York visiting my father-in-law, Francisco Mora Catlett, son of Elizabeth Catlett (1915–2012), one of the first Black women in the US to earn a master of fine arts from Iowa University in 1940. Catlett was a celebrated printmaker and sculptress, known for her depictions of motherhood, Black and Mexican working-class people, and the icons of the Black freedom struggle. My wife and I were in my father-in-law's living room apartment in West Harlem, and I was sharing stories of the people you will come to know over the course of reading this book. It was a heavy conversation, and afterward I decided to take a walk to release the weight that had gathered at the center of my chest. I had recently reread Ellison's *Invisible Man* with some close friends so I decided to walk to Ralph Ellison Plaza, just a few blocks north on Riverside Drive.

Riverside Drive runs parallel to the Hudson River on the west side of Manhattan and provides passageway between 72nd Street to the south and 181st Street to the north near the George Washington Bridge. A great number of historic buildings and coveted addresses can be found along its route. This stretch of New York City was once home to Babe Ruth, Hannah Arendt, Saul Bellow, George Gershwin, and Ralph Ellison. Between Riverside Drive and 150th Street is the carefully maintained Ellison Plaza, filled with red, pink, and white azaleas and surrounded by oak, maple, hickory, and elm trees. While the plaza's footprint is modest, its tribute to Ellison is not. At its center stands a towering fifteen-foot sculpture, *Invisible Man* (figure 1.5), created by Elizabeth Catlett. Her five-thousand-pound monument takes its name from Ellison's 1952 novel, whose anonymous Black protagonist is haunted by the realization that Americans can only see their projections when looking at him—never can they see a complete person. Catlett's bronze sculpture joined New York City's monument landscape in 2003.

It was an oppressively hot and humid day in early July with hardly any clouds or wind. It was the kind of heat that made me question taking this

FIGURE 1.5 Elizabeth Catlett's *Invisible Man*, bronze, Riverside Drive, Harlem, New York

Photo credit: Sofia Piana, 2024

walk; it also made me wonder what summers would feel like in New York thirty years from now. As I approached the monument, I was struck that day by the size of the hollow silhouette Catlett placed at the center of her *Invisible Man*. It was a magnificent representation of the message at the heart of Ellison's novel—you can see right through his body. His head had the African form popularized during the New Negro Movement of the 1920s. Harlem was the epicenter of that unprecedented change in Black life; it pulsed with the energy of artists, writers, scholars, dancers, and musicians. Their creations embodied the ingenuity of Black people, whose cultural references had been fragmented by transatlantic slavery and then were renewed by common struggles in the New World. As I continued to take in the monument, with death records still on my mind, I realized that the silhouette inside Catlett's *Invisible Man* was placed in a side profile like the Renaissance sketches of Italian anatomists. The same anatomical forms appear in the trauma figures used today by medical examiners on autopsy reports (figure 1.6). But unlike the

FIGURE 1.6 Autopsy diagram—male lateral view

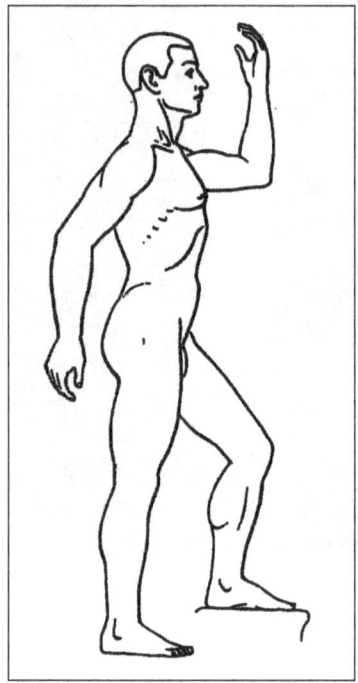

Source: Defense Health Agency, Office of the Armed Forces Medical Examiner

medical diagrams of death records, the lead hand of Catlett's silhouette is facing away from his body and pushes toward the outer edges of the sculpture; this man is very much alive, and his hand guards against the dehumanizing gaze of a nation that has placed him into a life-denying frame.

And then I recognized the duality of Catlett's monument: there were two bodies inside the work, and both helped me understand how death investigators, and many of us, see the victims of police violence. When I looked at Catlett's monument facing east toward Harlem, the Black figure was filled with buildings, streetlights, car emissions, hurried New Yorkers, tree foliage, azaleas, birdsong, and edges of the Manhattan skyline. From this direction, what appeared inside this Black man's body was obviously human-made—the structures inside were the consequence of legal, political, and economic decisions. And yet they were not natural in the sense of something divinely ordained, permanent, or native. They were instead the sum total of our interactions with the things we design or neglect. It was undeniable from this vantage point that society appeared inside his body.

When I faced west toward the Hudson River, the silhouette inside Catlett's *Invisible Man* was filled with brown branches, green leaves, and blue sky. In this direction I could not see Manhattan inside his body, just nature. Very little that appeared, however, was simply natural. Dutch and Anglo-American colonists transformed what Lanape people once called Manahatta, or "hilly island," from a rugged oyster-harvesting and fishing landmass into townships and eventually the sprawling metropolis we now know. The native scene on the New Jersey side of the Hudson was also lost long ago to the timber and agriculture industry that thrived in the region during the eighteenth and nineteenth centuries. While the flora that can be seen inside Catlett's *Invisible Man* are surely nature, they reflect centuries of careful and at times haphazard decisions, laws, and economic projects championed by agriculturalists, industrial tycoons, politicians, city planners, and the middle class with their private property. Even the vista allowing me to look at this Black silhouette was made possible by humans flattening lands, clearing trees, building streets, forging walking paths.

This is when I realized that death investigators often only see nature, or the illusion of nature, inside a victim's body. Like looking at Catlett's *Invisible Man* while facing the Hudson, they see a body detached from society and believe their observations are unaffected by history or the surrounding political environment.

In all of the autopsies I reviewed for this book, almost never did I find a medical examiner or coroner attribute an in-custody death to larger systemic issues within law enforcement, our criminal justice system, or inequities within our society. I did not find, for example, medical examiners integrate into their discoveries well-established truths about police not being properly trained to care for people suffering from mental illness, making law enforcement more likely to mistake actions of distress for aggression or noncompliance. Or that Black and Latino populations carry the pressure of living in overpoliced neighborhoods, which is likely to result in elevated heart rates and stress hormones while simply encountering law enforcement. Or that these heightened biological responses, set into motion by police, then played a role in a death during the use of a prone restraint maneuver, pepper spray, or a chokehold limiting blood to the brain—actions taken by police that add more stress to a body already weathering the absence of care in our society.

But the habit of only seeing nature inside us is not limited to physicians and scientists. Many believe that being healthy, sick, or dead is determined by the sheer luck of our genes or decisions that align our bodies with the laws of nature. Human biology, from this vantage point, is often understood as something bound only by natural law and therefore indifferent to human-made legal regulations, economic plans, or the political strivings of a nation.

Fortunately, there are others who see our health as the result of social structures that give texture and form to our bodies. Society, from this perspective, interacts with our biology, filling us with more than just nature—heart rates, cortisol levels, fat, mental illness, asthma, and even cancer are viewed as transactions between ourselves and the cities, states, and nations where we live.[8] These interactions include our access to healthcare, how far we must travel for doctor visits, air pollution that surrounds schools, homes, and public parks, laws that increase interactions with police, food deserts and heat islands, being unemployed, unhoused, Black, or Latino/a—all of these social creations weather endocrine and immune systems, place stress on hearts, minds, and souls.

When I began reading the autopsies of people who died while in the custody of law enforcement, I could see that their bodies contained biology *and* society, along with the virtues and failures of America. I had long understood that medicine and science were not simply the instruments of progress but could also be tools of discrimination and violence. I had cultivated this vision from an early age. My mother, who had suffered unspeakable childhood trauma living in American cities that were still segregated, died at the age of thirty-seven after a decade of battling an autoimmune disease and then cancer. Both had been misdiagnosed because of her age, her skin color, and the fact that our family could not afford physicians capable of thinking beyond the assumption that Black people naturally had lower white blood cell counts or that young Black women didn't get breast cancer. I had always believed there was a link between her difficult childhood, the lupus, and then the malignant tumor that took her life. But it was only after I became a historian of science and medicine that I came to understand that the indifference and limited imagination of her doctors were part of the reason my mother died so young—and that her experience was not unique. Far too many people of color, especially women, who came of age during racial segregation in America carried the record of their survival in their immune systems, cells, and behavior.

When confronted with autopsies that erased the agency of law enforcement and blamed the bodies of victims for their own deaths, I recognized the same unwillingness to think creatively and with wisdom about the many factors in America that shorten the lives of Black people. These deaths, along with my mother's, were the result of layered political and economic decisions, old racist designs that held a fast grip on the hearts and minds of American scientists and physicians.

Shortly after the murder of George Floyd, I was meeting with Helen Jones and with families in Los Angeles who had taught themselves how to evaluate autopsies with medical textbooks, legal dictionaries, and their own experiences with the law. They asked questions about hematomas, lacerations, and bone fractures on loved ones who supposedly died of natural causes. I learned about thirty-year-olds restrained by police and then dying from heart conditions that usually end people's lives in their late sixties. Families spoke to me about husbands and fathers denied access to medication for chronic conditions in jail, dying shortly afterward and then having their deaths classified by a medical examiner as natural. It became clear to me that these families were tracing the effects of structural violence on the bodies of their loved ones; they were uncovering forms of hostility embedded in systems, laws, and medical practices that produced and maintained the unjust treatment of vulnerable people. And when this violence appeared within or on the body of a person of color, families were exposing structural racism. Each of the stories I encountered involved someone who might still be alive if not for the actions of police and jail staff, the indifference of lawmakers and state officials, and our overwhelming need for safety in parts of America where poverty and undesirable people are never too far away.

Soon thereafter I created the UCLA Lab for BioCritical studies, which is dedicated to studying the complex interactions of society and the human body—especially the bodies of vulnerable people. Taking a close look at in-custody deaths was our first task and one that revealed the toll of political and legal violence on the bodies of individuals who should still be alive. In the beginning I met with Helen Jones every week. She would bring a death record of someone who had lost their life while in custody and share with my students and colleagues the questions and insights that she believed were most important to see and understand. Helen had a wealth of knowledge and expertise about the faults and virtues of our death investigation system that would have taken too long for most academics to acquire.

For example, she taught us how to compare the synopsis of events found in the summary of the forensic investigator, or coroner, with the technical assessment of injuries noted by the medical examiner. It was common for an investigator to describe a violent encounter resulting in injuries that the medical examiner would not incorporate into the cause of death. I also learned from Helen how death investigators weaponized details about the criminal history of the deceased, or their troubles with substance abuse, or, even worse, their health history, making the case that they were going to die regardless of the actions of police. She drew my lab's attention to the places in the autopsy where illegible handwriting, unchecked boxes, missing files, and vague language obscured or distorted what happened to the victim and why.

In time, my lab turned Helen's experience, wisdom, and vision into research questions that could be used to study and analyze any death record. We asked about injuries that did not have an explanation, whether police were in the room during autopsy, the types of drugs that investigators screened for Black people and not for whites, the age, weight, and height of victims, and if death investigators bothered to verify claims from police that the deceased suffered from mental illness or some other heath condition. Those questions were then reviewed and evaluated by Helen. This was a revolutionary collaboration unlike any I had experienced as an academic. Our work was a manifestation of what Ruha Benjamin has called "viral justice," where my lab took seriously "all of the ways people are working, little by little, day by day, to combat unjust systems and build alternatives to the oppressive status quo."[9] Knowledge and expertise from impacted community directly informed my vision and assessment of the tragedies you will learn about in this book. Without Helen, this work would not have been possible.

It was not long before my lab used Freedom of Information Act (FOIA) requests to gather nearly one thousand autopsies of people killed by police from around the country. Each record would be read and analyzed by young researchers who desperately wanted to change things. We had forensic files with technical details about how someone's cardiovascular or immune system had failed but without the medical examiner or coroner naming the human actors or institutions that trigged this failure; many cases read as if the people who died had not actually been in custody.

Most of the autopsies you will encounter in this book were written by death investigators who reduced the interactions of a complex life to a single moment, choosing to see only nature within. But to see society inside our bodies requires a willingness to question and judge the systems of power governing our lives; this capacity should be part of the toolkit of any death investigator who strives to be a reliable witness and tell the truth about how someone could lose their life during arrest or while in the custody of the state.

MAPPING THE SILENCE

American police kill on average 1,200 people a year during arrest or while attempting to place them into custody. In the seventy-one-year history of law enforcement in Iceland, one person was fatally shot by an officer. The incident occurred in 2013 and made international headlines.[10] In Stockton, California—which has approximately 25,000 fewer residents than Iceland—there were three officer-involved deaths in the first five months of 2015. News of these deaths barely reached beyond local media.

The number of Americans who lose their lives inside our jails, prisons, and detention centers paints an equally troubling picture. This is because most of these deaths are hidden—from public witnesses and from government agencies charged with tracking this information. Those who die within carceral spaces are watched and recorded by their captors, and there are few consequences for facilities that fail to report these cases.[11] This is an astonishing oversight when you consider that America has the world's highest incarceration rate with 810 people held in state custody for every 100,000 adults over the age of eighteen.[12] This means there are roughly two million people at any given time within our labyrinth of federal, state, and county carceral facilities.[13] It also means every single state in the US incarcerates more people than almost any other independent democracy in the world.[14]

John Horton's death contains tragic details I have found in hundreds of autopsies involving police: the targeting of vulnerable populations by law enforcement and the erasure of this calculated violence through forensic records that turn the deceased into the agent of their own death. The autopsy report is central to this process. It contains details of dismembered bodies, scene descriptions, and claims about the physical or mental state of the victim—but often very little about the actions of police. It is also a record of responsibility with the power to hold the state accountable and be the impetus for justice and change. John's case is not only one of violent loss. His story, and many others, contains the seeds of an abolitionist dream shared by countless families who want to bring an end to dying in custody. To get there, the practice of death investigation must be established as a privileged and honored responsibility, not a venue for erasing the moral and political failures of the worlds we authorize.

This book tells the story of how in-custody deaths happen. It also explains why death investigators fail to expose the social and political conditions that are ultimately responsible for people dying during arrest or while in jail. Having looked at nearly a thousand cases, it is my belief that autopsies written for unarmed people killed by police are pushing up against the limits of American competence. Dying in custody, whether in jail or on the street, means dying because of custody.[15] To see the effects of government on our bodies is a skill that has to be cultivated. It requires physicians, forensic scientists, and the larger American public to understand that our health and death are a consequence of the societies we design—not separate from the laws and political decisions that govern, police, or presumably protect us.

In this book I explain how the loss of records—from county files, medical documents, and police reports to specimens removed from bodies during autopsy—creates the conditions for law enforcement to take lives while avoiding accountability. It is nearly impossible to hold police and the state accountable for deaths in custody if there are no records.

I also show how the classifications used to study in-custody deaths have become insufficient. By telling the stories of people killed in custody from around the country, I explore the virtues and limits of the idea of a natural, undetermined, suicide, homicide, or accidental death, their legal and social significance; and ultimately how these designations allow death investigators to displace, erase, and in some cases clarify the responsibility of local government or law enforcement for the loss of life in custody.

Last, I explain the efforts of impacted families and social justice organizations around the nation who are challenging the authority of our death investigation system. They have taken on the difficult work of pushing for legislative changes that limit the power of law enforcement and make death investigators accountable to the public. I have been inspired watching everyday people become what Eddie Glaude has called "the leaders we have been looking for" to halt a crisis threatening us all.[16] It is terrifying to witness a criminal justice system that can take someone's life, a system in which the safeguards designed to tell us what happened cover up the truth, redact files, and stonewall families, reporters, or anyone searching for answers. I fear that the discriminatory political decisions we've inherited from our nation's violent past continue to enchant the imagination of most Americans and lawmakers, setting the country on a death-obsessed trajectory where we will be forced to endure an unspeakable number of lives lost to police custody while new leaders try to steer the nation to more worthy shores.

Ending in-custody death is going to require a commitment to change without evidence of progress. It is going to require leaving parts of ourselves behind to believe in something we haven't seen yet—a world where no one dies during arrest, in jail, or before trial.

CHAPTER 2

ILLIBERAL INVESTIGATORS

Medical examiners and coroners use science to arrive at seemingly objective conclusions about untimely and mysterious death. They stand within a liberal tradition where truth and fairness are supposed to create equity and safety in society. The work of death investigators, however, also exists between competing visions of justice. On one side stands the state and its interest in law and order. On the other are "the people" who carry long memories of injustice and police violence gone unpunished.[1] The weight of both constituencies is felt by death investigators aware of their obligations to the public. Not all care to balance the scales evenly, choosing instead to turn against the people and abandon the liberal values that protect the freedoms of civil society. For those who resist this impulse, there are consequences when they try to stand with the people. I witnessed this firsthand in Los Angeles.

On June 18, 2020, eighteen-year-old Andres Guardado was shot by Los Angeles Sheriff Deputy Miguel Vega in the city of Gardena, California. The incident happened less than thirty days after the murder of George Floyd—and several months after the killing of Breonna Taylor who died in March of that year. Guardado had no criminal record and was working security for a small autobody shop that had been recently vandalized. Deputy Vega was one of two deputies surveilling the heavily policed area near West Compton. They were in a marked patrol car and saw Guardado speaking to someone parked in front of a driveway near the shop. Deputies say they saw Guardado "produce a gun"—which could mean anything from drawing a weapon to simply one appearing from underneath his clothing. Witnesses say he was unarmed. Deputy Vega and his partner, Chris Hernandez, confronted Guardado with their pistols drawn. "The police came up, and they pulled their guns on him and he ran because he was scared, and they shot and killed him," reported Andrew Heney, owner of the shop where Guardado worked.[2] Vega and Hernandez were not wearing bodycams, and the county Sheriff's Department (LASD) removed security cameras from the car shop weeks earlier while investigating an unrelated incident in the area; no video of the shooting exists.[3] Guardado died that evening face down on West Redondo Beach Boulevard.

Four days later the Los Angeles County Department of the Medical Examiner completed Guardado's autopsy and ruled his death a homicide. Only six states in the US explicitly mandate that an autopsy is to be performed following deaths that take place in the custody of law enforcement (figure 2.1). In places like California, state law requires an autopsy following a violent, mysterious, or sudden death, but the law does not explicitly name police violence as a type of death requiring an autopsy. In contrast, state law in Illinois mandates that "where a death has occurred while being pursued, apprehended, or taken into custody by or while in the custody of any law enforcement agency, it is declared that the public interest requires that an autopsy be performed."[4] Each of the five bullets fired by Deputy Vega traveled through Guardado's back toward the front of his body, leaving a trail of catastrophic injuries. There were no controlled substances in Guardado's blood. Sheriff Alex Villanueva filed a request to place his autopsy on security hold, claiming that LASD's investigation into the shooting was still pending. California is one of eleven states where autopsies are part of the public record, but state law grants police the ability to deny public and media access.

In a rare move, Chief Medical Examiner-Coroner Dr. Jonathan Lucas rebuffed LASD's security request, choosing instead to publicly release Guardado's autopsy, along with a written statement claiming that "the administration of justice [and] the public's right to know" were not mutually exclusive. "Both are important, particularly amid the ongoing national discussion about race, policing and civil rights," wrote Lucas.[5]

FIGURE 2.1 States that explicitly mandate that an autopsy is to be performed when an individual dies in law enforcement custody

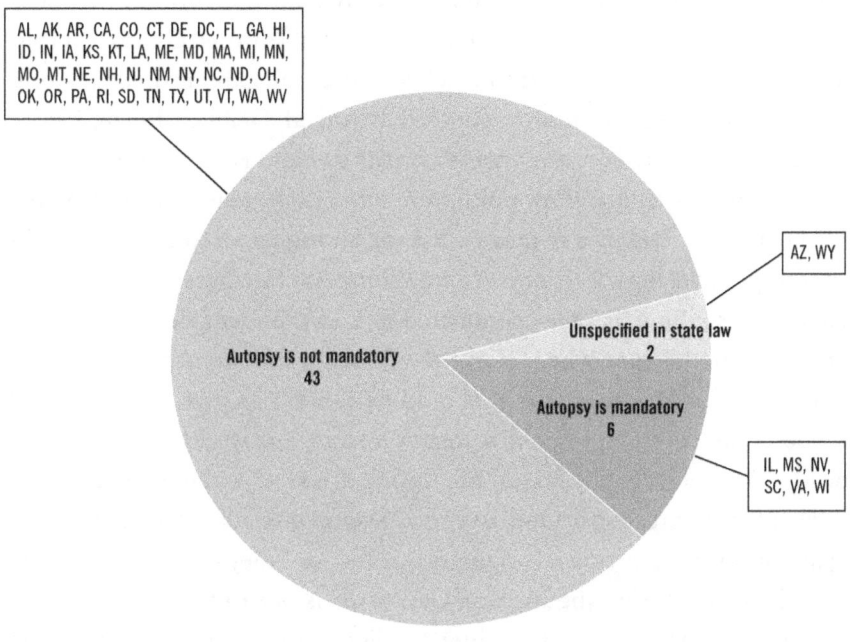

Source: UCLA BioCritical Studies Lab, 2025

While California state law allows police to withhold autopsy records from the public, it is the medical examiner who makes this final determination. In the years prior to Guardado's death, security hold requests from LASD were largely rubber-stamped by the medical examiner.[6] But rising public demand for police accountability and transparency following the death of George Floyd put pressure on Chief Medical Examiner Lucas to countenance the people's vision of justice. LASD was not pleased. Sheriff Villanueva released a statement claiming the medical examiner broke protocol, threatening that "this move will now force the Sheriff's Department to use court orders to enforce security holds."[7]

Community organizations and a handful of local officials were united in their outrage at Guardado's murder and LASD's attempt to withhold his death record. The city was already teeming with marches, rallies, and protests in solidarity with George Floyd and Breonna Taylor. Within days of Guardado's death, hundreds gathered in front of the Compton sheriff's station in protest. "I feel it in my soul that my brother was murdered, and this was covered up," his sister Jennifer Guardado told local media.[8] LASD refused to disclose any details about their pending investigation, which to many appeared unethical. Democratic protestors searching for answers were met with tear gas and rubber bullets.

In response to growing public unrest, Los Angeles County board member Mark Ridley-Thomas called for an inquest into the Guardado shooting, declaring, "It is beyond troubling that the investigation of Mr. Guardado's killing has been conducted by LASD under a deliberate cloud of secrecy. In this time when reform should bring more transparency rather than less, LASD insists that it should be trusted to investigate itself."[9] Inquests, are simply public investigations into a suspicious or untimely death. This includes the loss of life during arrest or while under the custody of law enforcement. Only twenty US states give coroners and medical examiners the discretion to originate an inquest if they believe it warrants a public investigation (figure 2.2); California is one of those states.

On November 30, 2020, Chief Medical Examiner Jonathan Lucas responded to local pressure and held the county's first inquest in over thirty years inside the Kenneth Hanh Hall of Administration in downtown Los Angeles. Inquests in California must be overseen by a justice of the peace. Retired justice Candace Cooper directed the hearing. I witnessed the proceedings through an online portal created by the county still in the grips of the COVID-19 pandemic.

At the outset, Justice Cooper limited our expectations. She declared that her findings would be "inadmissible in any civil or criminal proceeding" according to California state law. This meant her ruling would have no bearing on any criminal or civil lawsuit that Guardado's family might bring against the county for his death. She explained that this inquest was not designed to identify guilt or determine who was responsible for taking Guardado's life. Rather, its purpose was to ensure that law enforcement and the medical examiner were fastidious and law-abiding during their respective investigations. Justice Cooper also disclosed that she had exclusive access to LASD investigation files, and their content

FIGURE 2.2 States in which medical examiners-coroners have the power to call an inquest within the US. Locations with an * indicate that the medical examiner–coroner can only originate an inquest under certain circumstances.

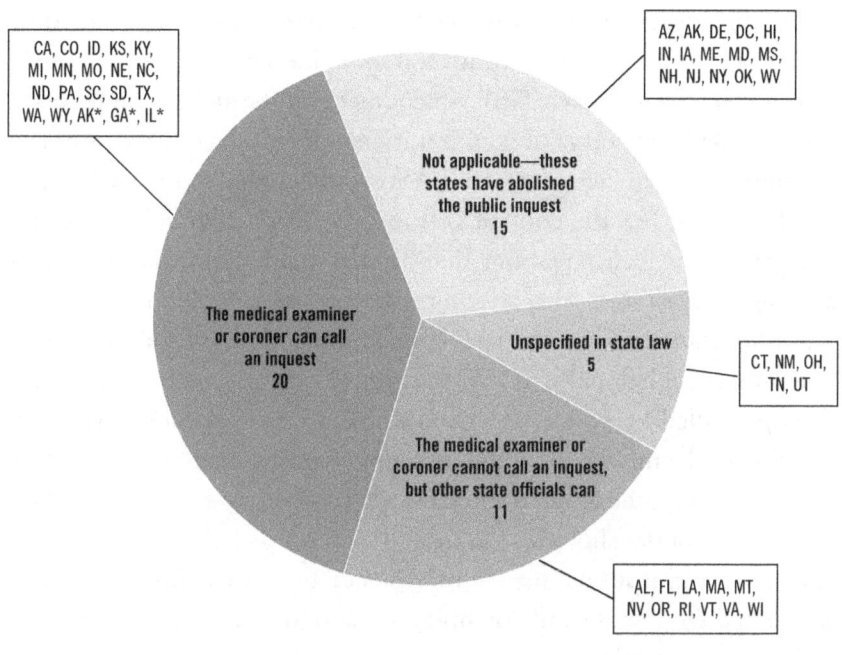

CA, CO, ID, KS, KY, MI, MN, MO, NE, NC, ND, PA, SC, SD, TX, WA, WY, AK*, GA*, IL*

AZ, AK, DE, DC, HI, IN, IA, ME, MD, MS, NH, NJ, NY, OK, WV

Not applicable—these states have abolished the public inquest
15

The medical examiner or coroner can call an inquest
20

Unspecified in state law
5

CT, NM, OH, TN, UT

The medical examiner or coroner cannot call an inquest, but other state officials can
11

AL, FL, LA, MA, MT, NV, OR, RI, VT, VA, WI

Source: UCLA BioCritical Studies Lab, 2025

would not be discussed during the hearing—it would remain sealed from the public record.[10] Lawyers working on behalf of Guardado's family and LASD were the only parties allowed to submit questions, and Justice Cooper had sole discretion over which were relevant to the proceedings and which were to be stricken from the record.

Justice Cooper first questioned Kevin Young, deputy medical examiner and board-certified forensic pathologist who conducted Andres Guardado's autopsy. Young walked us through the granular details of each of the five bullets LASD shot inside Guardado's body and the irreparable damage they did to his lungs, abdomen, and liver. Although subpoenaed, Deputy Vega did not appear at the inquest; he was out of the country and chose instead to exercise his Fifth Amendment rights. Congresswoman Maxine Waters would later call Vega's absence "unacceptable, outrageous, and . . . nothing short of an affront to justice for Andres, his family, and our community."[11] His partner, Hernandez, was also absent.

Justice Cooper called the coroner who investigated the scene of Guardado's death, members of the fire department who attempted to revive him, two detectives from the Homicide Division of the LASD who chose to exercise their Fifth Amendment rights, and a local reporter who recorded interviews of community members at the scene after the shooting. Sealed documents from LASD were handed to Justice Cooper in public view, but the content of those records remained a mystery. LASD shared a video explaining that the investigation into the Guardado shooting was pending. Also offering testimony was Dr. Bennet Omalu, a forensic pathologist and neuroscientist famous for his work on chronic traumatic encephalopathy (CTE) and for offering secondary autopsies of people killed by police. Dr. Omalu, measured and confident, drew attention to the misclassification of wounds to Guardado's body by Los Angeles County, the relaxed standards of its investigation, and the fact that the first bullet shot into Guardado's back was lethal—making the other four a gratuitous display of violence by LASD. Justice Cooper interrupted Dr. Omalu and downplayed the significance of his criticism. Justice Cooper explained:

> I understand that you may have disagreements with the autopsy, or the autopsy protocol or certain conclusions in the autopsy. But I don't think we're going to need to go into great detail as to each of those, because my primary concern is your ultimate conclusion as to the cause of death. Because that's the limited conclusion that I have to affirm.[12]

Cooper's comments had the effect of making Dr. Omalu's expertise appear superfluous for a justice hearing intended to be narrow in its scope.

The mood inside the court was tense and formal, with witnesses hidden behind surgical masks and barely audible. Justice Cooper, stoic and seasoned by a life of upholding the law, was exacting and efficient. The proceedings felt clinical and detached from the humanity of the situation—there were no statements from family or community members that knew Guardado. This feeling was amplified by the absence of the deputies who took Guardado's life and the refusal of homicide detectives to go on record about their investigation.

Those of us watching—whether online or in the courtroom—were spectators to political pageantry. The inquest was conducted with sealed investigation files, no direct engagement from the public, police officers unwilling to stand by their actions, and a judicial process that would neither identify who was responsible nor result in criminal charges. The hearing, along with Guardado's autopsy, was reassuring to only the least discerning—residents of the county who could be persuaded by the performance of justice and democracy, but not its substance. Again, what laws had Guardado broken? Was he more threatening to public safety than any other security guard who may be armed? Why wasn't he simply questioned or arrested? What purpose did this inquest serve if it could not determine who was guilty or responsible for killing Guardado?

When Justice Cooper announced the results of her investigation months later, she declared that "the manner of death was by the hands of another person other than by accident." Surely a public inquest was not needed to establish such an obvious fact. Cooper also affirmed that LASD and the medical examiner's office acted lawfully during their investigations. Her findings said nothing about whether Guardado's death was necessary, unavoidable, or just. A separate investigation by District Attorney George Gascón determined no charges would be brought against Officers Vega and Hernandez—they were found to be operating in self-defense and their use of force was deemed lawful.[13] Guardado's family and local residents paying attention were outraged but not surprised by the county's denial of justice. Examiner Lucas—who sided against LASD by publicly releasing Guardado's death record and initiating the county's first inquest in decades—resigned before Gascón announced he was clearing officers of criminal misconduct.

In this chapter I call attention to the medical examiners and coroners who investigate in-custody deaths. We will learn about the origins of their profession, the forms of investigation they conduct, and their role in helping legitimize the lethal actions of local government. Death investigators often occupy a space in our imagination as impartial forensic scientists concerned with truth and not politics. This perception is the result of legal reforms beginning in the nineteenth century. We will see how coroners were once powerful mediators of democratic accountability, performing the roles of investigator, prosecutor, and politician. They organized inquests and worked with juries made largely of free white men who aided them in determining how deaths occurred and who was to be arrested, charged, and brought before a criminal court. When the coroner system modernized between the end of the nineteenth and early twentieth centuries—turning death investigators into forensic experts armed with the tools of science and medicine—they were relieved of their prosecutorial powers and the nation lost a unique form of community oversight of the criminal justice system. This shift coincided with the rise of racial segregation and the reactive politics of white supremacists who used violence and systemic discrimination to disenfranchise Black people and limit who belonged to American democracy after the end of Reconstruction. Modernizing the coroner, restricting public influence over its investigative work, and diminishing the influence of Black and other nonwhite people over American public life were synergistic forces. By the end of the twentieth century the once formidable and direct partnership between state and public on matters of mysterious or violent death had been completely dissolved, leaving us with our current system that imagines justice through the narrow and technical lens of a physician rather than the wisdom of everyday people of a pluralist democracy.

DYING IN DEMOCRACY'S SHADOW

The role of the coroner originated in medieval England, with the first clear evidence dating to 1194. During the twelfth century King Richard I established what were called crowners to represent the interests of the Crown in local areas and generate revenue for the royal military—from the word "crowner" we get "coroner."[14] Knights and trusted aids of the king were often appointed to the role. The coroner's primary duty was to investigate violent or unnatural deaths through inquests. The process involved local officials notifying the coroner of a death, after which the coroner would convene a jury. Unlike modern juries, these were composed of local people familiar with the circumstances of the death and the needs of community. Medical men were not usually involved in the process, and only the most superficial body examination was conducted. This was because death investigation, even examining the body of a dead person, was a decidedly open process. And it would be the coroner's jury, made up of men from the region, that was responsible for determining the cause of death and deciding if it was felonious (including suicide or homicide), accidental, or natural. This system helped maintain royal authority while involving local communities in the death investigation and justice administration.[15] Coroners were crucial brokers of social order, bringing criminals to justice during the thirteenth and fourteenth centuries, combining what we now consider executive and judicial functions.

American colonists adopted the coroner system from their English forebears. Early American coroners, like their English counterparts, could not initiate their own investigation of a dead body. Instead, they directed the local sheriff to summon ordinary citizens from the county where the body was found to serve on the inquest jury. According to English law, only free white male citizens who owned property could serve as jurors—a restriction that persisted in America throughout the nineteenth century and extended into the twentieth because of systemic efforts to disenfranchise Black Americans and other nonwhites.[16] In the colonial era the coroner operated like a religious elder, moderating the inquest jury but not determining its outcome or verdict.[17] This was a remarkable example of political pluralism: the wide distribution of power and decision-making spread throughout members of society, rather than having power concentrated among elites and experts. Inquest jurors were free to use their own reason, judgment, and skills acquired from life experience to help coroners determine what caused an untimely death, who was responsible, and who was to be arrested and charged. The reach of this political pluralism was limited, however. Women in early America were excluded from serving on inquests as they were for most legal proceedings until the ratification of the Nineteenth Amendment— the exception being Wyoming in 1870. Enslaved people had no legal standing in the courts and could not serve on inquests until after 1865; in the political climate of Jim Crow, as we will see, Black Americans faced many legal barriers when they tried.

As for the bodies of the dead, medical examinations in the colonial era were left to the discretion of the coroner. They were free to enlist the help of a physician if the cause of death could not be determined by a jury or the coroner themselves. Colonial physicians sharpened their dissection skills on the bodies of executed criminals who were condemned to be postmortem specimens as punishment—many of these corpses were publicly displayed and left hanging as a postmortem reprimand.[18] Once the coroner established responsibility for a death with the help of a jury, their task was to inform local law enforcement, most often the sheriff, to the arrest the guilty party.

During the early republic there were no standard qualifications for becoming a death investigator and hardly any had specialized training. Still, the tasks and statutory responsibilities of the American coroner were more or less uniform throughout the colonies: work with a jury of citizens to identify the cause of death, identify the guilty party, and declare charges against them with the aid of the justice of the peace or local law enforcement.[19] With each colony operating as an autonomous political entity, there were no shared laws determining how coroners were appointed, the number required in each county, terms of service, how inquests were to be run, and if their records were sealed from the general public.[20] Colonial America was suspended between English law and political independence. Likewise, death investigations embodied the inertia of tradition and the creative energies of science and medicine not yet fully organized by the spirit of nation building.

Coroners as a profession and inquests as a practice continued after the American Revolution. With its newfound freedom the early republic became more concerned with the life and death of its population. In August 1790 American statisticians tabulated the country's first census, using social categories that reflected the racial and gendered hierarchies of a budding nation: "head of the household," "free White males over the age of 16," "free white males under the age of 16," "free white women," "all other free persons," and "slaves."[21] The number of inquests recorded among the nation's four million inhabitants increased in frequency during the early years of independence, though the deaths of men of distinction were most often preserved on the onion-paper ledgers from this time.

For example, when Alexander Hamilton was gunned down on July 11, 1804, by Aaron Burr after their legendary duel, John Burger, coroner for the City of New York, convened an inquest that determined Burr and his accomplice William Van Ness "feloniously willfully and of their malice aforethought, did kill and murder against the peace of the people of the state of New York and their dignity."[22] Note the jury's ability to name the intention of Hamilton's killers and how their acts were an affront to the moral sensibilities of the broader community—who found Burr and Van Ness guilty.

The power to investigate deaths in the early republic was diffuse. When Americans found a dead body in a county without a coroner, they appointed one and gave him the power to host an inquest.[23] This act speaks to a time when members of the public armed with reason and the skill of observation knew they could wrestle meaning and justice from tragedy with their own hands. They did this because the men of the early republic lived in a world where reason and science were within reach of all free Americans. This was the era of the Enlightenment, which initiated a shift from unquestioned religious beliefs to rational thought. The physical world was viewed as the primary reality—the one thing that could be truly comprehended—governed by natural laws and patterns awaiting discovery through empirical observation. Death was also subject to Enlightenment thinking. While the early science of anatomy was an invention of the Italian Renaissance, the men of the early republic were influenced by British and French forensic traditions believing that death, like plants and animals, could be observed, studied, and classified.

But in early America a very specific type of person could wield the tools of science and contribute to building a nation: white men. Reason, it was thought, was not to be found among Africans or Indigenous people, who were ruled by the laws of nature instead of being its master. Science allowed Europeans to have sovereignty over displaced Native people and the natural resources that circulated with enslaved Africans throughout the Atlantic. The role of the American coroner embodied this spirit of mastery, being at once a political, legal, scientific, and moral position—traits that whites believed Africans and their descendants could not obtain. Unlike their English counterparts, the American coroner was more powerful, serving colonists in a political environment with few government officials and an evolving democracy that required power sharing between civil servants and those who were counted as citizens.[24]

The uniquely democratic and American version of the coroner would later present issues in the nineteenth century, when political enfranchisement extended to Black Americans and then women. I could not find any record of a Black coroner prior to 1865—even within the free communities of the North—and there were only a handful of Black physicians in the entire nation during the nineteenth century. And while the mysterious deaths of enslaved people appear in the nation's ledger before 1865, they were included often because they had been killed by their owners, were murdered by another, or because their freedom insulted white supremacy. America's violent history often placed death investigators at the center of larger political struggles over truth, freedom, and equality.

THE HAMBURG MASSACRE

White Southerners after the Civil War—most especially white men who fought against the Union—resented losing their traditions for the freedom of Black Americans. The South's surrender did not engender remorse for slavery; neither did it inspire respect for the dignity of Black people. Confederates may have denounced the rebellion, but they continued to believe the land settled by their forebears remained theirs and African Americans had no legitimate claim to it—even Blacks elected to office immediately after the war or those that fought for the winning side. Southerners during the second half of the nineteenth century felt the balance of power shift against them. The social order that had given meaning, dignity, and purpose to their lives was collapsing, the veneer of their greatness lost—a sentiment that can be heard in recent calls to "make America great again." Violence and discrimination have a way of balancing the scales of a nation looking to return to the past.

In the sweltering summer of 1876, as the United States celebrated its centennial, the small town of Hamburg, South Carolina, became the stage for a violent tragedy that would reverberate through the corridors of power and the consciousness of a nation divided over the freedom of Black Americans.[25] Hamburg was once the center of the cotton trade in the region; after the Civil War, with the town's slave-based economy in ruins, free Blacks fled to Hamburg and other cities like it. They turned them into vibrant towns, with Black marshals, judges, and other elected officials, thriving businesses, city councils, and the kind of pride that would inspire celebration for the centennial of American freedom.

On July 4 an all-Black unit of the state National Guard, Company A Ninth Regiment, marched down Main Street in Hamburg in celebration of Independence Day. The troop included boys as young as sixteen and men whose fighting days were long behind them. While their uniforms were up for the occasion, the group of roughly forty men did not have the resources to waste live ammunition in the walnut and wrought-iron rifles that looped in their hands. But this did little to diminish the grand spectacle of their procession.

Around 6 p.m. two white men, Henry Getzen and his brother-in-law Thomas Butler, attempted to drive their horse and wagon through the parade, and specifically between the military men whose skin color, coordinated movements, uniforms, and weapons were symbols of the South's defeat and the dawning a new social order. While they were too young to have fought in the Civil War, Getzen and Butler inherited the South's resentment of free Black people. Captain D. L. "Dock" Adams asked the white men to pass around the procession. They refused, with Getzen insisting that he would not step aside "for no damn niggers!" Hearing this roused the members of the National Guard, with most refusing to cede any ground. Dock Adams, a man of pride and even temperament, diffused the situation by commanding his troop to let the white men pass. The incident brought what was a jubilant celebration to a sour end.

The following day Getzen and Butler returned to Hamburg with retired Confederate General Mathew Butler to file a complaint against Dock Adams and his National Guard. They met with Prince Rivers, the town's trial justice, legislative founders of Aiken County, and members of the Radical Republican Party that helped create the first majority Black state legislature in South Carolina.[26] Butler argued that Adams and his men were guilty of obstructing a public road. They insisted the National Guard forfeit their weapons and issue an apology. Hoping to avoid bloodshed, the town council convinced Justice Rivers and Marshal Jim Cook to set a trial for July 8 to allow time for tempers to settle. But the stakes were too high. General Butler's demand was not only unreasonable—the weapons were the property of the state of South Carolina and could not simply be seized by a civilian calling himself a general during a time of peace—but an insult to the very freedom the National Guard Armory was there to celebrate during the nation's centennial. Besides, the Butlers and Getzen were bad faith actors; while they consented to a trial and using the formality of the justice system to settle the dispute, in truth they wanted blood. General Butler had sent word of the confrontation to the white supremacist paramilitary group known as the Red Shirts. On the day of the trial, nearly two hundred Red Shirts from Georgia and South Carolina descended onto the small town, armed with bitterness and memory of a time before Black men were free to carry arms in public.

An ultimatum had been given to the National Guard to forfeit their weapons by 6 p.m. They refused and retreated into the town armory. Roughly an hour later, white men began firing into the building. The National Guard returned fire, killing a young white man named Thomas McKie Meriwether with a single shot to the head—a monument in his honor stands to this day in North Augusta, South Carolina. Matters escalated, as the Red Shirts were determined to take over the armory. They brought a cannon, adding its fire to the countless rounds thrown at the brick edifice where the National Guard had taken cover. It wasn't long until twenty-five Black men from the National Guard were captured—the others managed to escape and lived to share their story. A "dead ring" was formed around the Black men who remained. The Red Shirts called the names of National Guard members Allen Attaway, Dave Phillips, Hamp Stevens, Albert Myniart, and Pompey Curry. One by one the white militia executed them as they were summoned—only Curry survived his wounds. Two other guardsmen, Nelder Parker and Moses Parks, had been killed earlier during the conflict.

When the dust and blood settled on the morning on July 9, seven Black men and one white man had been killed over a conflict that began because Black freedom was an insult to white supremacy. Prince Rivers convened a coroner's inquest. The jury, made up of Black residents, found "seven persons guilty of murder, namely: E. J. Butler, Henry Getzen, Thomas Butler, Harrison Butler, John Lamar, Thomas Oliver, and John Oliver."[27] The jury determined that "forty-four citizens of Aiken County, S.C.; thirteen of Edgefield County, S.C., and thirty Georgians were accessories before the fact." Rivers issued arrest warrants for the eighty-seven men involved in the massacre, which included Mathew Butler, who would later become a South Carolina senator, and Benjamin R. Tillman, who became governor of South Carolina in 1890. None were detained or put on trial, even after a Senate subcommittee traveled to South Carolina in 1876 and 1877 to investigate the Hamburg massacre, along with the reports of voter intimidation and election fraud following the 1876 presidential election. In that contested presidential campaign, Republican candidate Rutherford B. Hayes was awarded the presidency over Democrat Samuel Tilden after Republicans agreed to withdrawal federal troops from the South, effectively ending Reconstruction (1865–1877).[28]

The Compromise of 1876 led to the restoration of white Democratic control of the South and helped inaugurate the beginning of Jim Crow laws that established racial segregation and the political disenfranchisement of Black Americans. Historians have labeled this moment in American history as the start of the great Redemption—a period where whites in both the South and the North worked together to revoke the legal gains of Black Americans and reassert white supremacy over American lands, institutions, and law.

Several years after the massacre, Senator Benjamin R. Tillman, who was tied to the incident, shared his thoughts in front of Congress on March 23, 1900, about the necessity of white men in South Carolina disenfranchising Black Americans and retaking the state. Tillman explained:

> We were sorry we had the necessity forced upon us, but we could not help it, and as white men we are not sorry for it, and we do not propose to apologize for anything we have done in connection with it. We took the government away from them in 1876. We did take it. If no other Senator has come here previous to this time who would acknowledge it, more is the pity.[29]

Hamburg lost many residents following the 1876 incident. The town eventually washed away when it could not afford to update its levee system, leaving it vulnerable to catastrophic floods in 1888, 1911, and 1927. Today the River Golf Club stands in North Augusta where the free Black town of Hamburg once thrived.

THE STATE OF DEATH DEVOLVES

The Hamburg massacre was part of the opening act for the political terror that shrouded the nation until the Civil Rights Movement. What happened in Hamburg also signaled changes to death investigation, inquests, and criminal justice throughout the country after Emancipation. White mob violence, lynching, and violence were omnipresent, and many crimes against Black Americans and other racial groups did not result in justice but were met instead with indifference from statesmen and local officials, much like in Hamburg.[30] Black people could hardly find justice in states resentful of the fall of the Confederacy and their perceived preferential treatment by the federal government. States decided the reach and application of the amendments—what democracy looked like in each of their territories.[31] While the federal government today constrains the states to guarantee the constitutional rights of citizens, matters looked much different during our nation's early history.

Originally, the Bill of Rights, which includes the first ten amendments, did not apply to the states at all. In 1833, the Supreme Court held that the Bill of Rights only applied to constrain the federal government.[32] This meant that the states were not limited by the amendments. They could, and did, violate the Bill of Rights, exercising the freedom to decide if they wanted these rights to apply to their people, who, when, and to what extent—we will see in future chapters how the assertion of states' rights and the autonomy of local government hampers efforts to collect national data on in-custody death. The ratification of the Thirteenth and Fourteenth Amendments inaugurated the battle within the American legal system to afford unified rights to all people in America.

Blatant legal and political discrimination ruled late nineteenth- and early twentieth-century America as states decided which rights would apply to its citizens. Black men could serve on juries in South Carolina following the Civil Rights Act of 1875, which prohibited discrimination in jury selection based on race. But the 1875 act did little to stop discrimination. In *Strauder v. West Virginia* (1879), the Supreme Court ruled that African Americans could not be excluded from juries on the basis of race. But it was nearly impossible for Black litigants to prove that this discrimination had happened. With the end of Reconstruction, South Carolina and many other Southern states implemented Black codes and jury qualification standards that effectively prevented Black people from participating in the process of criminal justice.[33] It was truly remarkable that the Black officials in Hamburg initiated an inquest, enlisting members of their own community to determine who was responsible for the massacre and who to arrest. That none of the eighty-seven white men who terrorized and killed members of the National Guard were brought to justice merely confirms how white racial resentment so easily undermined the constitutional rights of Black Americans and constrained the reach of democracy.[34]

On the matter of constitutional rights, there is a troubling resemblance between the Hamburg inquest and the Guardado case of 2020. While these incidents took place in different centuries and under dramatically different circumstances, at the center was lethal violence perpetuated by men who believed they represented the law. Armed militias, the ancestors of today's police, were once considered lawful agents of the state and were employed throughout the Union to suppress slave rebellions, hunt runaways, and carry out genocides against Indigenous people.[35] Even though the attorney general of South Carolina, William Stone, declared that the men who terrorized Hamburg were "without lawful authority" to demand that the National Guard surrender their arms, the Red Shirts did not recognize the authority of the "carpetbagger" government of Black leaders they claimed Republicans forced on them.[36] White men were the measure of the law. Sen. Benjamin Tillman said as much after the massacre: "We of the South have never recognized the right of the negro to govern white men, and we never will. We have never believed him to be equal to the white man, and we will not submit to gratifying his lust on our wives and daughters without lynching him."[37] While the chastity of white women was not at stake in Hamburg, the failure of the attorney general or local officials to prosecute the men found responsible by their Black peers is a tragic concession to the worldview of the Southern Democrats after the Compromise of 1876.[38]

In this respect, both the Hamburg and Guardado inquests were never going to bring the men responsible to justice. Precedent and tradition had settled this in advance, effectively creating a hollow democratic process far removed from the people's justice. The odds of arresting eighty-seven white men for murdering seven Black people in 1876 were roughly the same as arresting two police officers for killing an eighteen-year-old Latino man in 2020. The question is, why?

A part of the answer can be found in the changes to death investigation that took place while states were deciding which amendments were going to apply to its citizens. Free Black people with the full guarantees of the Constitution were a threat to white supremacy. Be it the courts or the inquest, Black enfranchisement meant that justice and the law would be shared. In an environment where whites were actively taking the power of government away from Black Americans, the coroner and the inquest were one of many political institutions with the potential to increase the reach of democracy. Segregationists in the South and white Republicans in the North who backed away from protecting the rights of Black Americans moved democracy toward contraction. In this sense, the transformation of the coroner into a licensed physician detached from criminal prosecution and the justice concerns of everyday citizens was aligned with larger national efforts to limit democratic participation under Jim Crow segregation. By the middle of the twentieth century the coroner-turned-medical-examiner was no longer the institution of direct democracy that had thrived in the centuries before Black political freedom.

ANTIDEMOCRATIC REFORM

Modernization of the coroner is often understood to be the consequence of moral, legal, and scientific progress in America.[39] This progressive story, compelling in many respects, allows our image of the coroner—a person of objective medical science uninterested in politics—to emerge over the course of the twentieth century as a trustworthy agent of truth and justice, unscathed by the racism and antidemocratic politics of the nation after the end of Reconstruction. And yet, the great contraction of American democracy during Jim Crow left its mark on the practice of death investigation, even though changes to the profession were motivated by scientific innovation and rooting out political corruption. The forward march of science and technology does not always carry democracy along the way. Modernizing the coroner abolished this once-important institution of direct democracy in America.

Near the middle of the nineteenth century, lawmakers looked to end the political corruption that had taken over the profession of the death investigator.[40] Becoming a coroner had provided men of ambition an entry point into American politics; they were often elected like other officials, and most were paid based on the number of deaths they investigated. This created a political environment where coroners grew partial to the constituents who placed them in power and the authorities that put food on their tables. Getting involved in the business of death for the political opportunities it afforded seemed inevitable for a role designed to serve a king in a land with no crown.

Alpheus Hodges, for example, became the first coroner of Los Angeles after Americans wrestled the territory away from the Mexican government following the Treaty of Guadalupe Hidalgo in 1848. Hodges was also the first mayor of Los Angeles and found his way into politics after heading west to San Francisco in 1849 hoping to score during the Gold Rush.[41] Like many educated white men of his era, he failed upward and acquired the dual role of mayor and coroner of a very small Los Angeles County. With an active statewide genocide waged against the Indigenous peoples of California, Hodges was paid by then governor Peter Burnett $100 for every "Indian" autopsy that he oversaw.[42] While he surely presided over the deaths of locals from the region, Hodges had an incentive to work closely with law enforcement and local militias enlisted to eliminate Indigenous people from the Los Angeles basin.

Death investigators faced criticism for not utilizing medical experts sufficiently.[43] Physicians who led the emergence of American medical schools during the nineteenth century trained newly minted doctors to become interested in death investigations and the connections between the law and medicine—what is known as medical jurisprudence.[44] American coroners had the subpoena power to summon physicians at inquests, conduct postmortem examinations without pay, and testify in court. Physicians resented the power of the coroner as it made a mockery of their professional autonomy, forcing them to be beholden to government officials who were less credentialed but backed by strong political allies. During the middle half of the nineteenth century, tensions between coroners and physicians grew, with doctors challenging the expertise and legitimacy of the lay coroner entrusted to investigate causes of death with no medical training. American physicians, who were growing in prominence in America and were well organized under the American Medical Association, argued in print and with state lawmakers that proper medical experts were needed to conduct modern autopsies and produce investigations that could stand up in court. They believed that poorly trained coroners and physicians in the courtroom were a threat to the entire medical profession. In 1860 Maryland became the first state to require coroners to be physicians, with Baltimore appointing a practicing doctor to the role in 1868; Massachusetts followed in 1877.[45]

By the start of the twentieth century, the argument for requiring coroners to be medical examiners trained as physicians had become persuasive in many states.[46] The population of American cities had swelled due to the migration of Black Americans from the South and the arrival of immigrant groups from Europe. During the Progressive Era, American industries such as manufacturing, meatpacking, coal mining, and textile mills expanded dramatically, and reformers grew concerned with the devastating impact these industries had on American life. In response, private citizens, charitable organizations, and public health officials fought successfully to reform how Americans worked, where they lived, and how they received medical care along with other general social welfare from local, state, and federal government. During this time, the field of medicine and public health witnessed rapid advancement, particularly in the field of bacteriology, which helped physicians and public health experts fight infectious diseases such as typhoid and cholera, which had once decimated towns and crippled industry. The rapid growth of American industrial production left the nation particularly vulnerable to communicable illnesses as workers operated in close proximity to one another and lived in densely populated urban centers where clean water and fresh produce were rare—modern sewage systems were still in their infancy in major American cities. Coroners were increasingly relied upon to track and record deaths from infectious disease, aiding public health officials and physicians in the fight against the spread of lethal illness. They were also called on to monitor accidental deaths due to industrial poisoning, injury, and tragic vehicle accidents.

To be effective at helping manage the livelihood of a local community, many reformers called for coroners to be trained in forensic science, anatomy, and the newest techniques in medicine. In response, states began to draft laws that either abolished the coroner entirely or required counties to employ physicians in a role that was once open to the layman. This meant that death investigators were expected to have scientific skill and could no longer be men whose major talent was following the whims of local and state politics. The need to protect the public's health expanded the science of death investigation.

Efforts to require coroners to become physicians gained momentum with the reform of New York City's coroner system in 1918. The same year that New York changed its death investigation system, the National Research Council (NRC) released a report mailed to coroners around the nation advocating for the abolishment of coroners on the grounds of political corruption and insufficient skill in the areas of medicine and science.[47] The NRC wanted to replace coroners with doctors credentialed in forensic medicine. They also wanted to relieve coroners of their judicial powers to convene physicians and jurors for an inquest. Soon after, state legislators began to adopt new codes that required death investigators to be appointed by government officials and local county boards. Their roles as legal arbitrators and medical investigators were also divided in most states, as the profession moved more firmly into the nonpartisan space of forensic pathology and further away from adjudicating criminal justice.

By the late twentieth century, about half of the US population was served by medical examiner systems, primarily in major cities.[48] In time, death investigation became a diversified practice in the hands of individual states. And with virtually no federal oversight, the science of death became a politically diversified practice, with varying laws and complex bureaucracy determining if populations were served by coroners or medical examiners, whether or not the role was an elected position or made by appointment, if there were term limits, what deaths fell under their jurisdiction, whether or not they were required to perform autopsies, if investigators could hold inquests, and if their records were public.

ILLIBERAL INVESTIGATORS

After the end of Reconstruction, the antidemocratic politics of white supremacy flourished throughout the states, limiting the legal and political power of Black people and other vulnerable minorities.[49] Institutional racism terrorized, fractured, and diminished the public's power over American democracy at a time when the threat of violence stifled the civic engagement of Black people and other nonwhite communities.

Lynching was one form of this violence. The late 1880s and early 1890s marked its peak in the American South, with annual reports exceeding one hundred and sometimes two hundred incidents. Lynching was an old American tradition that placed justice in the hands of everyday white citizens who believed they were agents of the law.

While primarily a Southern phenomenon, lynchings also took place in Northern and Western states. Over time, they became increasingly concentrated in the South and predominantly targeted Black people. Lynchings were most common in rural counties facing rapid population growth and migrant Black populations with the power of the vote and the potential to change electoral politics in the new places they called home. They could be triggered by minor offenses like breaching racial etiquette; most involved murder accusations, while fewer still were related to allegations of rape. The violent spectacle was often carried out in spaces of exchange and travel in order to publicly reinforce Black subordination and send a message about who controlled law, order, and American democracy. Before World War I, local communities generally supported lynchings, with attempts to prosecute perpetrators being rare and convictions almost nonexistent. Mass public lynchings attracted hundreds or thousands of white spectators, including children. Body parts were often taken home as souvenirs.

Lynching declined as a result of anti-racist activism and white supremacists using the law and local politics to perpetuate discrimination. Ida B. Wells, the NAACP, and many other civil rights leaders launched anti-lynching campaigns that raised public awareness, shifted popular support of the practice, and put pressure on the federal government to denounce this violent spectacle.[50] Anti-lynching activists and civil rights leaders also pressured the federal government to be more proactive in protecting the civil liberties of Black Americans, especially in the South.

Other forms of violence and intimidation were used to disenfranchise politically vulnerable communities. In 1865 the all-white Seattle Board of Trustees passed anti-Indigenous ordinances that prevented Duwamish Nation people or any "Indians" from living on a "street, highway, lane, or alley, or vacant lot" within the town limits—turning the city into a sundown town where white vigilantes and police were free to capture, fine, and subject them to forced labor.[51] State leaders stopped the immigration of Chinese people in 1882 in an effort to ensure white settlers in Western states had employment opportunities promised by the federal government—a restriction not lifted until Congress passed the Immigration Act of 1964.[52] The sheriff's department forcibly removed Mexican

Americans from their homes in the Chavez Ravine to make space for Dodger Stadium in Los Angeles in 1959.[53] During the 1964 Democratic Convention, Fannie Lou Hamer explained that she suffered lifelong injuries after being beaten nearly to death inside Winona County jail for helping organize Black voters in the South.[54] White urban planners worked with local police to clear residents along Claiborne Avenue in New Orleans to build the I-10 freeway through Tremé in 1968 without a public discussion, destroying one of the oldest and wealthiest Black communities in the nation.[55]

When people of color fought back and insisted that they were worthy of dignity, countless lives were taken by white mobs who left their victims bloodied, disfigured, and unburied in Tulsa, Atlanta, Chicago, Knoxville, and Detroit.[56] Reforms to the American death investigation system and criminal justice also left them defenseless.

Political pluralism after emancipation presented death investigators and lawmakers with an ethical and political dilemma: the deaths of nonwhites mattered, and they had a right to be active participants in inquest juries and the broader criminal justice system. According to the letter of the law, the Fourteenth Amendment to the Constitution guaranteed the rights of citizenship, equal protection, and due process. This meant, among many other things, that Black Americans and other racial groups could serve as public jurors on inquests that determined the cause of a death and punishment for the crime. They could take on more official roles, becoming marshals, sheriffs, and deputies directly involved in criminal justice—as we saw in the Hamburg massacre.

However, the movement to turn the coroner into a figure of science and relieve them of their prosecutorial functions minimized public access to this once-venerable democratic institution. Modernization would orient death investigators away from the justice concerns of local communities and toward the requirements of clinical expertise, forensic science, and law-and-order politics. It also made the coroner a neutral party during a time when politically vulnerable populations needed institutions of justice and accountability in the wake of racial violence.

After state lawmakers demanded that coroners be trained in medicine and forensic science, death investigations came to be seen as a proper scientific endeavor. This brought the science of death into alignment with the Enlightenment values of reason, observation, and expertise. But only a small number of men were believed to have the capacity, temperament, and training to be a coroner or medical examiner—talent for science and medicine was found among the elite, not the everyday citizen. By the end of the twentieth century the science of death evolved into a medical practice carried out with state officials insulated by scientific expertise and detached from the wisdom and concerns of the public.

There was legal pressure for this insulation. The coroner's findings became elevated within criminal law court as the disciplines that made up forensic science grew and organized into national associations with technical journals and specialized training. As death investigations became more closely aligned with forensic science, the information they gathered and the autopsies they produced were increasingly seen as value-neutral and objective. This in turn meant that the autopsy and the death record could meet the court's evolving standards for reliable evidence, particularly in criminal cases.[57] This development further anchored death investigation to matters of law and order. The standard of proof in an inquest is generally a "preponderance of the evidence," which is lower than the "beyond a reasonable doubt" standard required for criminal convictions. Having death investigations led by scientific men who conducted their work without police involvement or the concerns of the public—merely collecting the facts of human biology, as it were—meant that their findings could be admitted into criminal court without violating the confrontation clause of the Sixth Amendment.[58] According to the Sixth Amendment, "the accused shall enjoy the right . . . to be confronted with the witnesses against him."[59] The courts have interpreted this clause to mean information gathered in support of a criminal charge and brought before a jury is considered "testimony" (or testimonial) against the accused, therefore entitling them to test the veracity of this information in the crucible of a cross-examination in front of a jury.[60] Potential violation of the confrontation clause was effectively eliminated after states adopted the position of the medical examiner, a role that was no longer linked to criminal court.

The abolition of the coroner was part of the shifting ethical and legal landscape of the country. State law no longer required death investigators to determine culpability in cases of mysterious, violent, or untimely deaths. While the courts benefited from this, so too would law enforcement and local governments. As forensic practices modernized, coroners and medical examiners lost their authority to declare whether or not violence carried out by rifle clubs, white vigilantes, or police was necessary or in the interest of the common good. Gone were the days of the coroner offering judgments, with the help of everyday citizens, about the effect of violence and murder on the moral sensibilities of local communities and the broader public—like in the murder of Alexander Hamilton or what was attempted by the Black survivors of the Hamburg massacre.

With the coroner, and eventually the medical examiner, playing a less prominent role in criminal prosecutions, so too would the inquest change. Inquests were no longer tied to criminal justice and became instead nontestimonial hearings with no prosecutorial authority—a shell of what they were during the early republic or the nineteenth century before modernization. This meant the public no longer helped the coroner, now a medical examiner, identify how someone died, who was responsible, and/or what charges were to be made by local authorities. Currently, medical examiners retain the power to call inquests in only twenty US states; everywhere else this power resides with another official, is unspecified in the law, or the inquest has been abolished entirely (figure 2.2). A public inquest has no bearing on criminal charges in all states. While these changes affected all Americans, they disproportionately impacted newly enfranchised Black citizens and other marginalized groups who frequently endured police violence and white vigilante terror. The failure of the Hamburg inquest to produce convictions and justice anticipated what would become of the public's diminished power over forensic investigations in the twentieth century.

Eliminating the public's power over criminal charges during an inquest was complete in most parts of the country by the 1960s.[61] By this time criminal charges and prosecutions were almost exclusively under the power of state attorneys and solicitor generals—officials who were elected by the people or appointed by a governor. Death investigators, along with their public inquests, were officially detached from criminal justice proceedings. Turning the coroner into a politically neutral agent of medicine and science censored death investigators on matters of justice and the greater good and brought an end to democratic participation in the inquest.

Most would agree that a death investigator trained in evidence-based medicine is preferable to a coroner without these skills. Many would also agree, however, that an investigator capable of denouncing gratuitous violence is crucial for the health of the greater good.

We can hardly blame politically vulnerable communities for struggling to see the difference between the coroner's institutional silence and police who violate civic freedoms, equal protection, and due process rights. What they perceive is real: death investigators speak the language of democracy but restrict its reach in society.

The coroner's narrow focus on biological explanations carries the effects of a not-too-distant past where liberal civic values faced assault, segregationists looked to constrain American democracy, and state officials worked to eliminate political corruption by modernizing the science of death. Following these changes, medical examiners and coroners lost their ties to the public, the values of political pluralism, and direct democracy. We should not be surprised then that death investigators now struggle to see the societal forces inscribed on the bodies of the deceased or the justice concerns of grieving communities.

CHAPTER 3

SOCIETY LIVES IN THE BODY

J ohn Horton III was killed inside a Los Angeles County jail in March 2009, two months after Barack Obama was sworn into the presidency. In July of that year, Harvard professor Henry Louis "Skip" Gates Jr. was arrested by police in Cambridge, Massachusetts, when neighbors reported he was breaking into his own home. All three of these Black men, despite stark differences in their class and social status, were connected to a deep history of discrimination that made people sick and diminished the life expectancy of Americans.

Obama was asked about the arrest of Gates at the end of a primetime press conference on healthcare reform. It was early in his presidency and his thoughts still reflected the clarity of an Illinois senator who worked on the South Side of Chicago and knew what structural inequality does to Black people. Obama personalized his reaction, speculating what would happen "if I was trying to jigger into—well, I guess this is my house now, so it probably wouldn't happen. But let's say my old house in Chicago—here, I'd get shot." He added:

> What I think we know separate and apart from this incident is that there is a long history in this country of African Americans and Latinos being stopped by law enforcement disproportionately. And that's just a fact. As you know . . . when I was in the state legislature in Illinois, we worked on a racial profiling bill, because there was indisputable

evidence that blacks and Hispanics were being stopped disproportionately. And that is a sign, an example of how, you know, race remains
a factor in the society.[1]

It was the first time in American history that the president would
say he could lose his life to law enforcement just like any other person
of color.

Obama's comments drove media headlines.[2] The Left saw it as an
opportunity to revisit the significance of racism in America despite having a Black president. Conservative responses telegraphed strategies that
would be used to undermine Obama's healthcare reform bill, claiming
the president's comments were an overreach of power into what was
effectively a local issue. Others argued that talk of systemic racism
among law enforcement was a signal that President Obama could not be
an impartial leader of the free world. Rush Limbaugh said on his radio
show that "the president's reaction to this was not presidential. . . . We
got the militant black reaction, the Cornel West angry reaction. Basically,
we saw a community organizer in action last night. . . . Obama is not
a force for positive race relations in this country. He is not a uniter."[3]

Obama made a second statement on July 24, 2009, to calm the frenzy
that had taken the media's attention away from healthcare reform. "I
unfortunately gave an impression that I was maligning the Cambridge
Police Department, or Sergeant Crowley specifically," Obama explained
during a White House press conference.[4] There was a political calculus
at play here: if Obama's historic Affordable Care Act was going to pass,
it would require bipartisan support that could be jeopardized if the
nation's first Black president appeared biased against law enforcement
in support of Black and Latino people. The strategy did not work.
Conservatives continued to find reasons to oppose the bill throughout
Obama's presidency, despite his appeals across the aisle.

The greater missed opportunity, I believe, was the president's unwillingness to use this moment to help the nation understand the connections
between police discrimination and the health risks of the very people
who were going to benefit from the Affordable Care Act. Surely this
included Blacks and Latinos but also whites, the poor, the unhoused,

the disabled, and many others you will soon meet in these pages who died in custody during a health crisis.

There was precedent for an American president speaking publicly about the systems of discrimination that target Black people and impact society as a whole. President Lyndon B. Johnson, just two years removed from establishing Medicare and Medicaid, declared after the Detroit uprising in 1967:

> The only genuine, long-range solution for what has happened lies in an attack— mounted at every level—upon the conditions that breed despair and violence. All of us know what those conditions are: ignorance, discrimination, slums, poverty, disease, not enough jobs. We should attack these conditions—not because we are frightened by conflict, but because we are fired by conscience. We should attack them because there is simply no other way to achieve a decent and orderly society in America.[5]

After the Watts Rebellion two years earlier, Johnson reminded the nation that "the brave story of the Negro American is . . . a compound of brilliant promises and stunning reverses."[6] Paternalism aside, when the Negro was a social problem for the state to study and solve, American officials showed some capacity to see and discuss publicly the larger political, economic, and social factors diminishing Black lives.

The reaction to Obama's statements about police discrimination in 2009, along with his attempt to walk back criticism of law enforcement, showed how the myth of a colorblind America distorted public discussion of our nation's past. Obama's presidency simply provided the occasion for this myth to thrive in what was a fantasy of American postracial sensibility that could be found in both liberal and conservative media, political commentary, classrooms, and churches. NPR news analyst Daniel Schorr claimed, "The post-racial era, as embodied by Obama, is the era where civil rights veterans of the past century are consigned to history and Americans begin to make race-free judgments on who should lead them."[7] John McWhorter of the Manhattan Institute declared in *Forbes* magazine, "Racism in America is over."[8]

Liberal and conservative reflections at this moment were also aligned on the matter of law-and-order politics. Some liberals read into Obama's rise to power support for the colorblind belief that our political and legal institutions were finally capable of treating everyone equally before the law, allowing the Black son of a single mother to rise into the ranks of the presidency. Conservatives shared their own version of this view, arguing that Obama's election was further proof that state institutions did not see color, only citizens more or less willing to comply with the laws and beliefs that have always determined the success and life chances of Americans. Conservatives were also eager to fire back at "social justice warriors" by doubling down on the belief that crime, poverty, and unemployment within Black and Brown communities were caused by their culture, poor decisions, and lack of ambition. Their failures were not because of a legal or economic system limiting their movements, diminishing hope, and reducing life chances. These communities simply failed to take advantage of the opportunities available to them. Obama's presence in the White House was supposedly proof that systemic racism in America was a myth.

While the nation debated whether or not Obama's rise to power meant the end of racism in America, Helen Jones finally received her son's autopsy from Los Angeles County. It was July 22, 2009, just a few days after Obama first commented on the Gates arrest. The report from the Los Angeles County Department of the Medical Examiner-Coroner claimed John's cause of death could not be determined, meaning there were competing explanations for why he died. One was suicide from hanging, the other that he had sustained recent traumatic injuries during a physical confrontation while in solitary confinement. The contradictions in the county's report mirrored the nation's larger ambivalence about the existence of racial discrimination and the causes of illness and early death among vulnerable populations.

What we believe shapes the problems we are willing to recognize. In this chapter I explain that the health of Americans is a story that involves most people living in the absence of care, experts arguing over the causes of disease and early death, and states fighting the federal government for the freedom to neglect the well-being of any population it deems undesirable. It is a dark and troubling history filled with *brilliant promises* and *stunning reversals*. The neglected health of Black Americans is a central vein in this story, branching out to the nation as a whole. The unwillingness of America to embrace them as people worthy of rights, dignity, and care established a more general spirit of indifference about the health of everyone.

Very few Americans realize that we live and perish under a constitution that does not require local or state governments to invest in the health and longevity of the public. The United States Constitution is silent about our right to medical care or good health. State institutions, not legally mandated to care for the people, have worked with physicians, lawmakers, and social scientists to discriminate against undesirable communities and convince us more generally that governing our health would negate our freedom.

For example, in his book *Dying of Whiteness*, the historian Jonathan Metzl explains that white Americans, particularly in the Rust Belt and the South, with some of the highest rates of disease and lowest life expectancy, have stockpiled guns and blocked healthcare reform measures to prevent the advancement of Blacks, Latinos, and immigrant groups. These actions have adversely impacted white people's own life chances—choices driven by "racial resentment" and the desire to protect white privilege.[9]

Indifference to our own well-being and that of others is a deeply American way of seeing the world, shaping what many perceive when confronted with people who are sick, have substance abuse issues, carry mental illness, suffer chronic conditions, or die early. We often only see bad choices, poor genes, ignorance—not the legal, political, and economic decisions that create unhealthy people.

I make the case in this chapter that we struggle to recognize the appearance of society inside the bodies of vulnerable people—whether in a clinical space or in the custody of law enforcement—because our perceptions of health remain hostage to the discriminatory intentions that were braided into American medicine and the field of public health at the end of the nineteenth century. These intentions continue to haunt and divide us. The less invested we are in the health of others, the more we encourage government to retreat from its responsibility for the public's health. The more the state retreats, the less it appears accountable for the illness, disease, and loss of life under its watch—again, who exactly was responsible for John Horton's death in solitary confinement? And with this vague and distorted understanding of death in America, it becomes difficult to see and name the discriminatory politics shaping our collective life chances. It is a vicious cycle of misapprehension, racial animus, and misplaced accountability that bears itself out, perhaps most obviously, in the death records of people killed by police.

THE DEATH OF ALESIA THOMAS

Alesia Thomas was a thirty-five-year-old Black mother living in Southeast Los Angeles. Sometime after midnight on July 22, 2012, she needed help with a mental health crisis. Alesia took her children, ages three and twelve, to the Southeast station of the Los Angeles Police Department just before 2 a.m., but she did not stay with them. Police spoke with the children and soon gathered at their mother's address. LAPD followed Alesia back to her home to enforce a state law passed a year earlier authorizing law enforcement to arrest a parent for abandoning a child under the age of fourteen.[10] It is doubtful Alesia knew she was committing a crime and certainly not one that might result in the forfeiture of her life. Perhaps she believed, in this moment of crisis, that what she was doing was protected under California's "safe surrender" law, allowing mothers to leave their babies at police and fire departments without prosecution.[11] I choose to believe Alesia loved "*her* babies"—as Black mothers often say—despite the difficult decision of placing them in the care of police.[12]

County records claim that when police arrived at her home, Alesia resisted arrest. Those same records say that police used force to take Alesia into custody; footage from a patrol car shows a white female officer throwing Alesia into the vehicle and kicking her violently in the chest, abdomen, and groin. The video provides audio of Alesia complaining of not being able to breathe and then collapsing shortly after. Police called paramedics, who then took her to the emergency room at

Centinela Regional Medical Care's facility in full cardiac arrest. Medical staff attempted to revive her but were unsuccessful. Alesia never got the care she needed. Instead, she perished two hours after leaving her children at a police station in Southeast Los Angeles.

Official county records claim the cause of Alesia's death could not be determined. On the first page of the county autopsy is the following statement: "The decedent was a 35-year-old Black female who became unresponsive in a police car after arrest. She was transported to a hospital and pronounced. She had a reported history of mental problems including bipolar disorder and schizophrenia, drug abuse, and being suicidal."[13] This type of information at the beginning of an autopsy provides a summary of what happened to the person who has died; its prose is clinical, detached, and designed to orient readers toward certain details and not others. While California is one of the few states where public access to autopsies is protected under state law, very few of us will have the patience or desire to sort through pages of dense and highly technical medical analysis. The anatomic summary, then, like the one here for Alesia, interprets and distills for us the often unclear factors of death.

In Alesia's case, we learn that she lost consciousness in the back of a patrol car without knowing the details of her being assaulted by police. We are told of her mental health and substance abuse issues. Then there are medical statements alleging she was bipolar and schizophrenic, which create such a lasting impression that it rearranges in the mind of the reader the order of events, making Alesia's illness appear to be the first and most important feature of her death. The summary also invites questions about her character and decision-making: What type of mother leaves her children with police? How much cocaine was in her system? Did she pose a threat to others? Was Alesia's body too weak or too guilty to face justice?

Alesia's autopsy was twenty-three pages long. It included an anatomic dissection of her body, a toxicological analysis, a report from the hospital that attempted to revive her, and a case report written three days after her death. In most states a complete autopsy contains all of these files. While each component is important for making a case about what happened to a victim of police violence—or any other form of sudden and unexpected death that takes place without the care of a physician—the case report is the most significant. It tells the story of what happened before and after a person died. Its purpose is to offer a compelling story about the circumstances around the loss of life for medical examiners, police, state officials, and members of the public—though the context provided is often too narrow in its scope and temporality to do justice to the end of a life. The case report is by far the least technical section of a death record, written with details that often betray its neutrality.

The coroner who authored Alesia's case report was a forensic investigator trained to evaluate death scenes by gathering relevant physical evidence and interviewing law enforcement and witnesses involved. In death cases involving police this might include collecting bullets, visiting and taking photos of the scene, gathering specimens from the victim for laboratory analysis, and of course taking statements from the officers who had taken a life. Forensic investigators are not medical doctors and although most have some specialized training or certification in forensic science, few have advanced degrees beyond a bachelor's. The training and qualifications required to be a forensic investigator vary across each state, and there are no federal laws mandating the minimum expertise needed to do the job—counties and states make up these rules. In California the minimum requirements to be a forensic investigator, also known as crime science investigators, are a valid driver's license, certification in crime science investigation, a clean criminal record, and a passing score on the California Criminalist Examination.

The medical examiner very often receives a body days after a person has died with very little information about what has happened. This means that the case report provided by a forensic investigator shapes what the medical examiner sees within and on the body. The physician who conducted Alesia's autopsy read the following narrative before dissecting her:

In speaking with Detective Diaz, the additional information was learned: On the early morning of 07/22/12 at approximately 0145 hours, decedent reportedly dropped off her (2) minor children, ages 3 and 12-years old, at the LAPD-Southeast Station, having left them with a basket of clothing. Obtaining information from the child(ren), Southeast officers responded to decedent's residence as they were going to take her into custody for child negligence; however, responding officers found decedent as appearing incoherent, noting an angered demeanor, with report she resisted arrest. Hence, officers employed minor use of force in taking her into custody, having used a leg sweep to gain control of her. She was subsequently carried downstairs and once placed into the back of the police unit, was noticed to have become unresponsive, no longer breathing, at which time officers summoned for a rescue ambulance. Officers had been at her place of resident approximately 10-15 minutes in duration. Additional history included a bipolar disorder, schizophrenia, with decedent also known as suicidal as was reported by decedent's mother. Diaz also confirmed a reported history of alcoholism, reporting a history of prior meth use as well/ possible current use per mother.[14]

In this statement we see Alesia had her children's safety and care in mind when she left them with a basket of clothing. We also see the amount of force law enforcement believed was an appropriate response for Alesia's indiscretion: they used "a leg sweep to gain control of her" and noted that she was "subsequently carried downstairs." Again, there are details about Alesia's history of mental illness, although the narrative does not make clear what doctor or health professional was consulted to confirm her diagnosis.

It took the Los Angeles Department of the Medical Examiner-Coroner four months to complete their investigation into Alesia's death. Her autopsy included a Y-shaped incision across the front of her body to remove her heart, lungs, spleen, liver, kidney, and pancreas in search of evidence of physical trauma and abnormalities. Her brain was also removed, analyzed, and weighed. A Y-shaped incision and organ removal is standard practice for medical examiner-coroners working in California. In other states, like Maryland, Pennsylvania, and New York, for example, body cavity incisions and organ removal are not necessary and instead fall under the discretion of the physician conducting the autopsy. The surface of Alesia's body was scanned with a fluoroscopic light to identify evidence of bruising and bodily fluids. X-rays were conducted to confirm injuries, and photographs were taken to document the condition of her body when it was brought into the dissection room. Blood from her heart and fluid from her eyes were sent to a laboratory to identify the possible drugs in her system and her glucose and electrolyte levels. And then finally there were two detectives from LAPD to witness her dismemberment in the name of science and truth.

After consulting Alesia's body, the medical examiner could not determine what killed her. In his opinion, the "effects of cocaine intoxication appear to be a major factor in the death. However, we are unable to exclude how much her struggle with law enforcement officers by resisting arrest contributed to her demise. Therefore, manner of death is undetermined."[15] The medical examiner also added that a screen of her blood for disorders revealed a "positive for sickle cell trait." This last statement is suspended above the medical examiner's signature on Alesia's autopsy, and there were no attempts to explain how or why this detail might be relevant to her death. But the reference was loaded with meaning.

Sickle cell disease is a genetic disorder where the blood cells in a person's body take on a sickled shape and become incapable of carrying appropriate amounts of oxygen in the blood and vital organs. It is not a terminal illness but a chronic condition that often produces severe swelling and debilitating inflammation that can be managed with medical care. One can certainly die if the condition is not properly treated, but there have been no studies confirming that merely having sickle cell disease, absent other factors, causes early death. The disorder is also wrongly assumed to be a disease specific to Black people. While sickle cell anemia is prevalent among people with West African ancestry, it emerged independently within populations found in the Mediterranean, the Middle East, and Southeast Asia. The African Americans who have the disorder, which is estimated to be 10 percent of the US Black population, are the descendants of enslaved West Africans who were trafficked from regions where the condition was prominent.

Alesia had one copy of the genes involved in the disease—meaning she was a carrier of sickle cell trait. But to have the full-blown blood disorder one has to carry two copies of the genes that cause the disease.

Carriers of sickle cell trait are generally asymptomatic and tend not to experience severe or life-threatening health complications. Nonetheless, the suggestion that Alesia might have had a blood disease adds more evidence to the idea that her body (or nature) was to blame for why she died—not the police who arrested her, or the California state lawmakers who authorized law enforcement to apprehend families facing a crisis of care.

RACISM IS A PUBLIC HEALTH ISSUE

Dr. Rochelle Walensky, director of the Centers for Disease Control and Prevention (CDC), released a public statement in April 2021 declaring racism in America a threat to public health and safety. Her comments were made while the country was reeling from the deaths of more than five hundred thousand Americans from the COVID-19 pandemic. Public data showed that these deaths were concentrated within Black, Latino/a, and Indigenous communities. The reason, Walensky explained, had nothing to do with genes, family history, or individual decisions of the victims. She argued instead that "the pandemic illuminated inequalities that have existed for generations and revealed for all Americans a known, but often unaddressed, epidemic impacting public health: racism."[16] Walensky's comments were a revelation, but only to those unfamiliar with the work of public health scientists who have produced countless studies measuring the effects of racism on American health.[17] Walensky claimed:

> Racism is not just the discrimination against one group based on the color of their skin or their race or ethnicity, but the structural barriers that impact racial and ethnic groups differently to influence where a person lives, where they work, where their children play, and where they worship and gather in community. These social determinants of health have life-long negative effects on the mental and physical health of individuals in communities of color. . . . As the nation's leading public health agency, CDC has a critical role to play to address the impact of racism on public health.[18]

Walensky described what Obama did not during his presidency: there were long-standing social, political, and legal conditions that determined who lives and for how long in America. And those conditions targeted Black Americans and other communities of color.

Walensky's calling racism an epidemic was a complete reversal of how state officials discussed disease and illness when the notion of public health emerged during the late nineteenth and early twentieth centuries. After the end of Reconstruction, in 1877, the federal government retreated not only from the civil rights of Black Americans but also from their medical care, marking a defining moment in the history of "the people's" health and setting the nation down a trajectory of neglect and indifference that now distorts how we look at people who are ill, unhealthy, and dying young. During the twentieth century, "the people's health" largely meant the health of white Americans and was driven by racist concerns about the cleanliness and hygiene of inferior groups, the spread of disease and illness among Black communities, immigrants arriving from parts of Europe and Asia into congested urban centers, and the health hazards of industrialization.[19]

Most of our history has been marked by an abundance of disease, illness, and early death; Americans have simply learned to live with the perishing of others.

HEALTH FROM WAR

Not a single state institution was prepared for what the Civil War would do to the health of formerly enslaved people, military men fighting the war, or the cities that became sanctuaries of freedom. Neither the Union nor the Confederate army anticipated an extended struggle, and each viewed the war largely in terms of military strategy and resource acquisition. As a result, neither side bothered to bring into the conflict physicians, medical supplies, or convalescent shelters that could respond to the injuries sustained during the fight, or the outbreak of malaria, yellow fever, pellagra, and other illnesses set loose by the largest displacement of Americans in the nation's history.[20] Disease and illnesses loomed over the lives of the nearly four million slaves freed by the end of the war. The collapse of the plantation system during the conflict meant that formerly enslaved people were often estranged from the family and kinship networks that Black people created for themselves to weather the violence of slavery. Those networks had provided shelter, clothing, food, and medical care. As often happens during war, families were displaced and fractured, sometimes permanently. This not only left Black Americans vulnerable to homelessness, starvation, and illness; it also created the conditions for epidemics and preventable death to thrive in the towns and cities where they found refuge.

During Reconstruction (1865–77), the US government developed a response to the health crisis created in the wake of the Civil War, taking some responsibility for the sordid state of affairs facing the new citizens of the nation. On March 3, 1865, President Lincoln signed an act to establish what was officially called the "Bureau of Refugees, Freedmen, and Abandoned Lands.[21] Commonly known as the Freedmen's Bureau, it was charged with rebuilding the South and protecting the health and safety of Black people. This was the first time the federal government would be directly committed to the well-being of the American public at this scale. But this unprecedented health intervention remained a modest response to a crisis that would require long-term investment and coordination between federal and state governments—something difficult to achieve in the wake of a war where the nation disagreed over the freedom and personhood of Black people.

Avoiding reenslavement after Emancipation was dependent on the ability to work and provide for oneself and one's family. Many Black people could not achieve this independence and were forced to return to plantations or were sent to labor in work camps and prisons.[22] Congress intended for the bureau to offer only limited support along a path toward self-subsistence. This was clear given the limited reach of the bureau; it operated in just fifteen cities in the South, and the hospitals they created were designed largely to deal with local outbreaks—the medical care provided fell significantly short of the vision that Black people and reformers hoped for near the end of the Civil War.

This unprecedent investment in the public's health ended in 1872 when Congress abolished the Freedmen's Bureau. Historians often explain that the Freedmen's Bureau was dismantled as states in the South grew impatient with federal institutions operating within territories that should be under the control of states. While there is truth to this, it fails to capture the heart of the issue: Southern states wanted the freedom to neglect Black people—and any other population they deemed undesirable. Health and education are the tools of power, and an investment from federal institutions into the well-being of the formerly enslaved was tragically seen as a threat to the supremacy and freedom that white Americans enjoyed. The Freedmen's Bureau established institutions that attempted to integrate Black people into the nation as proper citizens worthy of dignity and care. White Americans, in the South and the North, were insulted by this effort and rejected the idea that the federal government might constrain states into being concerned with the health, education, and well-being of Black people or any project designed to view them as members of American democracy. Black health continues to suffer the consequences of the federal government's retreat from their life chances.

Racist ideas about the inferior health and longevity of Black people played a role in this opposition to federal investment into their health. Circulating at the turn of the twentieth century were the vile beliefs of the eugenics movement, which had spread rapidly in western Europe and the United States.[23] The eugenics movement was set into motion by the influence and reception of Darwinian evolution among Anglo-speaking anthropologists who believed that the course of human development could be improved by controlling which races reproduced. Men of science and medicine believed that the talents, intelligence, moral behavior, and physical health of humans were fixed and bound to the biology of their race. Racial groups that were unfit or inferior, it was believed, would fall ill, die young, and gradually perish. Far too many American leaders believed in the infamous mantra of social Darwinist Herbert Spencer that the survival of the human species would be determined by the fittest. Why, then, should the federal government or any state institution be concerned with a population one generation removed from slavery and not likely to see the end of the twentieth century?

This was the position of the late nineteenth-century statistician and health scientist Frederick Hoffman. As an employee of the Prudential Life Insurance Company, Hoffman published *Race Traits and Tendencies of the American Negro* in 1896. The book presented a data-driven case that the high rates of illness, early death, illegitimacy, and criminal activity were heritable racial traits unique to Black people—not a reflection of a society where government institutions had retreated from their well-being and healthcare. Hoffman believed that the looming disappearance of the race should discourage the use of state resources for providing Black people with improved access to medical care, better housing, or education.

Hoffman's claims about Negro extinction complemented other myths about Black inferiority that had been circulating in medical textbooks and legal arguments against enfranchising Black people since before the time of slavery.[24] The fact that Hoffman's case was based on data—which he willfully misconstrued to support his position—and that he was German-born gave his theory an air of impartiality that allowed it to thrive in the minds of many Americans.

Myths about the impending death of Black people and their assumed biological differences from whites were parroted in fifteen-cent illustrated monthlies like the *North American Review*, *Century Magazine*, and *Popular Science*, which were read in millions of white middle-class homes.[25] Although these racist ideas were used to justify slavery, they took on increased political and economic significance as the nation pondered what to do about the so-called Negro problem in the wake of Reconstruction. The great American sociologist W. E. B. Du Bois wrote in *The Philadelphia Negro*—one of the first sociological studies of Black life in the US—that "the most difficult social problem in the matter of Negro health is the peculiar attitude of the nation toward the well-being of the race. There have, for instance, been few other cases in the history of civilized peoples where human suffering has been viewed with such peculiar indifference."[26]

At the end of Reconstruction Black people were left, once again, to care for themselves or rely on the wavering political will of local governments to construct segregated, poorly resourced public hospitals and social services that provided access to care, shelter, and other provisions vital for sustaining health and well-being.

HEALTH PROGRESSES

American ideas about health took a partial step forward during the Progressive Era (1900–1930).[27] Progressives believed that state institutions should be active in the lives of Americans and committed to the use of science to improve government and the health of populations. Out of this belief emerged an uneasy, paternalistic, but productive alliance of reform-minded doctors, housing developers, advocates for the poor, chemists, civil engineers, labor unions, and activists who were committed to elevating the lives of Americans.[28] Reform at this time, however, moved in two different directions.

At one level reformers thought seriously about how the infrastructure of a city, state, or nation influenced who was healthy, who was ill, and who might die early. Progressive reformers focused on creating clean water, better housing, a shorter work week, access to fresh produce and meats, waste removal, and basic education as paths toward a healthier and more advanced society. This attention to conditions within the control of local, state, and federal power reflected the larger goals of reformers who tried to mitigate the detrimental impact of industrial growth and capitalism on health of the nation.

For example, in 1902, Congress changed the United States Public Health Service (USPHS)—which since the eighteenth century had been concerned with the health of the military—into a public-facing investigative unit charged with researching the causes of communicable disease, sanitation, and water safety. Progressive reformers also fought successfully for the passage of the Pure Food and Drug Act of 1906, which aimed to protect the American public from dangerous substances in food and drugs by requiring manufacturers to label their products. The act would later lead in 1930 to the creation of the Food and Drug Administration, whose task has been to regulate the safety of food and medications available to consumers.

At the same time, however, ideas about American health during the Progressive Era were thoroughly influenced by the eugenics movement, racial hygiene, and more generally the sentiment that there were populations in America who did not belong to the nation and could even perish without raising much concern. During this time Progressives supported the separation of racial groups, redlining practices that limited the quality of and access to healthcare, and even sterilization and birth control measures intended to limit the reproduction of the least fit. Progressives were quite comfortable with beliefs about the inferiority of non–Anglo-Saxon populations and the misguided notion that many races would suffer until their stock was improved through coercion and the leadership of the most talented within a given race—the inspiration for Du Bois's well-known slogan for the Black elite, the Talented Tenth.[29] Progressive economists and social scientists were especially prolific in their backhanded assessment of the cultural factors involved in "the Negro problem" in America.[30] For example, the renowned Progressive economist and Harvard professor Thomas Nixon Carver declared: "There is no instance in history of a race that has achieved an honorable position in the world until it had developed a feeling of race pride and race solidarity. In my opinion the greatest present weakness of the Colored race in America is the lack of this feeling."[31]

Carver's claim that the behavior and talents of Black Americans ultimately determined the destiny of the race reflected larger sentiments held by Progressives and racial segregationists who blamed the victims of discrimination for their low social status, cultural inferiority, and early deaths—the resonances between the past and present seem apparent here. The proliferation of this type of thinking left nonwhite communities vulnerable to urban development projects that exposed them to hazardous waste, landfills, and other known causes of illness and disease. It also constrained wages and limited access to unions, national organizations, and other democratic institutions that might offer cover from the discriminatory practices of the state and urban developers. The refusal to see Black people and other nonwhite groups as equal members of the nation and worthy of protection left these same communities exposed to high rates of unemployment, discriminatory policing, and disproportionate representation in jails, insane asylums, and labor camps.

The two sides of Progressive Era reforms, one broad and concerned with systems that improve quality of life and the other coercive and discriminatory, produced unequal effects on the life chances of Americans. On the one hand, average American life expectancy started an upward trajectory during the Progressive Era, with the life expectancy of Black Americans moving from 33 years old in 1900 to 72.3 years old by 2002 and that of white Americans during this same period moving from 47.6 years old to 77.7 years old.[32] On the other hand, countless lives were diminished, unborn, or lost due to the coercive reforms of this period: advocating for birth control within poor communities; hygiene education that discouraged the upper classes from having children with people from different racial backgrounds; counseling programs that discouraged young couples from having children with partners with a family history of disease, illness, immoral behavior, drug use, or alcoholism; the forced sterilization of mothers who could not care for their children; profiling and policing of social delinquents; anti-miscegenation laws; and the exclusion of Chinese immigrants and restrictive quotas for other immigrant groups. The face of coercive reform was not always white. Black people who were upper-class and socially mobile also championed progressive programs aimed at the poor, ill, and unclean.[33] Discriminatory ideas about race, biology, and health pervaded nearly every aspect of American life at this time.[34]

Still, when the Progressive Era came to an end in the 1930s, it seemed possible that the federal government might develop a comprehensive national health agenda that integrated public health science with advancements in medicine. This vision reflected the belief that modern statecraft should be led by scientific innovations that make government more technical, efficient, and active in the lives of Americans. Using science, the federal government could establish goals for the healthcare and life expectancy of the nation.

There was momentum for this unified health system. President Franklin D. Roosevelt's New Deal (1933–39) established the Social Security

Act and other measures designed to protect the financial future and well-being of Americans. In 1944 Congress passed the Public Health Service Act, which gave the federal government authority to establish quarantine mandates for each of the fifty states. It also made the USPHS responsible for managing the spread of communicable diseases from foreign countries. Then, in 1946, the federal government moved the Communicable Disease Center (the predecessor of today's CDC) under the USPHS, providing it with scientific resources to investigate outbreaks such as typhus, dysentery, rabies, and the plague. By 1951, the CDC had eliminated malaria in the US. At the federal level, government institutions were expanding and taking on a more active role in the lives of all Americans.

FRACTURED HEALTH

But the prospect of a health agenda led by the federal government that could coordinate the states and pull together the science of public health with individual medicine ultimately never launched. Although Roosevelt established Social Security benefits for vulnerable Americans and set the conditions for expanding the work of the USPHS, he stopped short of advancing national health insurance, which would have been the key to unlocking a healthcare system where the federal government could regulate the cost, access, and goals of medical care at the national level. Roosevelt said, "What we can do is lay a foundation on which we can build a structure to give a greater measure of safety and happiness to the individual than any we have ever known."[35] Roosevelt's use of the word "structure" here was important: national infrastructure for healthcare in America had been missing since the end of Reconstruction, and in its absence the public's health was subject to the whims and motivations of local governments. Roosevelt also seemed to recognize the necessity of coordinating federal and state institutions if American life expectancy was going to continue to rise.

But America in 1930 was racially segregated. The only way to establish "safety and happiness" would be to build healthcare systems that could work with state governments that were actively discriminating against Black and nonwhite residents. Federal power on the matter of American health could have reduced health inequities. Black babies continued to perish from pneumonia and influenza at elevated rates between 1949 and 1961, while white families lost significantly fewer babies from these same illnesses during this time.[36]

When Harry S. Truman became president in 1945, he started working on a universal national health insurance program that would offer Americans security from the economic effects of illness and disease.[37] Truman's proposal emulated universal healthcare policies in Germany, Britain, and many other European nations that by 1911 had passed national legislation using public resources to increase access to care and offer economic relief for wages lost to illness.

Three major obstacles stood in the way of realizing a coordinated vision between state and federal power on the matter of American health equity: the American Medical Association's (AMA) opposition to national healthcare, the Democratic Party's ambivalence over the rights of Black Americans, and growing bipartisan support for employer-based insurance.

Lobbyists for private health insurance, the American Hospital Association, and the AMA opposed the role of the federal government in setting an agenda for American medicine. The health insurance industry wanted to control their exposure to unhealthy patients that might raise premiums and cut into profits. Hospitals and medical professionals also wanted to remain free from government mandates and preserve the right to charge for services and refuse patients. AMA launched an aggressive campaign opposing Truman's healthcare reforms that framed his efforts as moving the country dangerously toward the path of socialized medicine and totalitarianism.[38] The AMA also argued that most employers were providing insurance for their workers as a result of the successes of the labor movement during the Progressive Era, making national health insurance redundant. Of course, Black people were less likely to be employed in settings where insurance was a benefit and often had to find domestic work or unconventional forms of labor to earn money, which prevented them from accessing insured healthcare.

Southern Democrats also viewed Truman's national health insurance proposal as an attempt to use medicine as a tool for desegregation—which indirectly it surely was. Southern Democrats feared that if national insurance was successful, it would grant Black patients in the South access to white doctors, and Black physicians in return would be free to treat white patients.[39] As the historian Daniel Sledge has explained, even though Southern Democrats were a core part of the New Deal coalition that pushed for greater federal intervention into public health, they passionately opposed national policies that aimed to address the health needs of Black Americans and other vulnerable populations.

By 1953 Truman and liberals within the Democratic Party had been defeated. Liberal advocates for national health insurance would take an incremental approach, finding their aspirations only partially realized in 1965 when Congress, under President Johnson, created Medicare and Medicaid, which established a national system of hospital insurance and physician care for the elderly, and coordinated federal and state government resources to provide insurance and healthcare for families with children and low-income populations.[40] But the ambitious prospect of unifying public health science with individual medical treatment for everyone was lost. Truman wrote in his 1956 memoir:

> Democracy thrives on debate and political differences. But I had no patience with the reactionary selfish people and politicians who fought year after year every proposal we made to improve the people's health. I have had some bitter disappointments as President but one that has troubled me most, in a personal way, has been the failure to defeat organized opposition to a national compulsory health insurance program.[41]

Truman was, however, optimistic about the future, acknowledging that "this opposition has only delayed and cannot stop the adoption of an indispensable federal health insurance plan."

Still, for the time being, concessions to conservatives and racial segregationists fractured the very idea of public health, dividing the nation between those with and without the means to access care and modern advancements in medicine and science.

In 1958, the Nationwide Family Medical Care Expenditure Survey interviewed three thousand US households about their health expenses and healthcare coverage. Although the survey was small, it was one of the first studies into the inequalities in American healthcare access. Only half of the Black households in the study had health insurance, whereas 75 percent of white households had coverage.[42] Black households spent less each year on medical care than white families, even though both groups reported similar rates of heart disease, arthritis, kidney disease, and high blood pressure. The study revealed that Black families without insurance simply did not seek care, spending 60 percent less on medical care than white families without insurance. This disparity was found even among Black families with insurance, who spent 44 percent less on medical care than insured white families. There were simply not enough medical facilities to meet the health needs of Black Americans who did carry insurance or had the means to pay for care.

White families not only had access to regular care, but the quality was better. They had use of vitamin supplements and fortified food to address health deficiencies, X-rays in hospitals, modern surgery techniques that were safer due to the availability of antibiotics, and new vaccines. The study shed light on the disparities between Black and white health. Between 1900 and 1948 Americans in the South continued to die from infectious diseases at a rate significantly higher than the North.[43] Driving this disparity were the large number of Black Americans in Southern cities and rural areas grappling with life-diminishing racism that remained after the end of Reconstruction. In the grip of racial segregation and white supremacy, Black Americans continued to live in outdated and unsafe housing, were the focus of very few social programs run by local governments in the South, had very little access to vaccines and other forms of modern medicine, and in many cases were unemployed or underemployed, which was the vehicle that provided access to healthcare.[44] Black families were forced to seek treatment in segregated hospitals with inferior facilities and not enough beds. If they attended hospitals that were not segregated, they were very often the last to receive care. Racist discrimination in medical school admissions exacerbated matters, as historically Black colleges could not produce enough physicians able to meet the health needs of Black and other nonwhite communities around the nation.

This fracturing of American health experiences coincided with significant changes within the science of public health. The fields of bacteriology, chemistry, virology, and the life sciences more generally underwent rapid advancement due to private and state funding. These developments gave rise to a new type of public health scientist who was committed to specialization rather than broad interdisciplinary work; unlike in the Progressive Era, public health scientists were increasingly less interested in the connections between the infrastructure of cities, labor, healthcare access, and food supplies. New academic journals, professional societies, and the growing prestige of life science and public health departments at Harvard, Johns Hopkins, and Cold Springs Harbor were all part of the growing specialization of public health science. While this trend was happening across nearly all academic fields during and after the World War period, it had the effect of diminishing the broad vision of health that had previously united Progressive Era reformers at the start of the century. The science that now studied "the people's health" was increasingly led by technical experts trained to speak and collaborate with one another rather than with the worker, layperson, or activist who advocated on behalf of vulnerable people. Even science writing changed dramatically during this time, with experts adopting an impersonal, quantitative, and detached prose that facilitated fact-driven technical analysis that dared not touch the moral, political, and societal issues implicated within "public health." Observations about microorganisms, cell biology, disease pathways, and eventually genetic mutations became the common vocabulary of public health scientists. This made it very difficult to sustain a vision of the people's health that could translate scientific discovery across different fields and remain clear about the political and moral stakes of such efforts—never mind issues of racial equity or social justice.

By the 1960s American health was increasingly seen on a petri dish rather than in the streets or the public square. Public health interventions had become politicized, and many scientists wanted to avoid having their work dismissed as socialist—like the AMA had done against the Truman administration during his push for national health insurance during the 1940s. Instead, public health professionals stuck to producing non-partisan truths about disease in the human body. This turn toward bench science inspired a technical view of health that was grounded by evidence and data but no longer connected to the concerns of everyday people managing health on their own—much like the medical examiner who replaced the coroner during this time. Federal funding also moved away from community-centered programs and instead toward basic sciences, opening the door for the pharmaceutical industry to offer technological fixes to illness, disease, and death that had social and political causes.[45] The prevention of disease took a back seat to federal funding priorities invested in finding pharmaceutical cures for health inequalities sustained by the resistance of the AMA, hospital associations, and officials that wanted the freedom to mistreat and ignore the health of Black people and any other politically vulnerable population.

Healthcare in Los Angeles during the 1960s offers a tragic illustration of the inequalities created and sustained in nonwhite communities.

FIGHTING SLOW DEATH

Helen Jones, the mother of John Horton III, explained to me that in 1959 John's grandparents, Pearlie Mae Ross and Clifton Ross, made their way to Watts, California, from Oklahoma City. They were looking for a better life than what was possible in the Jim Crow South. Los Angeles and Long Beach were home to the largest ports in Southern California, making both cities ideal for the defense industry that emerged there during the interwar period. Between 1940 and 1965 the Black population nearly tripled as the city attracted migrants from New Mexico, Texas, Louisiana, Mississippi, and Oklahoma.[46] Racial land covenants, however, limited most Black and Latino residents to South Los Angeles, a fifty-one-square-mile urban area south of downtown and six miles east of Venice Beach. Just over a half million Black people lived in South Los Angeles in 1965, making it one of the largest Black spaces in the county at the time.[47] They were machine operators, assemblers in manufacturing plants, craftsmen, clerical workers, domestics, and many were also unemployed.

In 1965 more than one-quarter of all families in South Los Angeles lived below the poverty line, with many families of four making less than $32,000 a year in today's currency. Black men and women living in Watts faced a 13.2 percent unemployment rate—more than double that of the entire Los Angeles–Long Beach Metropolitan Area and twice as high as the national average for nonwhites in 1965.[48] Black infant mortality in South Los Angeles was also twice as high as the citywide average, and very few children were immunized against diphtheria, whooping cough, smallpox, or polio. The healthcare infrastructure was all but broken: there were only 106 physicians for every 252,000 residents in South Los Angeles and only 454 beds available in the eight for-profit hospitals operating in the region.[49] The two public hospitals serving South Los Angeles residents, County General Hospital and Harbor General Hospital, were eighteen miles north of Watts and ten miles to the south, respectively—well over an hour of travel time on public transportation.

This was the situation faced by the Ross family—John's grandparents—when they made the Imperial Court projects their home in 1959. They witnessed the Watts uprising just a few years later. It was proceeded by protests that began in the summer of 1964 where Black people in Harlem, Rochester, Chicago, and Philadelphia had grown tired of the discrimination and white hatred thinning their lives.[50] The street rebellions that followed were ignited by violence often perpetuated by police and white citizens who believed they were guardians of systems that favored white families but consumed Black and Latino communities.

The uprising in Watts began with the arrest of twenty-one-year-old Marquette Frye and his brother Ronald at the intersection of 116th Street and Avalon—a mere two miles west of John's grandparents' first home. Like John's family, Marquette was originally from Oklahoma; he came to Watts as a teenager in 1957 after a brief stay in rural Wyoming. Marquette, Ronald, and their mother, Rena Price—who rushed to the scene when word traveled that her sons were in trouble—were all violently beaten by white police in what appeared to be a dispute over a traffic violation.[51] Police were clearly engaged in racial profiling, and Black bystanders joined in defense of the Fryes. Soon after, banks, retail stores, markets, and other establishments were the targets of unrest. Each represented white wealth, economic mobility, and political power that contributed to the slow death of Black and Latino residents in segregated Los Angeles. Literary scholar Lauren Berlant used the term "slow death" to capture the "physical wearing out of a population and the deterioration of people in that population that is very nearly a defining condition of their experience and historical experience."[52] Black protesters in Los Angeles were literally fighting for their lives.

The rebellion lasted six days, with police taking thirty-four lives and injuring countless others. Marquette would become the reluctant face of the uprising and an outspoken critic of injustice throughout Los Angeles. He also spent the rest of his life suffering from debilitating health conditions and being targeted by state violence; he was arrested a reported twenty-eight times and often beaten by deputies while in the Los Angeles County jail system. Marquette, now living under an assumed name, died from pneumonia at the age of forty-two with an immune system weathered by the city he called home.[53]

Media commentary, reports, and official investigations released after the uprising explained that segregation, unemployment rates, poverty, underserved schools, and hostile encounters with police had taken their toll on the spirit and well-being of Black and Latino people living in South Los Angeles. Jack Conway, deputy director of the Office of Economic Opportunity, told the House Appropriations Subcommittee on October 10, 1965, "If I were to try to place some responsibility on [the uprising], I would say that most of the programs in Los Angeles are administered in a very impersonal way, quite detached from the people and quite removed from the places where the problems are concentrated."[54] President Lyndon Johnson, who took a conservative stance on the unrest, claimed it "bore no relation to the orderly struggle for civil rights that has ennobled the last decade." Yet he could not deny its cause. "The bitter years that preceded the riots, the death of hope where hope existed, their sense of failure to change the conditions of life—these things no doubt led to these riots."[55]

In their interview with the Frye brothers on September 9, 1965, reporters at the *Los Angeles Sentinel* refused to call the uprising a riot.

Reporters explained, "A riot is senseless mob violence. . . . What happened in Watts in 1965 was a revolt, rebellion and certainly, civil unrest."[56] Whether Americans condoned the protests or not, it was clear to many that the uprising—along with the lives lost before and after—could have been prevented and were the consequences of systemic discrimination.

The Watts Rebellion was a response to death and violence hiding in plain sight.[57] It shared features with the scores of rebellions around the nation led by Black Americans and other aggrieved groups against systemic racism diminishing their lives.[58]

DECLINING HEALTH

At the end of the twentieth century plans for the people's health remained trapped in debates over the role of the federal government to establish a nationwide health agenda that improved access to care and aligned the nation's overall health with the plans of public health science. Between the Reagan and Clinton administrations physician associations, insurance companies, and lobbyists for the pharmaceutical industry continued to impede efforts to make health affordable and equitable for Americans. These obstacles, combined with a less regulated and less welfare-oriented economy, have left Americans dying earlier than citizens of other nations.

When President Obama signed the Affordable Care Act (ACA) into law in 2010, it was the most comprehensive federal investment into health services since Congress approved the expansion of Medicaid under the Johnson administration in 1965. The act included provisions requiring individuals to have coverage, helped states establish affordable care options covered by insurance, prohibited denial for coverage based on a preexisting condition, expanded Medicaid eligibility for the poor and low-income individuals, and also offered tax incentives for employers who provided health insurance.

The final version of Obama's ACA was a compromise—his original goal was to create a single national health insurance plan like the National Health Service in the UK, which would allow the US federal government to directly regulate the costs of insurance, hospital visits, and medications. The ACA would increase healthcare access but did not allow the federal government to regulate insurance and healthcare costs for everyone. Despite several legal efforts by conservatives and the Trump administration to dismantle the ACA, many of its provisions remain popular among Americans in both parties, and there is evidence that American health has improved since its passage.

Like Truman and Johnson, Obama faced charges of overreach by the federal government into health matters best left to the states and individual consumer choice. States that opposed the ACA challenged the constitutionality of the mandate that individuals have coverage and the expansion of Medicaid. The fiercest opposition came from Southern Democrats and Republicans who paradoxically represented communities devastated by the loss of blue-collar jobs, weakening labor unions, school systems in disrepair, opioid addiction, poor health outcomes, and a dissolving social safety net. The ACA contained provisions that would remedy some of these problems. But the forces of racial resentment that opposed equal access to healthcare in the previous century were now standing in the way of healthcare provisions that would benefit white Americans and the nation as a whole. As the historian Jonathan Metzl has explained:

> When politics demands that people resist available health care, amass arsenals, cut funding for schools that their own kids attend, or make other decisions that might feel emotionally correct but are biologically perilous, these politics are literally asking people to die for their whiteness. Living in a state or a county or a nation dominated by a politics of racial resentment then becomes a diagnosable, quantifiable, and increasingly mortal preexisting condition.[59]

The retreat of the federal government from the health of Black Americans evolved over time into a broader indifference for the health of vulnerable Americans regardless of race. Poor whites living in the Rust Belt or the South face the same structures of limited access and incompetent medicine that has long diminished the life chances of Black people. In the absence of state investment, we've grown comfortable living with illness, disease, and early death.

The data bears this out. Since the 1980s American life expectancy has steadily fallen when compared to other nations. In 1933 life expectancy in the United States ranked eighth behind the Netherlands, Norway, Australia, Sweden, Denmark, Switzerland, and Canada. By 1950 life expectancy in the US fell behind eleven other nations, with Americans living on average sixty-eight years. Between 1983 and 2009, the United States saw its most dramatic decline in life expectancy, falling from 15th to 32nd in the world's ranking. Just before the COVID-19 pandemic the US ranked 40th in average global life expectancy, with Americans projected to live shorter lives than populations living in Albania and Lebanon. In 2020 Americans were dying earlier than people in Greece, Hong Kong, Chile, Slovenia, and Thailand.[60]

Life expectancy within each of the fifty states varies.[61] Between 1959 and 2019, American life expectancy has declined most rapidly in Southern states and the Midwest where the politics of racial resentment and opposition to the rights and healthcare of Black Americans were strongest during and after racial segregation.

When US Mortality Database estimates began in 1959, South Carolina had the nation's lowest life expectancy. If South Carolina were a country, it would have ranked 34th in global life expectancy at that time.[62] According to CDC data, the average life expectancy in South Carolina in 2019 was 76.8 years, which was two years below the national average and placed it among the ranks of the ten least healthy states in the nation.[63] There was also a 3.5-year gap in life expectancy between European Americans (77.5 years) and Black Americans (74.1). The state's poor health can be explained when placed in historical context: it was the first state to secede from the Union, it had some of the nation's most aggressive racial segregation laws during the twentieth century, and it led the nation's opposition to ACA under the leadership of then attorney general Henry McMaster and later governor Nikki Haley. In 2019, South Carolina had one of the nation's highest rates of uninsured residents and faced ongoing healthcare-access issues, especially in rural areas.

Healthcare advocates and the business sector called on state leaders to expand Medicaid but were rebuffed.

In 1959, Kansas ranked first in national average life expectancy, making it comparable to the Netherlands and Denmark. In 2019 Kansas ranked 30th in national average life expectancy according to the CDC.[64] In recent years, Kansas has adopted tax cuts and defunded public education, which has hurt the economic mobility of the state's residents, including the white working class.[65] During the Obama administration Kansas joined the multistate lawsuit challenging the ACA's constitutionality and rejected state-based health insurance and Medicaid expansion; it was one of seventeen states that experienced the most significant decline in life expectancy between 2010 and 2019.[66]

Although all fifty states have contributed to the nation's drop in life expectancy, the South and Midwest experienced the most dramatic declines in health outcomes, making an outsized contribution to America's lower quality of life. Those declines were especially felt in states that were the former seat of racial segregationists, states that opposed the ACA, or states that sat along the Rust Belt with large white working-class majorities.[67] For example, Ohio and Mississippi challenged the expansion of Medicaid and the constitutionality of the ACA despite witnessing staggering declines in life expectancy between 2010 and 2019.[68] According to the CDC, Ohio and Mississippi rank 42nd and 51st, respectively, in national average life expectancy in 2019 before the pandemic.[69]

While we should celebrate that the majority of states initially adopted the ACA or changed their position in support of the expansion of Medicaid, one can't help but wonder about young children and babies yet to be born in states that continue to face inequitable healthcare access. Declining life expectancy keeps the score of how much our nation's racist and discriminatory past will cost us in the future.

JUSTICE FOR ALESIA?

We return now to the story of Alesia Thomas. What could we say about her death if we recognized the larger history of racial discrimination and state neglect for the health and well-being of Black Americans? What would it look like to see more than simply nature inside her body? These are questions we can answer. Contemporary public health has rediscovered its interdisciplinary roots and recommitted itself to health equity and broad visions for how to improve the people's health, much like at the end of the nineteenth century and during the Progressive Era. As a result, new collaborations have emerged between public health scientists, sociologists, physical and mental health professionals, and legal scholars to identify the social and political causes ending people's lives prematurely—especially the lives the Black people.

The medical examiner who conducted Alesia's autopsy cited bipolar disorder, cocaine, sickle cell trait, and struggle with police as causes for her death—factors that made it difficult to determine what killed her. Bipolar disorder, however, is not a terminal condition. It is a mood disorder whose symptoms include bouts of mania and depression. While studies show that people diagnosed with bipolar have an average life expectancy of sixty-seven years, Alesia was thirty-five years old when she died.[70] Studies show that reduced life expectancy for people with bipolar is driven largely by natural causes, which are deaths due to illness or diseases that most often manifest later in life.[71] Alesia was not ill or sick when she died. She was, however, in the presence of law enforcement.

Recent public health research also shows that a great number of people suffering from mental illness lose their lives during violent encounters with police. A joint study between researchers at the CDC and the John Jay College of Criminal Justice at CUNY published an article in the *American Journal of Preventative Medicine* estimating that 25 percent of fatal police encounters in the US involve people with mental illness, and 76 percent of people who lost their lives to police brutality had mental health treatment at some point.[72] They found that while not every interaction between the mentally unwell and the police results in death, a significant number of these transactions end in violence. These observations were confirmed by researchers at the University of Toronto and Yale University who published a study in 2021 analyzing six years of data on police use of force and civilian injury from multiple departments across the country.[73] Six of the police departments requested not to be named in the study, and data from the remaining departments came from Los Angeles, Dallas, and New Orleans. Researchers found that 20 percent of the people injured during police interactions had severe mental illness. They also found that people with serious mental illness were 11.6 times more likely to experience police use of force than people who are mentally well.

Simply not having adequate access to mental health resources, what researchers call unmet need, can also lead to violence at the hands of police. An interdisciplinary research team of public health scientists, criminologists, and sociologists published a recent study examining the relationship between people living in urban centers who had unmet mental health needs and the chances of these same people having violent interactions with police. To have unmet needs means someone is unwell but cannot access proper or consistent care. Unmet mental health needs are linked to lower quality of life, frequent emergency room visits, substance abuse issues, challenges at the workplace, and early death.[74] Much of the research has tried to explain this issue by examining flaws in the healthcare delivery system, limits to insurance, and availability of providers, along with the severity of the illness and trust in medical care providers. However, scholars are now beginning to recognize that law enforcement is in effect resolving the disarray created by health systems. People with unmet mental health needs are significantly more likely to have negative and violent encounters with the police than those able to meet with a mental health professional regularly or who had no mental health issues.

When mental health needs go unaddressed, Americans often self-medicate. Conservative estimates say that between 21.9 and 24.1 percent of Americans with mood or anxiety disorders are subsidizing unmet mental health needs with alcohol or some form of controlled substance.[75] These figures become even more concerning given the nation's spiraling epidemic of controlled substance and prescription drug abuse. According to the US Department of Health and Human Services, one in seven people in the United States are expected to develop substance use disorder; only one in ten people will receive treatment for their condition.

A postmortem toxicological analysis found 0.45 mg/mL of cocaine in the blood taken from Alesia's heart. There was also a 2.2 mg/mL of benzoylecgonine found in Alesia's system—which usually appears in the urine of someone whose liver has processed cocaine. These levels were well below the lethal dose for Alesia's height and weight. Alesia did not call a mental health professional during her crisis and instead went to police for help. The police who followed her home were not there to offer care or support—they were there to arrest her.

Alesia's family could not charge the white female officer involved in her death or the Los Angeles Police Department with homicide because her autopsy was classified by the Los Angeles medical examiner as undetermined. They were, however, able to bring felony assault charges in *People v. O'Callaghan*.[76] With help of civil rights attorney Benjamin Crump, Alesia's family revealed during trial the amount of violence she endured.

It was found that five officers arrived at Alesia's home, and she was restrained with a hobble tie, with her hands and feet bound together—this was why she could not walk down the stairs of her own volition. Use of force by police escalated when they attempted to place Alesia into the rear passenger side of the patrol vehicle. Officer and former marine Mary O'Callaghan told Alesia to move deeper into the vehicle. Alesia could be heard in the audio shared during trial saying, "I can't move" and "I can't breathe." The other officers pushed her deeper into the vehicle while O'Callaghan warned Alesia, "Knock it off, or I'll fucking cunt punt your ass." The door on the rear driver's side was open and Alesia's body spilled over into the free space—perhaps to get air or possibly from the sheer amount of force used against her. At this point Officer O'Callaghan told Alesia, "You better put your legs in or you're going to get fucking crushed." Again, Alesia's response was "I can't." O'Callaghan can be heard on camera calling Alesia "a fucking lard ass" and complaining that getting her into the car was like "roping cattle." At this point O'Callaghan used the car door frame and roof as leverage while she kicked Alesia repeatedly in the lower abdomen and groin, yelling, "Get the fuck in there!" The violence continued until the other officers told O'Callaghan to stop and reminded her that the dash camera was recording. When the attacks ended Alesia collapsed within view of the camera.

In court documents the physician who attempted to save Alesia's life is referred to as "the People's medical expert." They explained that Alesia's inability to move or breathe was consistent with signs that she was experiencing cardiac impairment. To the untrained and uncompassionate eye this could be viewed as defiance and noncompliance. O'Callaghan's defense attorney argued that her use of force was lawful and warranted. The jury disagreed and sentenced O'Callaghan to three years in jail for felony assault. In response to the sentence O'Callaghan argued that her lawyer was constitutionally ineffective on the grounds that they did not exclude evidence of Alesia's death and medical distress. O'Callaghan argued that this information would prejudice the jury in favor of Alesia. The court disagreed, arguing that Alesia's statements of distress should have been interpreted by any reasonable officer that she was not a threat to public safety or themselves. Felony assault charges are a rare victory—it is increasingly difficult to prove in court that police violence against civilians is unreasonable and excessive. Alesia's lawyers also agreed to a $2.5 million settlement with the Los Angeles City Council on behalf of her two children. The money of course will never fill the void of their mother's absence.

If Alesia lived in a different city, and perhaps another country, it is very likely that she would still be alive. Instead, political and legal dysfunction tallied in her body, creating the opportunity for her encounter with the law—Alesia went to the police for help and they responded with life-ending force. Long before the tragic day of her death, our nation's divestment in the health of Black Americans had taken its toll on Alesia's body. Her immobility in the face of the law provides us with a tragic symbol of what care looks like in America. In her final days—and certainly many moments prior—Alesia could not, through her will alone, manifest a healthier body or mind capable of meeting our society's unreasonable expectation that people should thrive in the absence of care.

The myth of American freedom has turned us into terrible caretakers. This is the first and most important thing you have to understand about dying in custody: the violent actions of law enforcement and the inadequacies of our death investigation system are not defects in state governance. Instead, they complete a process of neglect and indifference that have been steady features of American life. Americans have simply grown used to living in the absence of care and mistake this neglect for preexisting health conditions, mental illness, problems with substance abuse—as if those of us suffering were free to simply manifest better bodies or different decisions.

Any reasonable person would agree that a nation not fully committed to the well-being of the public will create unhealthy people. Yet, when confronted with unhealthy people, rarely do we think society is responsible. A state that convinces its people to believe it is not obligated to care for them—and that doing so would violate their freedom—is a dying republic.

CHAPTER 4

COLLECTING FRAGMENTS

The American historian Saidiya Hartman once explained that recovering the lives of enslaved Black women using records written by their captors was like telling an "impossible story." These stories were impossible because they required more imagination, compassion, and agency than what the archive would allow. The records were not created for us to know the victims. For Hartman, the point of telling these stories was not "to *give voice* to the slave, but rather to imagine what cannot be verified, a realm of experience which is situated between two zones of death—social and corporeal death—and to reckon with the precarious lives which are visible only in the moment of their disappearance."[1]

I believe Hartman's observation about telling impossible stories captures the difficulty of seeing the humanity of people killed by police using records written by the coroner and medical examiner. This archive is rife with contradictions. It is both sprawling and difficult to acquire. Its contents diminish the protagonist. Its prose favors police, jail staff, and lawmakers. Worse, these records leave readers with the sense that the victims were ultimately responsible, in one way or another, for their own deaths.

But if we take on the impossible task of recovering these lives taken by police—members of the public who are real only because their loved ones and allies insist they are—it is clear many have lived and died beyond the reach of democracy.[2] In fact, democracy has more than failed them; the terror of the law has made the chaos of death an enduring state of affairs for families and their communities, erasing the victims of police violence from our collective memory—like the deaths of enslaved women, men, and children lost to history.

Our blindness to these deaths is largely structural—though there are some who choose not to acknowledge people killed by police, much like there are those who refuse to confront slavery's horror and its enduring effects.

Knowing whose life has been taken by the law is not guaranteed by our Constitution. It is a privilege, determined by where you live and your access to power.

Only fourteen states in the US allow unconditional public access to autopsy reports. Whether the state is currently red or blue does not predict its policy on death records (figure 4.1). For example, New York, Delaware, and Massachusetts are all liberal-leaning states with a Democratic voting majority, yet all three exclude autopsies from their public records laws—these records are accessible only to next of kin, lawyers, and the medical doctor of the deceased. Alabama, Arkansas, and Texas are conservative states with a Republican majority, and their residents have full access to autopsy records. New Mexico and New Jersey sit somewhere between closed and open access, with each state allowing the public to acquire autopsies but only under specific conditions.

Communities thriving in spite of police violence helped me understand that autopsies offer a window into the health of a nation. The ability to read these records, sit with their implications, and evaluate for ourselves the missteps of the society we design is a source of power. The files are haunting, but bearing witness to them forced me to see the people we've abandoned in a nation that perpetuates inequality, the absence of care, economic uncertainty, and broken lives. Acknowledging the people lost to state violence is a pathway to political resilience—it empowers us to reject the unhealthy values poisoning our institutions and imaginations.

In this chapter we will see how lawmakers, police, and death investigators sustain public ignorance about the life-diminishing entanglements of our government. This is not an accident but an intended outcome of

FIGURE 4.1 States where autopsy files are protected by open records law

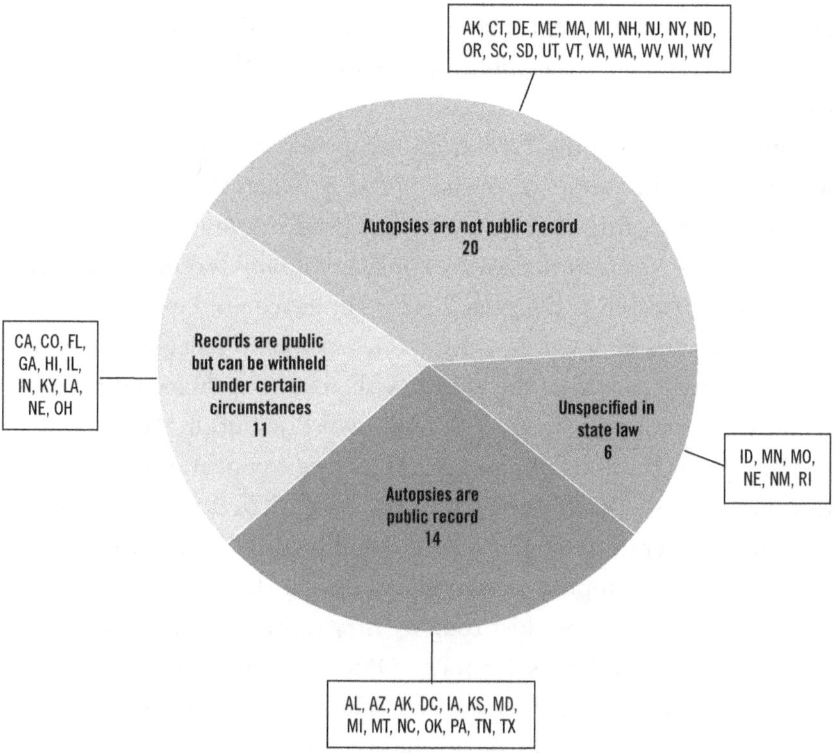

AK, CT, DE, ME, MA, MI, NH, NJ, NY, ND, OR, SC, SD, UT, VT, VA, WA, WV, WI, WY

Autopsies are not public record
20

CA, CO, FL, GA, HI, IL, IN, KY, LA, NE, OH

Records are public but can be withheld under certain circumstances
11

Unspecified in state law
6

ID, MN, MO, NE, NM, RI

Autopsies are public record
14

AL, AZ, AK, DC, IA, KS, MD, MI, MT, NC, OK, PA, TN, TX

Source: UCLA BioCritical Studies Lab, 2025

laws that have prevented public disclosure of autopsy records, increased policing, and neglected the infrastructure needed to gather data about state violence. Only a small number of us have the freedom to see the larger picture of when and how we are losing lives in police custody. This limited privilege reflects our nation's fears of direct democracy, an impoverished vision of who belongs to "the public," and the inability of Congress to mandate recordkeeping of lives taken by law enforcement. Dying in custody remains a silent crisis because record of the loss has been fragmented by design.

THE DEATH OF DANIEL PASTOREK

Living in an open-record state where autopsies are written for the public does not guarantee access. Local and state officials have the ability to redact, stall, and deny the public disclosure of death records even when mandated by law.

This is what Brittany Hailer, an independent journalist and fierce opponent of police violence, learned in 2020 when she tried to request the autopsy of an unhoused man who died inside a county jail in Pennsylvania—a state where autopsies are considered public record.[3] His name was Daniel Pastorek and he was a sixty-three-year-old white man who lived in Natrona Heights. It is a small town within Allegheny County, the former steel capital of the world, with about ten thousand residents living twenty miles northeast of downtown Pittsburgh. At the time of Daniel's death Pennsylvania ranked in the top ten of states whose residents had access to healthcare; it also ranked 47th in drug-related deaths and 34th in overall mental and behavioral health.[4] In 2020 Allegheny County faced a crippling economic recession that had started three years earlier. The county lost roughly fifty thousand jobs—more than any other county in Pennsylvania or Ohio over the same time period.[5] When jobs evaporate, shelter follows. The year that Daniel died there were 574 unhoused people in the county, and more than half of them suffered from substance use disorder or a mental health condition.[6]

Daniel was vulnerable to the broken parts of Allegheny County, and the wreckage eventually appeared inside his body. He was unemployed, without a home, coping with unmet mental health needs and using alcohol to self-medicate. Local police cited him multiple times for public drunkenness and hitchhiking. It was not long before Daniel amassed over a thousand dollars in fines and was sentenced to three months in jail when he couldn't pay. He was released on March 16, 2020, in an effort to reduce the incarcerated population during the COVID-19 pandemic. Daniel's public defender filed an appeal to reduce his jail time. But Daniel broke his foot shortly after his release and missed his court date. The county issued an arrest warrant and Daniel was returned to jail.

According to Hailer, who at the time was working for the *Pennsylvania Capital-Star*, Daniel had fallen ill inside jail, was put into solitary confinement, and then placed under suicide watch. Hailer spoke with other inmates who shared that Daniel cried out in agony for days, complaining of chest pains and vomiting. On November 26, 2020, after just nineteen days inside, Daniel was found dead on the floor of his cell.

Hailer wanted to know how and why Daniel had died. The Allegheny County Medical Examiner's Office, however, did not believe Daniel's death warranted an inquest; Pennsylvania state law gives medical examiners the discretion to decide if these public investigations are necessary. With no inquest for Daniel's passing, Hailer submitted a public records request for his autopsy and toxicology report under Pennsylvania's Right-to-Know (RTK) Law. The law stipulates that all state and local government agency records are presumed public unless stated otherwise. An official from the county's Office of Open Records denied Hailer's request for Daniel's death record, invoking the Coroner's Act of Pennsylvania. The act, originally passed in 1955, gave coroners the discretion to charge fees for "reports or documents requested by nongovernmental agencies in order to investigate a claim asserted under a policy of insurance or to determine liability for the death of the deceased."[7] Using a strained interpretation, Allegheny County argued that the act meant coroners were free to release autopsies only in situations involving an insurance claim or when establishing death liability. Lawyers for the county believed that the Coroner's Act excluded autopsies from public disclosure. Confident in their understanding of the law, the county sent Hailer a one-page email summarizing Daniel's death as natural and the result of "atherosclerotic cardiovascular disease." Hailer's investigation came to a dramatic halt.

SEALED RECORDS FROM THE BEGINNING

Each year US counties and states disclose how much they spend on repairing streets, firefighting, state employees, waste management, law enforcement, library book acquisitions, hospitals, and many other public goods. Releasing this information honors the belief that the state works on behalf of its people and is accountable for its service. These democratic commitments, however, are a recent political invention that required the imagination, will, and resolve of marginalized Americans and journalists.

America's founders were not champions of open government. They did not believe in state transparency or free access to state records. And they feared the idea of direct democracy. Nothing seemed more disastrous than placing political and economic decisions directly in the hands of common people. Our nation's founders dreaded the tyranny of the majority. After the ratification of the US Constitution, Alexander Hamilton proclaimed in June 1788: "That a pure democracy if it were practicable would be the most perfect government. Experience has proved that no position is more false than this. The ancient democracies in which the people themselves deliberated never possessed one good feature of government. Their very character was tyranny; their figure, deformity."[8] The historian Kathryn Carter argues in her work *Democracy in Darkness* that secrecy and concealment were central features of our nation's founding.[9] Experiments in transparency and disclosure often backfired, resulting in diminished public confidence in state government. Instead of a pure democracy, where the people influenced the direction of the nation, America's statesmen adopted federal and state constitutions where a voting majority chose officials who represented the public's interests. And it was only those officials who had intimate knowledge of how the state operated.

The officials who worked for the early republic mirrored the interests and desires of those with the power to vote. But this did not mean direct rule by the people or the ability of the public to shape government. It meant that from the very beginning the power of American democracy was fragmented. While elected officials at times appealed to the ideals of equity, freedom, and self-governance, they ultimately operated as independent actors accountable to their party and the more influential voters that put them into office. In the eighteenth century, most of the nation was not considered worthy to have their interests reflected by the state. The public, by which I mean the people who are recognized and protected by the state, was limited to free white men who were either educated, owned slaves, or had some form of inherited wealth. For those who could vote, printing presses were a mediator between the state and (white male) citizen.

In fact, during the American Revolution press houses played an enormous role in shaping sentiments about the rebellion through pamphlets and small books that disseminated its core ideas throughout the colonies and abroad. Printing presses were effective because they operated in a political climate that valued uncensored criticisms of the British Crown and then eventually the US government itself. Thomas Jefferson wrote in 1786 that "our liberty depends on the freedom of the press, and that cannot be limited without being lost."[10] The press that Jefferson and other founders spoke about was not newspapers, journals, and broadcasts of our present world, but actual press houses that distributed politically effective media to the educated voting class. Early beliefs about the free press were quite simple: printing presses that spoke openly about the state helped officials in a representative democracy establish trust and legitimacy in the eyes of a voting public who did not have direct control over state institutions. Press houses also gave the public whose interests were not represented by elected officials a venue for dissent.

This is what America's founders had in mind when writing about the freedom of speech in the Constitution. They believed government should protect the autonomy of the press to speak openly about government in public, empowering its voting members with enough knowledge that they either consented to being governed or channeled their discontent into civil forms of dissent and protest. Unrestricted access to state records, however, was not part of the bargain, even for printing presses. For the first 189 years of this nation's history, few Americans had access to our nation's official state records.

A PHILOSOPHY OF OPENNESS

Matters changed when Congress passed the Freedom of Information Act (FOIA) in 1966. FOIA offered the nation a general philosophy of far-reaching records disclosure, declaring that the American public had a right to information produced and recorded by federal agencies. The act entitled media, investigative journalists, and all citizens regardless of race, gender, or social status unprecedented access to government records.

FOIA was passed while the nation faced extraordinary cultural, political, and legal changes. This was the era of the Civil Rights Movement and the dawning of the New Left—a political force made up of young, educated radicals, civil rights activists, feminists, and members of organized labor. This group of diverse American voices had been left out of "the public" and pushed local, state, and federal institutions to reflect a new set of interests from an emerging social body dismayed by the failures of representative democracy. As the historian Michael Schudson has noted, FOIA captured a shared revolutionary spirit of transparency and disclosure where "American politics and society in this era became more fully democratic than they were before."[11] Open access to state records was a part of an effort to push American politics toward transparency, accountability, and pluralism.

American media were also instrumental in the movement for government transparency and accountability. As early as 1945 the Associated Press began advocating nationally for news journalists to have the freedom to pursue and access government information in their role as representatives of the public's interest. American journalists wanted to protect their craft from becoming state-controlled media like the Soviet Union. Open records and state transparency were paramount for this effort.[12] By the 1950s the American Society of Newspaper Editors also committed themselves to the cause of open records, forming an investigative committee interested in publicly disclosing government secrecy. The legal advisor of this committee was Harold Cross, who in 1953 published the widely influential book *The People's Right to Know*. The book revealed to the nation the poor state of record access and the complete lack of government disclosure.

Just a few years later the movement for an open government found advocates in Congress, with the work of John Moss—a relatively obscure Democrat from my hometown of Sacramento. Over the course of a decade Moss worked with the leaders in American news media and built allies in the Senate on the matter of open access to government information, democratic oversight of state institutions, and the role of the press in protecting the public's interests. These efforts paid off in 1966, when Congress passed FOIA.

Although FOIA represented the federal government's affirmation of the public's right to information, the actual pathway for public disclosure was largely left to individual agencies, which had the discretion to restrict and limit public access in the interest of security and privacy. More importantly, FOIA did not apply to records produced by individual states, Congress, the courts, or local government. Shortly after it was passed, states across the country wrote their own open-access regulations, often titled right-to-know laws, that specified which records were available for public discourse, which were not, and how members of the media or general public could access them.

DEATH IN CUSTODY REPORTING ACT

On July 11, 2023, Brittany Hailer won a lawsuit against Allegheny County for access to Daniel Pastorek's complete autopsy in the Commonwealth Court of Pennsylvania—nearly three years after his death in jail. She was represented by attorneys from the Reporters Committee for Freedom of the Press and the Yale Law School's Media Freedom and Information Access Clinic—two organizations carrying on the tradition of demanding government transparency that led to the passage of FOIA in 1966.

Pennsylvania is a state made up of many governments, municipalities, and townships that reflect the centers of power that emerged among white settlers during the eighteenth and nineteenth centuries. Counties and cities in Pennsylvania are organized by a class system based on population size. Each class of municipality operates under its own code of law. Larger cities or counties, like Philadelphia and Allegheny, belong to first- and second-class counties, respectively. Allegheny County claimed that its status as a second-class county, along with a very narrow interpretation of the state's Coroner Act, gave it the power to deny Hailer access to Daniel's autopsy. Less populated counties were able to obstruct the release of death records by charging $500 per file. This presented families with the terrible choice of either spending money on an autopsy or using precious resources to lay their loved ones to rest—too many chose the path of resignation and closure.

The Commonwealth court in *Allegheny County v. Brittany Hailer and Pittsburgh Current* reaffirmed that Pennsylvania's open records laws applied to all counties and that death records were written in the interest of the public good. Hailer's victory was historic. Judge Ellen Ceisler declared in the ruling opinion that releasing Allegheny County from Pennsylvania's open records laws

> would lead to the absurd result that a requester could receive autopsy records located anywhere in the Commonwealth, unless those records are located in [Allegheny] County or Philadelphia County. . . . There is no language in the [right-to-know law] or the Coroner's Act to suggest that access to certain public records depends on the county class in which the records are located.[13]

Hailer and I spoke shortly after the court's decision. I had been following the case carefully after filing and then eventually winning my own lawsuit against the Chester County coroner in southeastern Pennsylvania.[14] In 2022, I submitted a RTK request for the autopsies of seventeen people who died inside the county jail between 2008 and 2021. My request was denied by the Chester County coroner, who argued that autopsies were protected by HIPAA privacy rules and that the Coroner's Act empowered the office to refuse the public disclosure of death records during an ongoing investigation—Allegheny County made the same argument in the Hailer case. My case, *Chester County Office of the Coroner v. T. Keel, et al.*, was decided after *Allegheny County v. Hailer*; similarly, the court ruled that the coroner was obligated to uphold Pennsylvania's RTK laws and release autopsy records to my lab.

Being the first of its kind, the court's decision in *Allegheny County v. Hailer* was a victory for democratic transparency and accountability. Then Hailer saw what was missing in Daniel's death record. The medical examiner only conducted an external examination of his body. This apparently was enough to claim he had a lethal form of atherosclerotic cardiovascular disease. Hailer shared Daniel's autopsy with my lab. A mere four pages long, it was one of the thinnest death records I had ever seen. Hailer asked me, "How could the county say he died of heart disease without an internal examination of his body or even bothering to look at his heart?"[15] I was equally baffled by the medical examiner's lack of care and due diligence. I had seen dozens of autopsies where the person in custody supposedly died of heart disease, and most of those cases involved an internal examination of the body or the heart. While an external physical examination can reveal signs of cardiovascular illness, it is not considered the gold standard according to most physicians; the most reliable way to diagnose heart disease postmortem is removal and dissection of the heart, observing blockages in arteries and assessing the health of its chambers. No such examination was conducted for Daniel and the superficial assessment he was given appeared inconclusive in my judgment: Daniel's lower legs had no signs of swelling, his skin was free of blue or purple coloration, and there were no cholesterol deposits on the eyelids or other parts of his body—all common dermatological clues of serious cardiovascular illness. The county's toxicology report found no traces of alcohol, pharmaceuticals, or controlled substances in his blood. Also missing from the public record was an investigative report from the coroner who should have visited the scene of Daniel's death and provided an account of when he was last seen alive, who found him, the condition and placement of his body, whether resuscitation efforts were attempted, and the official time of his passing. Despite Hailer's victory for the residents of Allegheny County, Daniel's autopsy raised more questions than it answered. It offered only fragments of the truth.

Daniel's superficial autopsy mirrors the system the US uses to record in-custody death. On the surface death investigations appear concerned with recording the consequences of lethal police encounters. But a more careful assessment reveals that death records lack many details and are often unusable; the limited resources Congress has allocated to sustain it leave the impression that documenting police and custodial violence was an afterthought of state governance.

When I began studying lives lost to police violence, I tried searching for names. I knew several individuals but had no sense of how many other people locally and nationally also perished while in custody. At the time I believed that surely some agency within our government kept track of this information. Quickly I learned this was not the case. There is no comprehensive list of people killed by law enforcement for any given year in our nation's history. No government agency can tell you the exact number of people killed by police in 1965, 1972, or any calendar year. Investigative journalist Mike Masterson, of Ashbury Park Press, drew national attention to this shocking lack of information in 1995 when he released a study estimating that hundreds of people charged with minor offenses died in jail and detention centers each year around the country.[16] No one knew the true count, he argued, because the federal government did not track these data. Masterson shared his study with Congress, which within five years passed the Death in Custody Reporting Act (DCRA) of 2000. It required states to report every three months to the Bureau of Justice Statistics (BJS)—under the Department of Justice—the death of anyone who "is in the process of arrest, is en route to be incarcerated, or is incarcerated at a municipal or county jail, State prison, or other local or State correctional facility."[17]

DCRA, which became law in 2000, was ambitious but fatally flawed. Congress authorized an enormous data-gathering effort on a shoestring budget and provided little guidance on how to execute the law or ensure the compliance of law enforcement in reporting this data. As a result, the BJS relied on the voluntary reporting of police and correctional agencies. The BJS also had to use its own budget to float the act and track in-custody deaths. This was nearly an impossible task. In the US there are 1,566 state prisons, 3,116 local jails, 1,323 youth correctional facilities, 142 immigration detention facilities, and 80 Indian country jails.[18] According to the Prison Policy Initiative, these systems are responsible for the lives of 1.9 million people, or roughly three times the number of people living in Boston. There are also eighteen thousand law enforcement agencies around the country. To manage this incredible effort, the BJS had to rely on state and local governments to survey in-custody death on its behalf, resulting in patchy and inconsistent data. The BJS stopped gathering arrest-related data in 2014 after limited state participation.

In 2013, Virginia congressman Bobby Scott, one of the original authors of DCRA 2000, introduced a new bill, the Death in Custody Reporting Act of 2013, to help resolve some of the failures facing in-custody death data gathering. In the new bill Scott proposed that states would not receive federal grant funding if they did not comply with DCRA. Congress wanted the states to effectively be more proactive in policing the law enforcement agencies they relied on to get data about in-custody death. Predictably, law enforcement opposed these updates to DCRA, but it passed unanimously in December 2014 following the public deaths of Eric Garner and Michael Brown. Still, DCRA remained a flawed solution. The amendments to the bill were largely punitive and did not increase funding to states to help develop and cultivate uniform data-gathering practices—a crucial detail for comparative statical analysis of in-custody death across states and counties. Then during the first Trump administration, lawyers within the Department of Justice argued that the punitive amendments to DCRA turned the BJS into a law enforcement agency, which was a violation of federal law barring government scientific institutions from being used for political purposes. While this view was not shared throughout all of the DOJ, it was enough to compel officials to place in-custody data-gathering efforts into the hands of the Bureau of Justice Assistance (BJA)—an agency authorized to administer and withhold federal grants but lacking the expertise or people power to properly manage a nationwide data-gathering effort.

DCRA is seen in the eyes of many as a failure. On September 20, 2022, a subcommittee on Homeland Security and Governmental Affairs within the US Senate convened a hearing titled "Uncounted Deaths in America's Prisons and Jails." The purpose was to scrutinize DOJ's adherence to DCRA. During the hearing, Gretta Goodwin, director of Homeland Security and Justice, provided testimony revealing that the US Government Accountability Office (GAO) had discovered close to a thousand deaths in custody during 2021 that states had failed to report, thus technically violating DCRA.[19] Goodwin also shared that during 2020, 24 percent of the records collected by the BJA did not have an account of how the person died, 14 percent did not have a cause of death, and 6 percent of all records were missing date of birth for the deceased. Data quality did not improve in 2021: only 30 percent of all records sent to the DOJ included all necessary data fields (e.g., race, date of birth, gender, cause of death, description of circumstances prior to death) while 70 percent of all records received were missing at least one required element. Andrea Armstrong, a professor of law at Loyola University whose work has revealed the human toll of mass incarceration, also provided testimony during the hearing. Armstrong found 180 cases of in-custody death for the state of Louisiana that were not reported to the BJA in 2020.[20] Armstrong drew attention to the different data-gathering instruments used by the BJA, noting that unlike the BJS, the BJA stopped collecting information about the total number of inmates admitted into a carceral facility, facilities with no deaths, trial status of the deceased, location of death inside the carceral space, preexisting conditions of the deceased, and finally the details about the illnesses involved in "natural" deaths. Failure to collect this type of granular data, she argued, stifled efforts to study, understand, and infer the root causes of in-custody deaths. Senator Ron Johnson, representing the Republican Party, criticized the Justice Department, stating that it had "repeatedly failed to properly implement and carry out its responsibilities under DCRA" as mandated by Congress.

NATIONAL VIOLENT DEATH REPORTING SYSTEM

In 2002, just two years after authorizing DCRA, Congress also established the National Violent Death Reporting System (NVDRS). It was the nation's first violent death registry to pull together different types of information about violent death from each state into a single frame. Unlike DCRA reporting to the DOJ, the NVDRS is concerned with deaths caused by civilians against one another in addition to in-custody deaths. The NVDRS defines a violent death as one caused by the deliberate use of any method to injure or poison oneself, another person, or group of people.[21] The data it gathers includes death certificates, reports from medical examiners and coroners, law enforcement records, and information provided by local and state health departments.

The NVDRS is public in spirit but private in practice. The data it contains was intended to be released to the public indirectly through the media and academic researchers. These intentions are apparent in its design, which is nearly impossible to navigate for someone not well educated or lacking stable internet access or the technical acumen to download and evaluate the information they hold. The NVDRS only releases summary data to the public, meaning the original information sent to them by police and public health agencies has been processed by a statistician providing the best interpretation they can offer. Because the system is based on voluntary reporting, like DCRA, it is not uncommon for police to request that the name of their department or the location of an in-custody death be withheld in the data, making the information unusable.

At its launch the NVDRS fell short of providing the coherent national picture of violent death that Congress envisioned. Only six states (Maryland, Massachusetts, New Jersey, Oregon, South Carolina, and Virginia) participated when it began in 2002. It would take sixteen years before the rest of the nation, including Puerto Rico and DC, would share data about civilian and police-involved deaths to the NVDRS. The gradual enrollment of states into the registry makes it nearly impossible to compare deaths over identical periods of time, and in some cases across bordering states—for example, Ohio began reporting to the NVDRS in 2010, but its neighbor Pennsylvania did not join until 2015. Also, state-level data about violent deaths prior to 2000 cannot be found in the NVDRS.

Limited funding, lack of infrastructure, and wavering police cooperation limited the participation of large states. When California began reporting to the NVDRS in 2005, only a small number of counties participated. Federal funding offered to incentivize cooperation did not go very far, and many counties in California did not gain the support of law enforcement to produce the records needed to reapply for federal dollars. The state turned to the California Wellness Foundation—an organization committed to the health and safety of residents throughout the state—to fund its data-gathering efforts. Grant funding expired in 2010 and California stopped participating in the NVDRS for nearly a decade.

When it resumed reporting in 2019, only thirty of the state's fifty-eight counties participated. The data that law enforcement released within those counties was at the mercy of what police were willing to disclose.

LIST OF LOST LIVES

Stanley Wilson Jr. died on February 1, 2023, inside Metropolitan State Hospital, according to Los Angeles County. The celebrated Stanford graduate and former NFL cornerback for the Detroit Lions had been held inside Men's Central Jail for the previous five months after attempting to break into a home in Hollywood Hills during a mental health crisis. Law enforcement claimed that the forty-year-old suddenly died after falling out of a chair while being assessed by medical staff at the state-run psychiatric facility. The medical examiner who investigated Wilson's death declared he died from a pulmonary thromboembolism (or a blood clot) and other complications associated with chronic traumatic encephalopathy (CTE). When Wilson's family received his body, there were abrasions on his face and what appeared to be a boot mark on his forehead. There was also open flesh around both wrists from when he was handcuffed and restrained while being beaten inside Twin Towers in downtown Los Angeles. Stanley's official death record made no mention of the violence on his body and read as if he had not been in jail before his death.

Stanley's mother, Dr. Debora Pulane Lucas, wrote in a commentary for the independent news journal *The Appeal* that her son's death was not publicly disclosed in the Los Angeles Sheriff's Department online database of in-custody deaths from 2023—which is in violation of a state mandate signed into law by Governor Gavin Newsom on September 29, 2022.[22] Dr. Lucas explained that "by not counting Stanley's death, LASD is not only erasing his death and the circumstances around it from public record. They are also making it harder to protect other incarcerated people from suffering similar deaths."[23] Stanley's family filed two lawsuits against Los Angeles County: one for withholding information about his death and another for taking his life. If not for the persistence of Stanley's family, his death would have never been recorded as an in-custody case.

Numerous studies have shown that police routinely underreport the number of people they kill, which significantly limits what government datasets can tell us about dying in custody.[24] In 2017 a team of public health scholars at Harvard University conducted a national study of legal interventions between 2006 and 2007. Drawing on crowd-sourced data—which includes data gathered by media, nonprofits, and other nongovernment institutions—they identified in-custody death cases confirmed by official reports provided to the NVDRS. The Harvard study found that fewer than half of law enforcement–related killings were reported during this one-year period.[25] They also discovered that police accountability for death in custody was effectively erased by law enforcement and medical examiners-coroners by incorrectly labeling the cause of death as "natural," "accidental," or "undetermined." This distorts the frequency of law enforcement–related death and produces legal barriers for families seeking restitution from county and state agencies; it is very difficult to charge a police department with a wrongful death lawsuit if the manner of death is not homicide.[26] Moreover, the Harvard study have found that underreporting was most common in cases not involving firearms and occurred more frequently in counties with a large low-income population.[27]

While the Harvard study established the underreporting of in-custody deaths by law enforcement, I wanted to use crowd-sourced data to assemble the largest picture possible of who died during police encounters in our nation's streets between 2000 and 2020—inside the lab we would eventually call this the "list of lost lives." There was the Homicide Report from the *Los Angeles Times*, which began in 2000 as a blog and Google map, that continuously tracked the location of every death classified as a homicide by the Department of the Los Angeles Medical Examiner. We used data from a project run by *The Guardian* called The Counted, which at the time was one of the most comprehensive records of in-custody death in the US built on police reports, witness statements, regional news, research groups, and other open-source data projects. Mapping Police Violence was another data resource we consulted; it collected in-custody death reports by identifying cases using the Google News search engine and the *Washington Post*. Last, we used information from an online database called Fatal Encounters, run by independent journalist D. Brian Burghardt based in Reno, Nevada, which by far was the most comprehensive record of in-custody death in the nation. Its records dated back to 2000 and included deaths that are precipitated by police or that occur when police are present.

Assembling this list of lost lives was not an easy task. The collection timelines across the different datasets did not exactly match. *The Guardian*, for example, collected information about cases that happened between 2015 and 2016, whereas Mapping Police Violence had data beginning in 2013. The *Los Angeles Times* Homicide Report and Fatal Encounter each dated back to 2000, but only Fatal Encounters had information exclusively about police-involved deaths. Each dataset used different racial designations for people with Asian, Middle Eastern, Black, or Hispanic (Latino) ancestry. My lab also had to verify duplicate names, correct misidentified people, and exclude cases that did not involve law enforcement. The latter required us to either confirm that law enforcement had assigned the victim a case number or gather the autopsy in question and review the coroner's investigative summary about the circumstances that led to the death. Some cases could only be confirmed after we found local news reports about police being involved in the incident.

Manners of death did not align across every crowd-sourced dataset; some coded natural deaths as "medical," which could mean death from illness but also death from medical neglect. My lab had to categorize several hundred deaths as "unknown" because different data sources reported contradictory information about the cause of death for the same individual. These discrepancies were not always the fault of the research team who organized the data, but they were a reflection of the US not having uniform standards for police to report information about in-custody death. Many of the dead remained a mystery to us, either because law enforcement withheld their names, case numbers were missing, the manner of death was absent, or the race and age were omitted.

The death ledger we assembled was staggering. Between 2000 and 2020, police killed 32,104 during arrest (figure 4.2). For perspective, between 1608 and 2022 there were 16,047 executions. In just twenty years, police killed more than twice the number of all prisoners executed

FIGURE 4.2 Cause of death for reported lethal police encounters during arrest or pursuit between 2000 and 2020

CAUSE OF DEATH/ HIGHEST LEVEL OF FORCE USED	NUMBER OF VICTIMS	PERCENT OF VICTIMS
Gunshot	23,005	71.66%
Vehicle	6,112	19.04%
Tasered	962	3.00%
Use of Force (Asphyxiated, Beaten, Bludgeoned, Restrained)	481	1.65%
Unknown	462	1.28%
Medical Emergency	383	1.19%
Drowning, Fall from a Height, Burned/ Smoke Inhalation	297	0.93%
Drug Overdose	182	0.57%
Undetermined	97	0.30%
Other	65	0.20%
Chemical Agent/Pepper Spray	33	0.10%
Gunshot + Taser	25	0.08%
Total	32,104	100.00%

Source: UCLA BioCritical Studies Lab, List of Lost Lives, https://www.terencekeel.com/the-coroner-report-project

in US history. Dying in custody is the new capital punishment. White Americans made up the majority of all cases, followed by Black people and Hispanic/Latinos (figure 4.3). There were 505 deaths of individuals of Asian/Pacific Islander ancestry, 354 deaths of Native American/Alaskan people, and 54 people killed who had Middle Eastern ancestry. There were 8,279 names, almost 30 percent of the data, whose race could not be identified because either law enforcement did not disclose this information or their racial identity could not be determined by police. Law enforcement does not record the identities of mixed-race people, choosing instead to classify people based on how their race appears to them.[28]

While the average age of death was thirty-five years, people under the age of twenty-five were killed most often (figure 4.4). Men made up 90 percent of all deaths and women roughly 9 percent of the cases. We found there were twenty-three people identified as transgender and ninety-two

FIGURE 4.3 The racial demographics of reported deaths by law enforcement during arrest or pursuit between 2000 and 2020

DECEDENT RACE	NUMBER OF VICTIMS	PERCENT OF VICTIMS
White	11,210	34.92%
Unknown	8,279	25.79%
Black	7,249	22.58%
Hispanic/Latino	4,453	13.87%
Asian/Pacific Islander	505	1.57%
Native American/Alaskan	354	1.10%
Middle Eastern	54	0.17%
Total	32,104	100.00%

Source: UCLA BioCritical Studies Lab, List of Lost Lives, https://www.terencekeel.com/the-coroner-report-project

people whose gender was not documented (figure 4.5). California, Texas, Florida, Georgia, and Illinois had the most reported in-custody deaths over this period of time (figure 4.6).

Approximately 72 percent of people whose names we gathered (23,005) died from a police officer killing them with a firearm (figure 4.2). With the recent deaths of Eric Garner and George Floyd, I thought asphyxiation or restraint might be the second leading cause of in-custody death.

FIGURE 4.4 Ages of all reported deaths by law enforcement during arrest or pursuit between 2000 and 2020

AGE	NUMBER OF VICTIMS	PERCENT OF VICTIMS	AVERAGE AGE OF DEATH	MODE (ALL AGES)
<18	1,433	4.46%		
18–23	5,125	15.96%		
24–29	5,707	17.78%		
30–35	5,243	16.33%	35	25
36–41	4,287	13.35%		
>41	9,153	28.51%		
Unknown	1,156	3.60%		
Total	32,104	100.00%		

Source: UCLA BioCritical Studies Lab, List of Lost Lives, https://www.terencekeel.com/the-coroner-report-project

FIGURE 4.5 The gender demographics of reported deaths by law enforcement during arrest or pursuit between 2000 and 2020

GENDER	NUMBER OF VICTIMS	PERCENT OF VICTIMS
Male	29,043	90.47%
Female	2,946	9.18%
Unknown	92	0.29%
Transgender	23	0.07%
Total	32,104	100%

Source: UCLA BioCritical Studies Lab, List of Lost Lives, https://www.terencekeel.com/the-coroner-report-project

FIGURE 4.6 The five states with the highest reported number of in-custody deaths during arrest or pursuit between 2000 and 2020, along with that state's contribution to the nation's overall number of in-custody deaths during the same period. For example, in-custody deaths in California constituted 16.52% of the 32,104 in-custody deaths in the US between 2000 and 2020, according to our analysis.

STATE	NUMBER OF DEATHS	PERCENT OF ALL DEATHS
CA	5,305	16.52%
TX	2,916	9.08%
FL	1,946	6.06%
GA	1,175	3.66%
IL	1,116	3.48%

Source: UCLA BioCritical Studies Lab, List of Lost Lives, https://www.terencekeel.com/the-coroner-report-project

However, fewer than 2 percent of the reported cases on our ledger involved asphyxiation or restraint. I discovered instead that the second leading cause of in-custody death in the US involved police killing people with their cars during high-speed pursuits ($n = 6,112$), making up about 20 percent of the 32,104 cases on our ledger.

I thought our data sources had mistaken civilian-on-civilian vehicle accidents for police-involved car fatalities. So, my lab reviewed the 108 vehicle-related cases that occurred in Los Angeles County over this twenty-year period—California has the largest highway patrol force in the country, and in 2020, Los Angeles ranked second in vehicle-related injuries and death across the state.[29] We were able to verify that 37 out of 108 cases involved a person dying while fleeing police, usually by losing control of a car or attempting to jump from a vehicle; in 44 out of 108 cases people were killed by a car that was fleeing from police; in 16 cases the death record notes that the person fleeing police died because they were hit directly by a patrol vehicle. Finally, we found eleven cases where pedestrians were killed either by a patrol car or a vehicle that was running from police.

Tasers and "medical emergencies" constituted the third and fourth leading causes of in-custody death among the names we gathered. Drowning, drug overdose, use of force, and deaths that could not be determined rounded out the top eight leading causes of death.

Our list of lost lives was surely an incomplete picture. Names we discovered from our crowd-based sources drew largely from voluntary police reporting, much like the data gathered from DCRA and the NVDRS. This meant that our ledger offered a picture of reported in-custody death and not deaths that were withheld from public disclosure at the time of our study, misclassified, or simply not reported at all. Without national standards or federal mandates for reporting in-custody deaths, it is difficult to calculate death rates at the county or city level, which is a standard practice of public health science. To do such an analysis using our crowd-based sources would, for example, make counties that regularly report police killings appear more lethal than counties of equal size that avoid or undercount in-custody deaths. Lack of federal leadership around in-custody death reporting and short-sighted lawmaking at the state level is preventing us from seeing where the crisis can be found. Still, the 32,104 people killed over this twenty-year period remained an undercount not simply because law enforcement and medical examiners are unreliable at reporting these cases but because our list only included deaths on the streets. Our lab would need to rely on a different set of sources to see how many people might be dying inside our nation's jails.

THE HIDDEN

A few months after the death of George Floyd, reporters at Reuters published a special investigation covering death inside US jails. This was part of a report titled "Dying in Custody" published in October 2020.[30] It featured the harrowing stories of individuals who lost their lives in jails around the nation between 2008 and 2019. Reuters transformed raw data from jail facilities obtained through FOIA requests, combined it with death statistics from the BJS, and created a useful resource that allowed readers to draw their own conclusions about the staggering number of cases reported during this nineteen-year period. It was a remarkably user-friendly interface that allowed anyone to view and download summary death data via an online portal. Each of the fifty states was represented, and jail deaths were organized by the county where the facility was located. Nothing close to this level of public disclosure exists on any US state government website.

When my lab looked at the Reuters data, we saw for ourselves how little desire there was for law enforcement working in jails to share details about the lives lost under their watch. Names were inconsistently documented. Dates of when people were booked and taken into jail were often absent—a crucial detail for measuring how long people had been held before they died. Too many cases were missing the age, gender, and manner of death. Not every facility used the same racial categories; some classified people with Arab names as white while Chinese, Filipinos, and Samoans were all simply labeled as Asian, effectively making the risk of dying in custody appear to be the same for each group. Mixed-race people could not be seen in the dataset. Neither could transgender or nonbinary populations. A jail facility in one county could have sound data one year and then be careless the next.

Although limited, the data painted a disturbing picture of death inside US jails, much like what my lab observed for deaths involving police on the streets. Reuters found that there were 7,571 deaths across 523 jails between 2008 and 2019. Just over 65 percent of these deaths happened while the person was awaiting trial, which meant they died before having the opportunity to defend their innocence or plead guilty to the charges brought against them. More than 25 percent of the cases observed between 2008 and 2019 were deaths by apparent suicide, and about 10 percent of all cases in the Reuters investigation were associated with drugs and alcohol. White people represented just over 50 percent of all deaths, while Black people made up 28 percent of cases, which is twice the number one would expect given they are about 12 percent of the US population. This disparity was a reflection of the unequal rates of arrest and incarceration Black people face relative to other racial groups.

The racial inequalities surrounding policing, incarceration rates, and jail deaths are especially apparent in Los Angeles, home to the largest jail system in the nation. On any given day there are thirteen thousand inmates inside the four facilities that make up the Los Angeles County jail system.[31] Los Angeles County also reports more in-custody deaths than any other jail system in the country.[32] The health and well-being of these inmates are under the authority of the Los Angeles Sheriff's Department (LASD). In 2020 multiple social justice organizations working throughout the county launched a successful campaign to close Men's Central Jail after conditions of the jail were revealed by media to be inhumane and after a wave of deaths inside the facility.[33] A large number of people inside Men's Central Jail were previously unhoused, suffered from mental illness, and had committed nonviolent offenses. Local organizations working with the Departments of Public Health and Community Mental Health argued that the needs for most people in the jail could be met by providing temporary shelters, increased beds at mental health facilities, and drug rehabilitation programs, and by eliminating the cash-bail system for nonviolent offenses. In 2021 the Los Angeles County Board of Supervisors voted four to one to shut down Men's Central Jail within twenty-four months and use $1.7 billion to implement what was called a "care first, jail last" program.[34] The deadline came and went. As of 2025, Men's Central Jail remains open.

The campaign to close the jail was aided by the work of impacted community members. Many wanted to know who died and how. Near the end of 2019, Helen Jones of Dignity and Power Now (DPN) filed a FOIA request searching for answers. She wanted the names and autopsies of everyone who died inside all four of the Los Angeles County jail facilities between 2009 and 2019. Helen had seen firsthand the toll of jail deaths among residents of Los Angeles; she lost her own son, John Horton III, on March 30, 2009, inside Men's Central Jail, in a year that proved to be one of the most lethal on record before the COVID-19 pandemic.[35] Helen sent her FOIA request to the Los Angeles County Department of Medical Examiner-Coroner (DME-C), which preserves deaths records from the county jail and is responsible for responding to all public requests for the autopsies it produces for the county. DME-C gave Helen and DPN fifty-six records, but according to data provided by Reuters there were 260 deaths inside the county jail during the ten-year period they requested—meaning there were 204 undisclosed records.

My lab had been working closely with Helen to study and evaluate the autopsies written for people who lost their lives in jail or during arrest throughout the county. Working with my colleague Nicholas Shapiro at UCLA, we searched for the 204 people who died in custody in the DME-C public database. The county's website revealed only two additional cases not released to Helen and DPN; each of these two cases involved a wrongful death lawsuit filed by a family member against the county according to the proceedings of the Los Angeles County Claims Board.[36] The other 202 records were effectively hidden from public view. We determined that LASD and DME-C had circumvented the state's public record mandate by placing the withheld records under "security hold." California state law gives the county sheriff discretion to withhold completed autopsy records from public disclosure during an ongoing investigation involving someone under their jurisdiction.[37] These files can be withheld indefinitely. For an autopsy to be placed on security hold, however, law enforcement must file a request to the local medical examiner or coroner, making the case as to why public disclosure of death records would compromise the results of a pending investigation. Death investigators are under no obligation to grant the request.[38] However, the 202 records hidden from view at the time of Helen's FOIA request made it clear that DME-C had adopted a practice of indiscriminately limiting the public release of death records. DME-C does not provide the public any details about whether a file was currently or previously on "security hold." Records that law enforcement and the medical examiner chose not to release to the public simply did not exist.

Frustrated but not deterred, we released a public report in June 2022 examining the fifty-eight autopsies given to our community partners by

the county.[39] Black people were in the clear majority, making up 22 of the
58 cases (38 percent), followed by Latinos at 19 (33 percent), whites at 14
(24 percent), and then 3 Asians (5 percent). In a world where our criminal
justice system was free of racial bias, we would expect the death rates
of each population to reflect their overall percentage within Los Angeles
County. African Americans make up only 9.3 percent of the population in
Los Angeles County and yet were clearly overrepresented in our sample by
nearly four times the rate we expected. There were fifty-two men and six
women, with Black women (n = 3) representing 50 percent of the female
cases. We discovered that twenty-six of the fifty-eight deaths were classified as natural; there were eight times as many Black men who supposedly
died from natural causes than white men, and there were 2.5 times more
Black male natural deaths than Latino males. The deaths of all three
Black women included in the files released by the county were classified as
natural. The average age of all these jail cases was forty-three years old at
the time of death, which was much younger than the life expectancy for
all racial groups in Los Angeles County: in 2020 the life expectancy for
Asian men and women combined in Los Angeles County was 86.6 years
old, followed by 82.4 for Hispanic/Latinos, 82 for American Indians/
Alaska Natives, 80.6 for whites, and 74.8 for Blacks.[40] Most deaths (74
percent) occurred while the individual was in pretrial status, meaning
they died before having the opportunity to defend their innocence or be
found guilty of the charges brought against them. Finally, we found that
law enforcement from LASD were present during fifty-one of fifty-eight
autopsy examinations. While California law gives LASD the authority to
attend an examination, having the legal entity involved in killing someone
in the room while the autopsy was performed appeared to be a conflict
of interest that creates the opportunity for police to influence the results
of what is supposed to be an objective scientific study.[41]

Local and national media picked up our report in July 2022. ABC
News ran a story on primetime television featuring Helen and me dis-
cussing the violent conditions inside Los Angeles County jails and the
medical examiner's mishandling of death records. Then there were
several rallies organized by DPN and the LA Justice Coalition in front
of the Los Angeles Hall of Justice and the Department of the Medical

Examiner with families who lost loved ones inside the jail. But it would take two years and the appointment of a new chief medical examiner before the county released the remaining 202 files. When we received them there were significant redactions. Entire sections of the "Coroner's Investigation Report"—the portion of the autopsy that details what happened before and after the death—were blacked out.

Before our reports and the ensuing media coverage, my lab received records from Los Angeles County with hardly any redactions. For example, in 2020, two years prior to the release of our June study, I requested the autopsies of people killed on the streets of Los Angeles County by police during the year 2009. According to our crowd-sourced data, there were fifty-five in-custody deaths on the streets of Los Angeles that year. Seven of those cases did not involve the use of a firearm, making them similar to deaths inside the county jail where police are only authorized to use pepper spray, Tasers, and restraints. I was interested in these cases to compare their quality and conclusions with the records written for in-custody deaths that occurred in jail. My lab received these seven autopsies in the fall of 2020. The files had only minor redactions of social security numbers, cell phones, and the addresses of next of kin; there were no redactions to the medical history sections or the coroner investigation summary (figure 4.7). This was consistent with the limited redactions we observed in previous years from Los Angeles and in other counties throughout California.

When we tried collecting files in 2022 from deaths that also occurred in Los Angeles County jails in 2009—as I had done just two years before for cases that took place in the streets—there were significant redactions (figure 4.8). Much more than sensitive identifying information was hidden. We found redactions in the medical opinion of the autopsy where the medical examiner recorded conditions that influenced how they arrived at the manner of death. Entire sections of the witness statement found on the coroner's investigation report were blacked out, leaving anyone with the file to guess what happened before, during, and after the encounter with police. Even the hospital reports that confirmed time and cause of death were hidden. There seemed to be no logic to the amendments other than to limit our ability to see the truth.

FIGURE 4.7 Investigator's narrative demonstrating the absence of redactions in the coroner's investigative narrative by the Los Angeles County Department of the Medical Examiner-Coroner (LACDMEC) for the autopsy of Miguel Molina, who died in custody on the streets of Los Angeles County in April 2009. My lab requested this autopsy before the public release of our report on the mishandling of death records by LACDMEC.

County of Los Angeles, Department of Coroner
Investigator's Narrative

Case Number: 2009-05889   Decedent: MOLINA, MIGUEL

Information Sources:

1. Medical Records #N001043252 – Providence St. Joseph Medical Center, (818) 847-4043

2. Detective Blagg – Los Angeles County Sheriff's Department, Homicide Bureau, (323) 890-5500

Investigation:

On 08/26/2009 at 2352 hours, Detective Gonzalez of the Los Angeles County Sheriff's Department reported this apparent accident/homicide to the Coroner's office. The decedent was transported to the Forensic Science Center by Forensic Attendant Montoya on 08/27/2009. I was assigned this case on 08/30/2009.

The decedent's prior criminal history reflects multiple drug and prostitution arrests.

Location:

Location of Injury: Unknown

Location of Death: Hospital – Providence St. Joseph Medical Center, 501 S. Buena Vista Street, Burbank, CA 91505

Informant/Witness Statements:

According to the medical records, on 08/26/2009 at 2028 hours, the Los Angeles City Fire Department arrived at 5350 N. Lankershim Boulevard. Upon their arrival, they discovered the decedent supine on the floor in the mezzanine level at a redline station. The decedent was pulseless and not breathing with his hands handcuffed behind his back. The deputies on scene reported that the decedent was exhibiting erratic behavior and was tazed five times. The barbs were removed from the anterior chest and cardiopulmonary resuscitative measures were implemented. He was transported to the hospital where he arrived in full arrest. He was intubated and advanced life support medications were administered. Despite medical intervention, the decedent was pronounced dead on 08/26/2009 at 2104 hours.

According to Detective Blagg, on 08/26/2009 at approximately 2018 hours, the decedent was involved in a fight with a Sheriff's Deputy and was subsequently tazed approximately four to five times. He was later discovered unresponsive and transported to the hospital where he was pronounced dead. A meth pipe was also recovered from the scene.

Scene Description:

The scene was not visited in this death investigation.

Evidence:

While at the Forensic Science Center, Forensic Attendant Montoya collected a hair and nail kit. These items were booked as physical evidence at the Forensic Science Center.

Body Examination:

The body is that of an adult male Hispanic who was examined in the main crypt area of the Forensic Science Center. He has a shaved head, hazel eyes and the condition of his teeth is unknown. Lesions are noted on his torso. An endotracheal tube and tube holder are in place as are bilateral intravenous lines in his arms. A dressing is also noted on his right hand. The decedent's back was not examined due to the instability of the examination equipment.

Identification:

On 08/27/2009 at 2224 hours, the Department of Justice identified the decedent as MIGUEL MOLINA (DOB 03/05/1982) by way of fingerprint comparison.

Source: Los Angeles County Department of Medical Examiner-Coroner, "Autopsy Report of Miguel Molina," Case #2009-05889, Los Angeles, CA, 2009

FIGURE 4.8 Investigator's narrative demonstrating significant redactions to the coroner's investigative narrative by the Los Angeles County Department of the Medical Examiner-Coroner for the autopsy of Damon Tripp, who died inside Los Angeles County-University of Southern California Medical Center after being transported from Men's Central Jail by the Los Angeles Sheriff Department in April 2009. My lab requested this autopsy after the release of our report on the mishandling of death records by LACDMEC.

 **County of Los Angeles, Department of Coroner Investigator's Narrative**

Case Number: 2009-05561   Decedent: TRIPP, DAMON DION

Information Sources:

LAC+USC Medical Center, (323) 226-8011

Investigation:

On 8/11/09 at 0815 hours Detective Hall, LASD Homicide (323) 890-5500, reported this apparent natural, in custody, death to Richard Heath of the Forensic Science Center. Detective Hall reported that the decedent was transported to LAC+USC Medical Center from Men's Central Jail and was pronounced days later. History of alcoholic liver disease. Foul play is not suspected.

A routine criminal background inquiry revealed multiple narcotic related arrests.

Location:

Death: LAC+USC Medical Center- 2051 Marengo Street, Los Angeles, CA 90033

Informant/Witness Statements:

According to the medical record

Scene Description:

Scene not visited by Coroner personnel.

Evidence:

Coroner Forensic Attendant collected a hair and fingernail kit and booked it at the Forensic Science Center.

Body Examination:

The decedent was an adult, Caucasian male viewed at the Forensic Science Center, refrigerator, he was nude. An endotracheal tube, left subclavian line, and Foley catheter were in place. The decedent was jaundice. There were multiple tattoos: neck- "dead man rolling", right arm- half sleeve design, and left arm- unknown design. There was red discoloration to the right lower side just above the right hip. No scars or apparent signs of trauma noted. I did not view the decedent's back.

Identification:

LFIS fingerprints identified the decedent as Damon Tripp on 8/12/09 at 1201 hours.

Next of Kin Notification:

Unknown/Not notified at the completion of this report.

Source: Los Angeles County Department of Medical Examiner-Coroner, "Autopsy Report of Damon Tripp," Case #2009-05561, Los Angeles, CA, 2009

WHOSE VIOLENCE? WHICH DEATH?

Our nation's use of violence to enforce the law and then conceal where the bodies are hidden is a disorienting phenomenon to witness. The problem impacts more than just Black and Latino lives. Law enforcement violence has evolved, threatening to take anyone on the wrong side of the law—along with the record of their dismemberment.

I asked the former director of the BJS, Alex Piquero, why Americans know so little about who dies as a result of police violence. Piquero is a second-generation Cuban immigrant who was raised in Baltimore and developed a love for statistics following major league baseball—a very common pathway for many data scientists. Despite his straight black hair, long wiry frame, and angular European features, he does not identify as white. Piquero is widely considered one of the top criminologists in the world and holds a distinguished professorship in criminology at the University of Miami. President Joe Biden appointed him to direct the BJS in 2022. Piquero and I spoke in late March 2024 just a few weeks before we were scheduled to present at a conference convened by the National Academy of Sciences (NAS) on the crisis of in-custody death.

Piquero explained that national organizations like the NVDRS and the BJS are in theory independent scientific agencies that lack the power to force better reporting by law enforcement and local governments. While the Justice Administration Act in 1979 gave the BJS authority to use federal funding to influence noncompliant counties, the funding was too modest to compel better records. Piquero believes that many of our data problems, however, could be solved by Congress, which has the power to mandate that law enforcement offices report this information and also to set standards for what and how this data is reported. As things currently stand, "Americans know more about the number of flights delayed on any given day of the year than the number of people dying in police custody."[42]

I then asked if he thought our flawed death reporting system was performing as intended. We grant police immunity in almost all in-custody death cases, I explained, with law enforcement killing just over 1,200 people a year but fewer than 2 percent of these cases result in criminal charges.[43] Piquero pushed back on my suggestion that protecting law enforcement was the reason for our broken reporting system. He pointed to police departments around the country, particularly those serving small communities, that report in-custody deaths in good faith and see deaths under their watch as a tragedy and failure of justice.

But knowing the number of deaths undisclosed by police in Los Angeles and other counties made it difficult for me to share Piquero's belief that police could be trusted to share who they are killing and why. I knew that terror in the service of inequality was an enduring feature of American life and the inertia of this history weighs heavy, leaving habits deeply ingrained within ourselves, law enforcement, and our vision of justice. It seemed to me that law enforcement agencies that refuse to report in-custody deaths are not simply resisting a public disclosure mandate. Their non-compliance stems from a commitment to a much older tradition where violence maintains the local power of police, racial hierarchies, and calculated chaos.

This sort of violence was on the minds of some in the federal government during the middle of the twentieth century. Legal historian Naomi Murakawa explains in her book *The First Civil Right* that the Truman administration believed white mobs that targeted Black people and other racial groups at the close of World War II were nearly uncontrollable. In response, President Truman designated the "right to safety and security of the person" as the "first condition of all rights, and in so doing, fired the Democratic Party's opening salvo against white mob violence and racial prejudice in the criminal justice system."[44] Liberals within the federal government believed white Americans would accept being prosecuted for crimes against people of color only if the criminal justice system presented itself as not partial to the racial groups whose lives they ruined. This was the origins of the mantra of colorblind justice, a strategy designed to limit the terror of white violence.

As the movement for Black freedom grew stronger during the middle of the twentieth century, fueled by international outrage over the lynching of Black veterans and widespread anxiety about potential race conflicts, liberals took action to institute a law-and-order agenda. Their goal was to construct police and carceral systems capable of quelling white racial violence and implementing stricter measures to address racial biases within the criminal justice system.[45] This included the Law Enforcement Assistance Act in 1965, passed under the Johnson administration, which was the first federal anticrime effort designed to bring more resources into local law enforcement.[46] President Johnson had this to say after signing the act into law: "Until every woman in this land can walk the streets of her city at night, unafraid and unharmed, then we have work to do in law enforcement. . . . I have signed into law two important instruments in our search for better ways to insure the supremacy—not of fear but of the law."[47]

Police power was also expanded by President Johnson with the 1968 Omnibus Crime Control and Safe Streets Act. The act brought even more resources to local law enforcement offices through block grants. Local police during this time acquired military-grade weapons to suppress leaders of the Black Power movement and dissuade other forms of civil disobedience that had been effective during the civil rights era. Southern Democrats concerned with the gains of the Civil Rights Act added amendments to Johnson's bill that bolstered the autonomy of local police and empowered them to disregard federal mandates when it suited them. This included a provision allowing local law enforcement to receive federal block grants even if they refused to integrate police departments.

The historian Stuart Schrader has argued that the increased power and autonomy given to police under the Johnson administration "created the conditions for increasingly well-funded, networked, and armed citadels of localism."[48] Schrader explains that this localism, in which police gained tremendous power over what justice means in our daily lives, was free to ignore the anti-racist legislative changes of the civil rights acts. Modern policing in America was effectively given the task of keeping the nation safe while rapidly growing beyond the control of the federal government, which during the 1960s was making strides to increase the reach and power of a pluralist democracy. The disconnect between police working to maintain power over local communities and the federal government moving toward social equality helps explain why the systems designed to collect data about in-custody death are inadequate.

Matters worsened under President Nixon, who inverted the liberal policies of the Truman administration, turning the first right to safety into an explicit political campaign against Black-on-white crime.[49] Empowered by Nixon's leadership, state and federal governments used police departments and a growing number of carceral institutions to deal with the perceived threats of Black people to white safety, creating the pathway for the overrepresentation of Black people in jails and prisons we are witnessing during our own time.

National concerns about Black violence—a dramatic shift away from white violence that terrorized communities for the first half of the twentieth century—produced a federal data-gathering agenda that was too narrow in its focus and overly reliant on local police departments willing to resist national mandates. The crime and violence reporting systems that emerged in the wake of Nixon's 1970s justice reforms were not intended to protect minorities still vulnerable to white terror or police violence; they were designed to observe civilian violence, especially violence by Black people (figure 4.9). Spotlighting Black crime, however, redacted the not-so-distant memory of the terror posed by slave owners, militias, unruly white mobs, and law enforcement.

FIGURE 4.9 The rising rates of murder and police-related deaths among Black American men relative to other groups

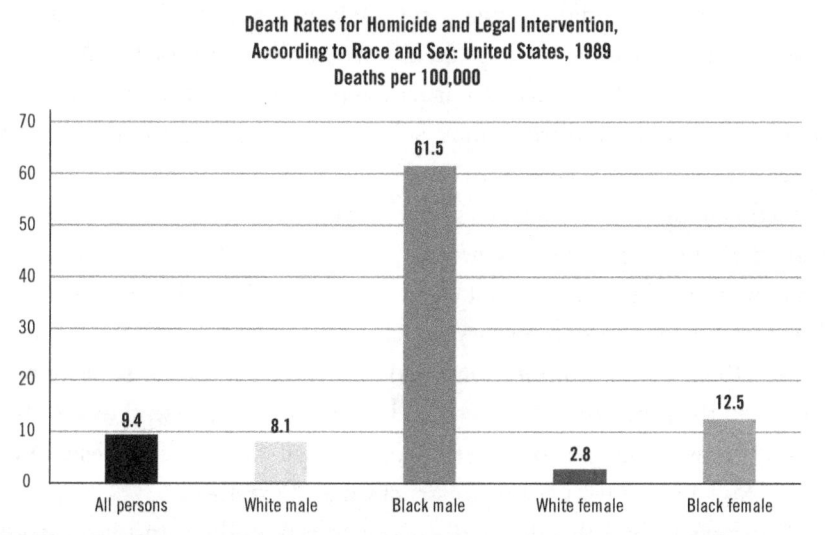

Death Rates for Homicide and Legal Intervention, According to Race and Sex: United States, 1989
Deaths per 100,000

All persons	White male	Black male	White female	Black female
9.4	8.1	61.5	2.8	12.5

Source: Jacob Feldman, Laura Montgomery, and Kathleen Turczyn, "Health, United States, 1991 and Prevention Profile," US Department of Health and Human Services, 1992

As many scholars have argued, the evolution of modern policing during the second half of the twentieth century is a complex story driven by the desire of local governments to solidify social hierarchies, manage civil unrest instigated by rising income inequality, offer punitive alternatives to our faltering education system, destabilize Black families, correct the excesses of capitalism, and supplement the erosion of America's social safety net.[50]

Still, American fears about Black crime limited how lawmakers saw criminal justice, placing us on our current course of over-policing and undercounting the victims of law enforcement violence.

In the early 1990s, Senator Joe Biden and, later, President Bill Clinton introduced criminal justice reforms that offered a colorblind vision of justice that in practice targeted racial minorities, poor people who committed nonviolent offenses, and individuals suffering with substance abuse issues. In 1994, President Clinton signed the Violent Crime Control and Law Enforcement Act. The bill had been conceived years before by Senator Biden, who had drafted the outlines of the act while working with top law enforcement officials and the National Association of Police Organizations in his role as chairman of the Senate Judiciary Committee.

Through this act, commonly known as the "Clinton Crime Bill," lawmakers expanded capital punishment, making it applicable to numerous federal offenses such as drug-related murder, terrorist attacks, and drug trafficking. The bill introduced a provision requiring life sentences for individuals convicted of a third serious violent or drug-related crime, routinely referred to as the "three strikes" policy. The bill also removed federally funded Pell Grants for prisoners seeking education, a move that liberals argued would eliminate educational opportunities that were crucial for rehabilitation. While the Violent Crime Control and Law Enforcement Act did offer funding for community policing initiatives through the creation of the Office of Community Oriented Policing Services, these resources increased the ranks of police nationally, providing approximately $8 billion in grants to law enforcement departments. The act also designated nearly $9.7 billion for prison construction and expansion.

Clinton's Crime Bill did address police misconduct and in-custody deaths, though the scope was limited. The bill authorized the Department of Justice (DOJ) to investigate police departments with an established pattern or practice of police misconduct and lethal violence that violates constitutional and federal rights. The DOJ was not given the power to investigate individual cases of police violence, nor did the Violent Crime Control and Law Enforcement Act offer standards for police use of force or resources and guidelines for establishing a national database to monitor police violence and in-custody death. It would take almost another decade for those provisions to be introduced by the federal government with the creation of DCRA.

After passage of the Violent Crime Control and Law Enforcement Act, social scientists and politicians became much more vocal about the fear of Black crime—revealing in the process an underlying spirit of the bill. Shortly after the act was passed, the criminologist John Dilulio coined the term "super-predator," which described a young violent male criminal who was "radically impulsive, brutally remorseless."[51] The idea was racially loaded and played on white American fears as Nixon had done in the 1970s. In 1995, Dilulio predicted in the *Washington Examiner*:

> On the horizon . . . are tens of thousands of severely morally impoverished juvenile super-predators. They are perfectly capable of committing the most heinous acts of physical violence for the most trivial reasons (for example, a perception of slight disrespect or the accident of being in their path). They fear neither the stigma of arrest nor the pain of imprisonment. They live by the meanest code of the meanest streets, a code that reinforces rather than restrains their violent, hair-trigger mentality.[52]

Dilulio's "super-predator" and its variants were adopted by Republicans and Democrats alike. In her 1996 speech at Keene State College in New Hampshire, First Lady Hillary Clinton parroted Dilulio's vision, claiming that the young men who drove crime rates in America were "not just gangs of kids anymore. They are often the kinds of kids that are called 'super-predators.' No conscience, no empathy. We can talk about why they ended up that way, but first we have to bring them to heel."[53] While Hillary Clinton would later regret her use of the term while running for president in 2016, the damage to Black and Brown youth in the 1990s had been done. US senator Bernie Sanders shared the same regrets during his bid for the presidency in 2020, having voted for the bill.[54]

Bipartisan support for the Violent Crime Control and Law Enforcement Act reflected a larger ethos of conservative criminal justice reforms aimed at civilians but not police accountability. During the 1990s New York mayor Rudy Giuliani and police commissioner William Bratton implemented zero tolerance for civil disorder—such as broken windows in neighborhoods, graffiti in public spaces, and other visible signs of crime—believing this was the best path for public safety. They implemented aggressive stop-and-frisk practices and profiling techniques that preyed on Black and Latino men. Also during this time prophecies about super-predators helped persuade state legislatures around the country to pass laws to prosecute and punish children as adults. These reforms had a disproportionate impact on Black youth who, having already been under the gaze of police surveillance as a result of nearly three decades of conservative criminal justice lawmaking, were prosecuted at rates higher than whites.[55]

And yet predictions about the rise of the super-predator would turn out to be incorrect. Data showed that violent juvenile crime rates, along with crime more generally, dropped in the middle of the 1990s largely due to changes that began in the 1970s, which included the legalization of abortion, increased numbers of police, rising rates of incarceration for drug offenses, and the decline of the crack epidemic.[56] The wave of young violent Black and Brown offenders never came, but the punitive laws remained.

The national turn toward conservative law and order politics during the second half of the twentieth century illustrates how we have made heavy investments into policing but have failed to invest in limiting the violence of law enforcement or disclosing death records. Lawmakers and the public more generally have been reluctant to imagine police as a threat to public safety, even though state-sanctioned terror has long threatened the health and security of Black people and other politically vulnerable groups.

This has left us at a crossroads. The legal systems designed to deal with (Black) civil disobedience and the threat of violent crime have empowered local law enforcement but without developing infrastructures of accountability to protect civilians from the overreach of local state power. A federal data set with names of people killed by police and unobstructed access to in-custody death records is as important to maintaining freedom from the tyranny of government as the Fourth Amendment or Miranda rights.

Using extraordinary resources, we have asked police in America to maintain law and order in addition to managing the problems of poverty, the unhoused, the mentally unwell, and people suffering with substance abuse. The record of when and how law enforcement has failed at these tasks is difficult to see because it lies in pieces. State and federal leaders are responsible for this. After the Civil Rights Movement, our criminal justice system became obsessed with the crimes of civilians—especially vulnerable communities that have been targets of state violence since the nineteenth century—but less concerned with the causes of social disorder or police accountability.

Our death-reporting system is not simply broken; it reflects America's increased reliance on police and our larger ambivalence toward racial equality and a pluralist democracy. Our dark and violent past has prevented us from building the systems we now need to keep everyone safe from the abuses of state power.

IMPOSSIBLE STORIES

As a nation we know very little about the lives taken by police. There are laws that prohibit the public disclosure of death records and create backdoor channels for police and medical examiners to avoid transparency. When government data is available, it very often is incomplete and less reliable than information gathered by media and everyday citizens concerned with our nation's growing death ledger—their tireless efforts offer a better example of democratic truth-telling than what is found in our state institutions.

There is no path beyond this current system without reaffirming the dignity of people taken by police, establishing our right to know the dead, and creating national mandates for law enforcement to divulge information about fatalities they create. Dying in custody persists as a concealed crisis because records are hidden, redacted, and fragmented by design. These records were not collected with the intention of helping the future make the past whole.

Someone who exists at the limit of our tolerance and compassion has already died in our imagination if their claim to life and dignity must be drawn from records that deny their humanity. This means they die twice, first in our minds while alive and then again through omission in our laws and records. Every autopsy I requested from a county that allowed a person to perish in police custody was a way to prevent them from dying a second time—it was an attempt to affirm with FOIA requests and court documents that these lives mattered, that they could not simply be skipped over and forgotten. Every denial, redaction, and effort to hide these people merely confirmed who was disposable in the name of safety and how few of us are the children of American democracy.

Coming to terms with our nation's death ledger helps us see the history of violence that informs the misguided and haunting perception we ask law enforcement to carry on our behalf: just about anyone in America can be a threat to your security and to social order. Collectively, we have decided that death is one way to deal with this risk to our safety and to shore up the hierarchies that sustain life in this country. Women, the elderly, white men, and Asians can be found alongside the bodies of Black people, Latinos, and Indigenous folk killed in custody. Telling "impossible stories" about lives lost to police violence—even if drawn from fragmented and imperfect archives—is how we bring the dead into the future and mend what history has broken.

CHAPTER 5

PERISHING

Recruiting physicians to make sense of death is an old practice in the West that has always betrayed the distinction between science and the supernatural, fact and fable, mystery and things within human control.

Early modern European Christians believed the bodies of nobles and church leaders could carry evidence of God's presence after death. Around the seventeenth century, a tradition arose of commissioning medical men and anatomists to exhume corpses to see if they had resisted rot and were incorruptible. Those who passed the exam were declared saints. Some of these bodies had been buried for centuries; when the bishop of Coimbra removed Queen Isabel of Portugal (1271–1336) from her grave on March 26, 1612, for her canonization, she had been dead for over 275 years.[1]

Christian theology at the time held that bodies that did not decay postmortem were proof that God had restored them to their original form. In the Creation narrative shared by the Abrahamic faith traditions (Judaism, Christianity, and Islam) Adam and Eve were fashioned by God in the garden of Eden where they lived in perfect harmony with the divine will; in this state they did not perish, rot, or decay. When Adam found himself on the wrong side of God's law after the crime of eating from the tree of knowledge, he and Eve lost their immortality and became temporal creatures governed by the forces of nature—so too did their descendants. Governed by natural law, they were no different from animals; they were also subject to an endless cycle of birth and perishing. Early modern Europeans believed, however, that people who carried God's will in their heart while alive would be rewarded with immortality and exhibit evidence of this divine presence in death. The church, physicians, and laypeople looked for a sweet-smelling corpse and flesh that remained supple, whole, and comely—signs that they were touched by the supreme force that governed their world.

It was left to physicians—who we might call the first medical examiners—to determine if these physical traits were caused by natural, preternatural, or supernatural forces.[2] Natural in this context meant occurrences that were normal, expected, and routine. It was, for example, ordinary for a body to become disfigured and smell foul in death. If a person exhibited these natural signs they were not touched by God or worthy of sainthood. Preternatural events were unusual but occurred through natural forces not fully understood; magic and the occult were sometimes believed to be at work here and could deceive people into believing a body was incorruptible. Supernatural signs on a deceased body occurred through divine intervention but could be observed empirically. The physicians who conducted a postmortem examination of Queen Isabel in 1612 found that her face was still covered in pink flesh and her hair looked as if it had just been washed. Her ears, eyes, and nose were whole and lifelike, her body fleshy.[3] These postmortem signs were supernatural. Medical examiners agreed Isabel had been touched by the divine and through her incorruptible flesh left all to witness a prelude of immortality for those of distinction who carried God's law in their heart and actions. The dead bodies of common folk, peasants, and laypeople were not a venue for discerning God's salvific presence in the early modern world. Sainthood was the exclusive privilege of people who lived extraordinary lives of leadership, power, and honor.

We inhabit a different world of living and perishing. The nation, capitalism, science, technology, and the categories of race and gender have replaced God as the most significant organizing forces in our society. Liberal democracy has expanded the type of bodies entitled to a postmortem investigation since the time of verifying the undefiled flesh of saints. The causes of mysterious death have also narrowed;

preternatural and supernatural are no longer options for understanding how we die—there are only natural events. Death investigators classify cases using concepts we assume capture biological truths that maintain their meaning regardless of the context. A modern death is either a homicide, a suicide, an accident, natural, or undetermined. There is a finality to these terms encoded onto official death records kept by local governments, which then determine, for better or worse, the legal rights of the aggrieved.

Unlike early modern Europe, our world is presumably free of ghosts, spirits, and mysteries governed by supernatural forces. Unexplained phenomena ought to appear to us now as the consequence of social and political realities within our control. This is not to say there are no mysteries. Some things are difficult to understand because we are asking the wrong questions, others because we need more information. Stumbling across a corpse in a forest may remain a mystery not because this is a supernatural phenomenon but because we may not have enough details to recreate the context of their death.

Fatal police encounters are unlike other mysterious deaths because they are enveloped in information—even if these details are not released publicly. Law enforcement violence concerns matters within our control and occurs within a context that can be documented and measured, if not observed directly. Still, death investigators record in-custody cases as though they were caused by forces beyond the influence of society—an enlarged heart, asthma, drug use, or some other unique physiological ailment—like the supernatural mysteries of early modern Europe.

In this chapter I share the stories of people killed while in police custody and classified under one of the five categories used by modern medical examiners and coroners (homicide, natural, accident, suicide, undetermined). I will show you what it looks like when medical examiners neglect the social, legal, and political realities that shape who perishes while in custody. We will see that death investigators allow the body of the deceased to bear the full weight of explaining their own death. This happens in a variety of ways: the refusal to draw direct and clear links between the actions of police and their effects on the deceased, attributing death to preexisting mental or health conditions, uncritically accepting narratives about the dead, and even failing to document that a death occurred as a result of an encounter with the law.

Context is a tool, and it is within the realm of science to use it. Failure to see and measure the social and political environment, to weigh its role in taking a life, makes a mockery of science and returns us to the world of ghosts, apparitions, and divine presences that leave traces on bodies that cannot be explained with appeals to the human-made systems in control of our modern lives.

To die in custody is nearly a supernatural phenomenon.

ENCHANTED BODIES

On July 27, 1844, in Spartanburg County, South Carolina, a local coroner by the name of Z. D. Bragg organized an inquest jury of twelve "good and lawful" white men to investigate the death of an enslaved woman named Roster. She was found dead on that day at the plantation of Fielden Clayton where she labored. According to the jury, Roster "had no marks of violence upon her, and died by the visitation of God in a natural way and not otherwise."[4] You can find this language in many inquests involving enslaved people during this period. Seven years earlier in Union County, South Carolina, the local coroner, Samuel Davis, held an inquest for the mysterious death of a slave named Dick. A jury of twelve found that he "had no perceivable marks of violence upon him and died by the visitation of God in a natural way, and not otherwise."[5] The men who investigated Dick's and Roster's deaths did not see or use context to determine how they perished. The inquest juries did not record if they appeared old or young, what type of labor they performed on the plantation, if they perished in the company of others, if they had been sick prior to death, precisely where they were found, and by whom. Neither did their investigations say if they appeared to be in good health, had recently healed injuries, or if there were any recent reports of illness or disease on the plantations where they toiled.

It does not take much to imagine why a state whose wealth was based on enslaved labor would fail to record how its laws and economy diminished the lives of the people who were the engine of their prosperity. Even if we were to afford some grace for the poor scientific standards of the time, the deaths of Roster and Dick still failed to tell us even the most basic details about the social and political environment surrounding their deaths; God simply came and took them, naturally.

We might believe natural deaths are now easy to decipher using modern science. However, they continue to present challenges for death investigators and require philosophical considerations to distinguish natural deaths from other types of perishing. According to the National Association of Medical Examiners (NAME), a natural death is one "due solely or nearly totally to disease and/or the aging process."[6] NAME recommends the use of the "but for" principle to distinguish natural deaths from other causes. Coroners and medical examiners have to ask themselves, if not for an injury or a hostile environment, would the person have died? NAME does not define or limit the meaning of a hostile environment, giving investigators room to determine and measure what an antagonistic setting might entail. To facilitate their assessment, investigators typically look for evidence of external factors, such as injuries, violence, or medications that may have "hastened the death of one already vulnerable to significant or even life-threatening disease."[7] When these influences are in play it is generally believed that the death is unnatural and properly defined by one of the other four classifications (homicide, suicide, accident, or undetermined).

Violent police encounters, by their very nature, create environments that are physically and emotionally hostile. To apply the "but for" principle to an in-custody death requires investigators to recognize law enforcement encounters *as* hostile. Death investigators, however, are reluctant to define police encounters as explicitly antagonistic and rarely are they explicit in their reports about the application of the "but for" principle in natural death cases involving law enforcement. And when the principle is applied, too often medical examiners and coroners come to the conclusion that the deceased was bound to die eventually from natural causes.

My lab found that between 2008 and 2019 there were 170 natural deaths involving violent police encounters during arrest and while in jail within Los Angeles County. Of all the carceral cases in our database, almost 53 percent were designated natural deaths, while only 2 percent of deaths on the street were classified as natural. Men made up 93 percent of all natural deaths. Of the total sample of deaths, 45 percent of decedents were Black, 31 percent were Hispanic/Latin American, and 19 percent were white (figure 5.1). The average age of all natural deaths in the sample was fifty-one years.

Early on in my research I discovered the supposedly natural death of Kenneth Wayne Adcock. He was a fifty-four-year-old white man given a five-year sentence inside a Los Angeles County jail for selling narcotics. He died after three months of incarceration on November 29, 2014, inside Henry Mayo Newhall Memorial Hospital. The medical examiner reported that Kenneth died from lack of oxygen to the brain, a heart attack, and coronary artery disease.

The forensic investigator opened their story about the end of Kenneth's life by explaining that he had "a medical history of using narcotic substances off and on for approximately 40 years" and also carried a "family history of heart problems and diabetes."[8] To corroborate this natural death the forensic investigator interviewed Kenneth's brother, learning that "their father had a quadruple by-pass" and also died of a heart attack. Kenneth had supposedly been addicted to speed since the age of twelve.

According to his brother, Kenneth was jailed in October 2012, two years prior to his death; the report does not specify where he was

FIGURE 5.1 Demographic data on natural deaths in law enforcement custody (during arrest or pursuit and within carceral facilities) in Los Angeles County from 2008 to 2019

IN-CUSTODY NATURAL DEATHS IN LOS ANGELES COUNTY, 2008–2019													TOTAL	AGE	
RACE															
Asian		Black		Hispanic/ Latin American		Middle Eastern		Unknown		White			Average	Mode
8		76		53		–		–		33		170		
GENDER														51	55
M	F	M	F	M	F	M	F	M	F	M	F			
8	–	66	10	53	–	–	–	–	–	31	2			

Source: UCLA BioCritical Studies Lab, Los Angeles County In-Custody Death Data 2008-2019, https://www.terencekeel.com/the-coroner-report-project

arrested, if he was sentenced, and/or the jail facility where he was held. While incarcerated Kenneth was brutally assaulted by jail guards who "crushed the decedent in one of the gate doors." The encounter left him confined to a wheelchair and needing fourteen months of physical therapy. Despite documenting these details, there was no evidence to suggest the investigator verified or disputed this story for the public record. Kenneth's official autopsy did not contain an incident report about the assault or hospital records from the jail infirmary about his injuries. Also missing was an assessment ruling out the possibility that this assault contributed to his death—Adcock perished only a year after his recovery. It is possible that these medical files were not provided in the death record out of privacy concerns. If this was the case, then it should have been noted along with a justification for why such an omission would be in the public's interest.

Details about Adcock's poor health and drug history helped make the natural death determination all the more real—that his body was ultimately to blame. Family and friends were conscripted into cosigning his natural death.

In my judgment, however, being incarcerated is what killed Kenneth. In the synopsis of events just prior to his death I found a single sentence that said: "The decedent was on a fire training hike when he complained of shortness of breath and collapsed."[9] This is the only location in his entire autopsy that mentions this rather important detail. Kenneth was a participant in the Conservation (Fire) Camp Program, which uses the labor of incarcerated people to combat California's growing fire season.[10] Individuals incarcerated in California who wish to join the program must pass a health screening, be a low security risk, have fewer than eight years remaining on their sentences, and complete a two-week training course. These all-prisoner teams reside in facilities known as fire camps, operating under the guidance of California Department of Forestry and Fire Protection (Cal Fire) staff. Their daily compensation ranges from $2.90 to $5.00, based on their assigned tasks, with a slight increase during active firefighting duties. Incarcerated firefighters typically operate in teams known as hand crews.[11] Their primary task is to construct firebreaks, which are gaps in vegetation designed to halt the spread of wildfires. These crews manually clear strips of land, removing all combustible material to create bare-earth barriers that deprive advancing flames of fuel. To accomplish this work, they employ various hand tools, including chainsaws for cutting through woody vegetation, shovels for clearing debris, and axes for chopping smaller plants and roots. The work is grueling and dangerous, and several inmates have died in the last decade in the program.[12] Inmate firefighters currently make up about one-third of California's total firefighting personnel.[13] The practice of using prison labor in the Golden State is not new; once it joined the Union in 1850, California used convict labor to build prisons, develop infrastructure for cities, and produce commercial goods.[14]

The investigators who wrote Kenneth's autopsy made no effort to consider possible connections between his death and the very program he was laboring for when he died. We cannot find in his autopsy information about whether the training hike involved a live fire exercise, what the air quality or temperature was that day, how far he had traveled, who was with him when he collapsed, how he was cleared to participate in this program to begin with, and whether Kenneth had recently seen fire combat.[15] These omissions were like the haunting silences I found in Roster and Dick's inquests nearly two hundred years ago.

The investigators who wrote Kenneth's autopsy did not explicitly use the "but for" principle in their assessment either. In this case, it could have meant asking, "If not for his being in jail, or his recent rehabilitation from being assaulted by jail deputies, or his participation in the dangerous Conservation Camp program, would he have died?" The answer I believe should have been no. Surely Kenneth carried mental if not physical trauma from his previous assault; we cannot imagine that being returned to jail—where he had been beaten into disability—would have felt safe. Rather than have his dependency issues treated with the care of a proper recovery facility, Kenneth was placed in a county jail system that reported twenty-eight deaths the year he died.[16]

Some may see the fire camp program as an opportunity and a path to freedom that Kenneth chose. But when faced with the risk of extended exposure to one of the nation's most violent jail systems versus the prospect of fighting fires for less than five dollars a day, the choice seems hardly one at all. If Kenneth's health history was severe enough to kill him during a training exercise, as the county medical examiner wants the public to believe, then the California Department of Corrections and the Department of Forestry and Fire Protection placed him at risk of death by allowing him to participate in the program. Kenneth's death should have been classified as a "homicide, medical negligence," with the responsibility falling on the shoulders of county and state officials. Instead of arriving at this conclusion, the death investigators placed the source of his death within his body, allowing a pathway around the difficult but important questions about the legal and social forces governing the environment where he perished—matters that modern science can measure and evaluate. The structures around his life were as influential in his death as his health history.

While Kenneth technically died from natural processes associated with lack of oxygen to the brain and heart failure, these factors alone cannot carry the full responsibility for his perishing. Evidence of a hostile environment was there to be found if only investigators had the will to see it.[17] When the end of Kenneth's life is placed in a frame where we can recognize society inside his body, his heart appears to be the final witness to a history of structural neglect, violence, and chaos—a vital organ enchanted by ethical and political failures of Los Angeles County and the state of California.

DYING FROM LEGAL IMMUNITY

Even if the Los Angeles County Department of Medical Examiner-Coroner had classified Kenneth Adcock's death a homicide, it is unlikely that criminal charges would have been brought against the county. When states began relieving coroners of their prosecutorial functions during the Jim Crow era, a distinction emerged between the meaning of homicide within the context of a death investigation and its legal definition within criminal courts. Homicide for death investigators became a neutral term, whereas homicide in the context of criminal law became associated with criminal intent and responsibility.

According to NAME, homicide is "a volitional act committed by another person to cause fear, harm, or death." Homicide within the context of criminal law technically means the killing of another, with varying degrees of culpability. Law enforcement and prosecutors have the additional responsibility of determining if this lethal act was intentional, unplanned, or an accident. Also complicating matters is the freedom given to police departments to lawfully and justifiably take someone's life; police routinely rationalize homicide as an extension of their duties.

Legal scholars Osagie Obasogie and Zachary Newman, in their study of seventy-five major American cities, demonstrated that excessive police discretion in justifying civilian deaths has undermined court rulings on in-custody death cases, effectively sanctioning these lethal practices. They argue that the failure to prosecute or bring criminal charges for lethal police violence erodes the guarantees of the Fourth Amendment, which gives "the people" the right "to be secure in their persons, houses, papers, and effects, against unreasonable searches and seizures."[18] The American public has little protection against lethal police violence, and the legal meaning of this type of death has increasingly been defined by law enforcement, not the Constitution, federal courts, or death investigators.

My lab found that between 2008 and 2019 there were twenty-one homicides in Los Angeles County involving police either during arrest or while in jail—the least common manner of death during the period. Approximately 3.5 percent of carceral deaths and 8 percent of street deaths during this time period were classified as homicides. Only one (Latina) woman died due to homicide in our sample. Hispanic/Latin American men made up half of all homicide deaths. The average age of all homicides was thirty-eight years (figure 5.2).

Two non-firearm homicide cases my lab reviewed were particularly haunting. In each case the amount of force deployed was staggering, as was the ability of police and death investigators to make these killings appear necessary.

The first case is that of Glenda Reymer, a forty-nine-year-old white woman killed by law enforcement outside her home in Long Beach, California, on June 22, 2001.[19] Glenda was a mother of three adult children,

FIGURE 5.2 Demographic data on homicide deaths in law enforcement custody (during arrest or pursuit and in carceral facilities) in Los Angeles County from 2008 to 2019

IN-CUSTODY HOMICIDES IN LOS ANGELES COUNTY, 2008–2019								
RACE						TOTAL	AGE	
Asian	Black	Hispanic/ Latin American	Middle Eastern	Unknown	White		Average	Mode
I	5	10	–	–	5	21		
GENDER								
Female			Male				38	36
I			21					

Source: UCLA BioCritical Studies Lab, Los Angeles County In-Custody Death Data 2008-2019, https://www.terencekeel.com/the-coroner-report-project

a sister, a long-term partner, and a bartender at a local watering hole. To the forensic investigator, Glenda had "a history of heroin abuse, seizure, mental illness, and a mass in her abdomen." Her death record does not make it clear if she was receiving treatment for her mental illness or the mass in her stomach. Her family shared with investigators that she had recently "lost over 30 pounds" and appeared to be "slipping mentally." Eighteen days before she was killed by police "she was carjacked and beaten severely" at a local park. Glenda suffered injuries to her face and neck, and she received medical treatment at Pacific Hospital in Long Beach. Those injuries had not healed at the time of her death. Unlike with the Kenneth Adcock autopsy, the medical examiner went on record to exclude their contribution to her death, noting that "there are no signs that the previous trauma contributed to death in any way." Her boyfriend explained that since the attack she "had begun to act very strange and erratic." While the injuries may not have immediately precipitated her death, the attack placed Glenda in the altered state of mind that brought law enforcement to her home.

The records of events on that day were chaotic. Officers were dispatched to Glenda's home on June 22, 2001, where she was apparently harassing schoolchildren. The police arrived and left shortly thereafter. Hours later, Glenda called police requesting medical assistance for her partner who she believed was suffering from an overdose. When they arrived with fire personnel, he appeared fine and not under the influence of any drugs or controlled substances. Police claim Glenda became disturbed once she learned her boyfriend would not be taken to the hospital for treatment. They asked Glenda to leave her home to "cool down." She agreed and got into her pickup truck parked outside. What transpired next was unclear according to the death record. The forensic investigator reports that instead of driving away, Glenda retrieved "a large kitchen knife" and threatened to "kill the officers, herself, and the boyfriend."[20] The death investigators made sure to note that these threats were accompanied with "slashing motions with the knife toward her throat and abdomen." Witnessing these actions, police threatened to shoot her with "a less than lethal beanbag." Clearly in distress, Glenda sat "on the back of a truck, emptied her purse, placed the purse across her chest, and began rocking back and forth." Was she trying to avoid being shot by police? Was she attempting to self-regulate a nervous system triggered a fight-or-flight response?[21] The public death record did not ask these questions, and no attempt was made to bring in a social worker or mental health specialist to de-escalate the situation.

According to police reports there were at least nine officers surrounding Glenda.[22] After fifteen minutes of unsuccessful negotiations, an officer used a Remington twelve-gauge shotgun to fire a beanbag round into her five-foot-five frame, which at the time weighed about a hundred pounds. He fired another round into her left arm after she appeared noncompliant. The distance from where the shot was fired was not recorded on the death report written by Los Angeles County. A spokeswoman for the Long Beach police later reported to the *Los Angeles Times* that the officer who fired the weapon was about thirty-five feet from Glenda. "Officers obviously felt they had to do something to end it peacefully," she reported.[23] Glenda's family disagreed. Her boyfriend was quoted in the same story, "There were so many officers around her, and she was so tiny, such a frail woman, I don't know why they couldn't have used pepper spray. She'd still be alive."

The beanbag round from Long Beach police broke her ribs. The second round severely damaged her arm. Glenda collapsed outside her home and an emergency thoracotomy was performed without success. Her heart practically exploded from the force of the shotgun round, forcing her ribs to break into her body, puncturing her heart. Glenda "died rapidly from markedly severe hemorrhaging from a tear in the heart caused by a powerful focused blunt force injury to the left lower chest."[24] Her death was classified as a homicide.

No one would dispute that the medical examiner arrived at the correct death classification. In the summary statement written by the forensic investigator, we find direct links between police actions and Glenda's death: "Officers shot her twice with less than lethal beanbags"; "she did not respond to the first hit so an officer shot her again."[25] The agency and intentions are clear in these less technical sections of the death record. This transparency, however, is lost in the medical assessment of Glenda's fatal injuries. There we find statements like "The woman's body died rapidly" and "There may be comingling of injuries." In these statements, there is a distance between the violence to her body and the actors responsible. "Injury caused by firearm projecting 'bean bag' missiles. Officer-involved shooting." Who fired the "bean bag" missiles? Was it the officers? One would hardly be faulted for not knowing after reading this sequence of statements without the accompanying investigative report.

The fact that Los Angeles County classified Glenda's death a homicide would have no consequences for the police that took her life. Then District Attorney Steve Cooley determined that the force used against her was "reasonable under the circumstance and Ms. Reymer's resulting death was neither intentional nor negligently caused."[26] To justify this position the district attorney's office cited California Penal Code § 835, which "authorizes a peace officer, who has reasonable cause to believe that a person to be arrested has committed a public offense, to use reasonable force to effect the arrest, to prevent escape or to overcome resistance."[27] While her death report did not specify what law Glenda had broken, Cooley also cited Penal Code § 417 (a)(1), which states:

> Every person who except in self-defense, in the presence of any other person, draws or exhibits any deadly weapon whatsoever, other than a firearm, in a rude, angry, or threatening manner, or who in any

manner, unlawfully uses a deadly weapon other than a firearm in any fight or quarrel is guilty of a misdemeanor, punishable by imprisonment in a county jail for not less than 30 days.[28]

Was Glenda acting in self-defense? Surely a hundred-pound white woman with mental illness would have felt threatened after being surrounded by armed police not long after calling them for help. Cooley declared that his office would not "initiate criminal proceeding against either of these officers."[29] Glenda's family found justice a few years later, but not from Los Angeles County. They won a lawsuit against Armor Holdings Inc., the Jacksonville-based manufacturer of the bean bag round that took her life.[30] Long Beach Police Department claimed that they expected the bean bag rounds to act as a "pain-compliance tool." Armor Holdings Inc. settled with the Reymer family for an undisclosed amount.

As in Glenda's case, there appeared to be no limits to the amount of force used against Michael Mears in 2015. His death showed how law enforcement subdual operates almost exclusively through the logic of additive violence, where force is only ever increased on a person in custody until the desired submission is achieved. Additive force is easy to justify, and its persuasive logic reverberates throughout death reports.

Michael was a thirty-nine-year-old white male, former marine, and native of Florida. He was discharged from the military in 1997 after sustaining a spinal cord injury during Operation Desert Storm. Michael was completely disabled and confined to a wheelchair for over two years before regaining the ability to walk.[31] He lived with chronic neuropathic pain in his right leg, suffered from posttraumatic stress disorder, and had been prescribed a series of steroids and pain medications to treat the symptoms of these conditions.

At the time of his death Michael was living with a sister in Los Angeles, west of the 405 freeway near Ladera Heights. On Christmas Eve in 2014 he experienced a mental health crisis; his sister reported that Michael abruptly started shouting, "They are coming to get me! They are coming to get me!" He then appeared to take cover in their living room and eventually fled the apartment. When he returned, his sister witnessed him experiencing convulsions and reportedly "banging his head against the wall in the hallway outside a unit on the third floor." She notified building security of Michael's altered state of mind and "the need for paramedics only." Building security and medical personnel encountered Michael in a hallway of the apartment where he had shattered windows and lights.[32] The medical examiner documents that in their opinion there was "concern that the decedent would hurt himself or others, and police were called."[33] District Attorney Jackie Lacy would later report that "paramedics believed Mears was under the influence of an illegal substance, such as PCP or cocaine, and due to Mears' behavior and size, they believed it was unsafe to approach him."[34] Michael was reportedly "over six feet tall and weighed 305 pounds."

When police arrived they claim to have found him in an agitated state and "bleeding heavily from numerous cuts on his body" from reportedly "rolling around on the floor of the hallway in broken glass." There was a brief period where Michael appeared to comply with police commands. Reports state that Michael laid prone on his stomach. But according to police, he kicked officers when they approached. They responded by striking him with batons, subjecting him to pepper spray, and then tasering him six times. This placed him in temporary shock and allowed police to pile on top of his body and apply hobble restraints, binding his legs and hands together. With his mobility limited, paramedics sedated Michael with an injection of Versed, also known as midazolam, a central nervous system depressant. He was transported to UCLA Medical Center and resuscitated twice after cardiac arrest. Shortly after, he was intubated, placed on a mechanical ventilator, and given continuous hemodialysis because of kidney failure. On December 26, he suffered a third heart attack and could not be revived. The medical examiner labeled his death a "homicide" due to "ventricular dysrhythmia," "cardiac enlargement with biventricular hypertrophy," cocaine intoxication, and "police restraint with use of taser."[35]

Michael's death was no more necessary or inevitable than Glenda's or Kenneth's. All were vulnerable and disabled people failed many times over by the institutions around them. When Michael's sister requested "the need for paramedics only," she wanted to protect him from law enforcement. Although paramedics arrived without police, they did not have the skill or training to manage his health crisis. They were not accompanied by a mental health professional or a social worker trained in peacefully resolving acute psychosis—someone who might have been able to connect with Michael during this episode.[36] The arrival of police escalated matters.

Finding the terms "altered" and "agitated" in Michael's autopsy suggested to me that the police and paramedics might have believed he suffered from "excited delirium." This condition emerged from the minds of police in the field; it describes a person in a state of severe agitation, or hyperarousal, often with an elevated heart rate and high body temperature.[37] There have been no clinical trials on the condition to confirm the existence of or parameters for this condition. It is not recognized in the *Diagnostic and Statistical Manual of Mental Disorders*. Several studies have found medical examiners using this diagnosis to rationalize excessive use of force by police.[38] It is a condition that allows police violence to appear necessary and, paradoxically, unrelated to the cause of death. In 2023, California governor Gavin Newsom signed a bill prohibiting the use of excited delirium in autopsies with the hope of producing more accurate death reports.[39]

Michael faced the full gamut of supposedly nonlethal weaponry. This included pepper spray and Tasers, which in isolation have proven to be lethal.[40] In 2023 I published with my colleague Jonah Walters one of the first studies on the history of pepper spray.[41] We found the use of chili peppers as a weapon can be traced back to American slavery, and modern clinical trials on mouse models prove the active agent in pepper spray (oleoresin capsaicin, or OC) is lethal in small doses when contact is made with the skin, eyes, and olfactory system. Police-grade pepper spray is unregulated by the federal government, and manufacturers use proprietary formulas that include potent concentrations of OC combined with synthetic lachrymator phenacyl chloride (CN), commonly known as tear gas, to produce increasingly more potent formulas that help them monopolize their hold on the police weaponry market.

Death investigators noted in their report that the amount of pepper spray used against Michael was so significant that it "affected the paramedics and officers in the hallway" as they attempted to arrest him.[42]

And when the weapon did not achieve the desired effect, police tased Michael, exposing him and officers to even greater danger as many pepper spray devices use a flammable isopropyl alcohol base solution, which can create a fire with the introduction of electricity.[43] In 2021, Catskill police officers killed a man in their custody who was covered in hand sanitizer, tased, and subsequently caught fire.[44]

The hobble restraint position that officers used against Michael has also proven lethal, as it can restrict breathing, increase pressure on the circulatory system of the captive, and induce cardiac arrest.[45] And then finally, the sedative given to Michael, midazolam, carries side effects that include depleted levels of oxygen in the blood, agitation, and a comatose state.[46] The totality of restraining force applied to Michael's body was staggering.

Despite all of the violence, law enforcement reported his death as an accident to the medical examiner.[47] While the death investigator would reject this classification, choosing instead to designate his death a homicide, they authored a medical opinion that read as if Michael's biology was the principal cause of his death: "It is my opinion that this 39-year-old man, Michael Frederick Mears died as a result of Ventricular Dysrhythmia due to Cardiac Enlargement with Biventricular Hypertrophy and Four Chamber Dilatation with other significant conditions of Cocaine Intoxication and Police Restraint with Use of Taser."[48]

Hypertrophic cardiomyopathy is a genetic condition where the heart muscles thicken, making it difficult to circulate blood and oxygen. The condition is fatal only in a small percentage of people.[49] A blood screening taken while in the hospital produced a "presumptive positive" result for cocaine, which meant it may or may not have been in his system at the time of his death; still, it appeared in his autopsy as a contributing factor. And as with Glenda's homicide, the report was narrated to create distance between the action of police and their effects on the body: "police restraint with use of taser" is not the same as saying "police restrained and tased Mears." This linguistic ambiguity appears elsewhere in the technical sections of the autopsy: "In order for the decedent to be restrained, police allegedly used pepper spray, and allegedly used a taser." Allegedly? A few sentences later, however, when describing the actions of paramedics, we find "he was given an injection of midazolam by the paramedics." The language here is clear, and the actions of medical personnel on Michael's body are obvious and plain.

No criminal charges were brought against the officers who arrested Michael. District Attorney Jackie Lacey would cite the US Supreme Court decision in *Graham v. Conner* (1989), which established an objective test for evaluating if an officer's actions were reasonable or excessive and therefore in violation of the Fourth Amendment. In *Graham v. Conner* a police officer in Charlotte, North Carolina, confronted, arrested, and detained a diabetic Black man named Dethrone Graham who was exhibiting unusual behavior during a health crisis involving low blood sugar. The courts ruled that the Fourth Amendment authorizes law enforcement to make an arrest or investigatory stop, which "necessarily carries with it the right to use some degree of physical coercion or threat thereof to effect it."[50] The courts explained, "The 'reasonableness' of a particular use of force must be judged from the perspective of a reasonable officer on the scene, rather than with the 20/20 vision of hindsight." They also added that the context and circumstances surrounding an arrest should determine whether the force was sensible. The courts ruled that despite his injuries Graham's Fourth Amendment rights had not been violated according to this objective reasonableness standard. District Attorney Lacey argued that Michael was a threat to himself and others, and that the force applied to his body did not violate his Fourth Amendment rights, despite killing him. She also cited the court decision in *Hill v. Miracle* (6th Cir. 2017) 853 F. 3d 306, which determined that use of force was appropriate in the event of a medical emergency.[51] The county determined that the officers "applied lawful force in detaining Michael Mears and are not criminally responsible for his death."[52]

The homicides of Glenda and Michael show us how law enforcement violence not only shortens lives but also distorts the language we use to describe it, imposing an artificial distance between acts of brutality and their effect in the world and on bodies. There is a strange refuge in statements like "The woman's body died rapidly" or "Injury caused by firearm projecting 'bean bag' missiles" rather than saying "Police fired a shotgun that her killed her instantly."

Transparency is not simply about access to death records. It also involves the language used to describe lethal police violence. I believe Glenda's and Michael's deaths should have been classified as "homicide, negligent arrest," disclosing for the public record that the outcome might have been different and these losses could have been avoided. Reports that evade naming the agents of harm merely protect police and ourselves from acknowledging connections that would be apparent in any other social confrontation.

Reading medical examinations of police homicides is like following a story where the protagonist is haunted by an adversary the narrator has implied doesn't exist—as though law enforcement was a specter or some supernatural entity.

ORGANIZED CHAOS

Police encounters with civilians are resolved in one of three ways: freeing a person (with or without a citation), arresting them, or death. All three outcomes are routine despite the tragic nature of the latter, which on average occurs three times a day. When a medical examiner identifies an in-custody death as an accident, their charge is to discern if the force used was intended to kill. They also have to determine if the outcome of the encounter deviates from the expectations we have about police encounters—beliefs that extend far beyond matters of science and medicine. Unlike police, death investigators are not legally bound by an objective universal standard from which to evaluate whether police violence was intended to be lethal or was merely an accident.

Randy Hanzlick, John Hunsaker, and Gregory Davis offer some guidance on this question. They have argued that the accident classification "applies when an injury or poisoning causes death and there is little or no evidence that the injury or poisoning occurred with intent to harm or cause death. In essence, the fatal outcome was unintentional."[53] This guidance, however, is not always sufficient for law enforcement encounters—like, for example, when on August 27, 2008, a Highland City police officer ran over fourteen-year-old Justin Ames who was on his bicycle at an intersection in San Bernardino County, California.[54]

Police did not intend to kill Justin, but they were chasing another suspect at the time of the collision. This detail makes the case more complicated; exposing people to harm falls within the line of police duty, as district attorneys repeatedly argue in homicide cases. This exposure includes not only an alleged suspect but bystanders and witnesses as well.

Did police have their lights and sirens on before they hit Justin? Was there dashcam or surveillance footage of the accident available to the coroner to use in their evaluation? What were the driving conditions that day? Had the patrol vehicle been recently serviced? What was the emergency that officer was rushing off to? How many hours had they been working before the collision? How many other vehicle deaths have happened in this police department? Answers to these questions cannot be found on the public record. Justin's death was reported as a traffic accident, not an officer-involved death. The preemptive labeling of Justin's death as merely a traffic accident obviates a real death investigation. This is poor science, but not entirely surprising; the San Bernardino County coroner sits under the administrative jurisdiction of the San Bernardino County sheriff.

My lab was able to identify Justin's case from a crowd-sourced dataset that operates with a more capacious understanding of an "officer-involved" death than the ledgers kept by state and federal officials. Returning again to Los Angeles County, there were 165 accidental deaths involving police between 2008 and 2019 (figure 5.3). Accidental death ranked second in all manner of deaths during this period.[55] Men made up the vast majority of the accidental death cases, representing 82 percent of the data. When gender and race were considered, Hispanic/Latin American individuals ($n = 71$) and white people ($n = 49$) were most often reported as dying from an accidental death, followed closely by Black individuals ($n = 31$).

The guidelines provided by NAME are simply inadequate for evaluating ambiguous or borderline accidental deaths involving police. Many cases show this to be true. For example, twenty-four-year-old Eric Poland stole a Toyota Camry in South Long Beach during the early hours of April 4, 2000.[56] It was dark and the marine layer blanketing

FIGURE 5.3 Demographic data on accidental deaths in law enforcement custody (during arrest or pursuit and in carceral facilities) in Los Angeles County from 2008 to 2019. This data includes vehicle-related cases.

IN-CUSTODY ACCIDENTAL DEATHS IN LOS ANGELES COUNTY, 2008–2019							TOTAL	AGE	
RACE									
Asian	Black	Hispanic/ Latin American	Middle Eastern	Unknown	White			Average	Mode
8	31	71	1	5	49		165		
GENDER									
Female			Male					38	23
31			134						

Source: UCLA BioCritical Studies Lab, Los Angeles County In-Custody Death Data 2008-2019, https://www.terencekeel.com/the-coroner-report-project

Long Beach was dense. Not long after, Eric was spotted by police and became involved in a high-speed chase. Poland lost control of the car and jumped from the driver's side moments before he and the Camry collided with a highway guardrail and a building. Eric died instantly from catastrophic head injury. Thirty-one-year-old Terelle Thomas was pulled over by police for suspected drug activity in Dauphin County, Pennsylvania, on December 17, 2019.[57] He swallowed a bag of cocaine at some point during the traffic stop. He seized an hour later while inside a jail cell and died at a local hospital. Edward and Gracie Contreras were traveling home from Knotts Berry Farm with their thirteen-year-old son when their car was suddenly struck by the driver of a stolen Jeep fleeing from law enforcement.[58] Edward and Gracie were killed after being ejected from their car; their son survived with severe leg and arm injuries.

Place these deaths into a broader understanding of "officer-involved," one that makes plain the links between the laws we authorize and the police that enforce them, and what initially appears to be an accident looks more like "structural homicide"—a death born out of the nexus of beliefs, legal codes, and political decisions that order our society. Was it necessary for police to chase Eric Poland given traffic conditions that day in Long Beach? Would Edward and Gracie Contreras still be alive if Los Angeles County followed the direction of cities like Chicago, which no longer mandates police to pursue suspects in stolen vehicles?[59] Had Dauphin County decriminalized minor drug possession in 2019—like Philadelphia attempted under District Attorney Larry Krasner or Baltimore under State's Attorney Marilyn Mosby—would Terelle Thomas have swallowed the drugs that took his life?[60] Some will say these questions are beyond the scope of a death investigator's task. But they are the right questions, ones asked by communities seeking justice in the wake of police violence. It remains within the power of contemporary science to think through the larger philosophical and political issues surrounding accidental police deaths.

After all, an accident is not a natural category hardwired into our minds at birth. Accidents are socially and politically unstable phenomena, carrying different meanings given the context and latent beliefs about what is normal and unexpected. Accidents are something we are taught to recognize. To label an in-custody death an accident, I believe, means coming to terms with our education on police interactions within the confines of the law. District and state attorneys have insisted we accept the judgment of police in the heat of an arrest to determine what is a reasonable use of lethal force, what is a homicide, what is an accident. Through this instruction we have been swept into a feedback loop of justified violence that desensitizes us, raises our tolerance and apathy for the next reported violent encounter—moving our collective acceptance of police violence to further extremes. In such an environment, can police even kill accidentally?

Or is it possible that creating accidents is an enduring quality of law enforcement? Might policing itself be an accident of history to which we remain tethered?[61] Many community advocates say yes to these questions and point to in-custody deaths and police violence as the grounds for liberating communities from the overreach of law enforcement.

One needs a generous view of human nature to imagine America without police. But one needs only to be a realist to see that police are failing to solve social problems that could be addressed more humane and honorable institutions of care and accountability.

ANOMIE

People in America are ending their lives at unprecedented rates. Suicide rates in the last decade have risen dramatically across all demographic groups, especially among men between the ages of eighteen and thirty-five.[62] Taking one's life within the custody of police, whether in jail or during arrest, is also one of the leading causes of in-custody death. Again, the refusal of law enforcement agencies to consistently report manner of death makes it difficult to evaluate the frequency of suicide during arrest or while in police custody at the national level. The local picture, however, is a bit more clear on this issue, especially in Los Angeles County, where the autopsies of victims can be gathered to confirm manner of death. My lab discovered fifty-four suicides while in the custody of police in Los Angeles between 2008 and 2019. Suicides ranked third in all death classifications used by investigators over this period, but the number of suicide deaths differed depending on the setting. While only about 3 percent of street deaths were classified as suicide, almost 16 percent of carceral deaths were. In terms of raw numbers, more men (*n* = 50) committed suicide than women (*n* = 4), and white individuals (*n* = 24) had the most reported cases, followed by Hispanic/Latin American individuals (*n* = 22), Black individuals (*n* = 5), and Asian individuals (*n* = 3) (figure 5.4). The reported hanging

FIGURE 5.4 Demographic data on suicide deaths in law enforcement custody (during arrest or pursuit and in carceral facilities) in Los Angeles County from 2008 to 2019

IN-CUSTODY SUICIDES IN LOS ANGELES COUNTY, 2008–2019						TOTAL	AGE	
RACE								
Asian	Black	Hispanic/ Latin American	Middle Eastern	Unknown	White		Average	Mode
3	5	22	–	–	24	54		
GENDER								
Female			Male				39	31
4			50					

Source: UCLA BioCritical Studies Lab, Los Angeles County In-Custody Death Data 2008-2019, https://www.terencekeel.com/the-coroner-report-project

of Sandra Bland inside a Texas jail cell in 2015 is the most prominent example of this otherwise hidden crisis.

Within this climate of rising suicides—in custody and among the free population—Americans are also losing faith in political institutions. Trust in government institutions has steadily declined since the Johnson administration in 1964.[63] Pew reports that in 2024 only one in four Americans said they "trust the government in Washington to do what is right 'just about always' or 'most of the time.'" Families are losing faith in public schools, with surveys reporting that half of the country believes K-12 public education is moving in the wrong direction.[64] American trust in scientific and medical institutions is also in decline.[65] And more people have reservations about police and the criminal justice system, with 60 percent of Americans believing civilians should have the power to sue law enforcement for excessive force, according to a national Pew survey.[66]

What lessons can we learn from in-custody suicides happening during a time when suicide is on the rise more generally and Americans appear to be losing faith in the institutions that govern and bring us together? Can and should law enforcement be held accountable for custodial deaths that might also be symptoms of a larger social or political malaise? If so, how can medical examiner-coroners convey this responsibility through biomedical discovery?

Suicides challenge the legitimacy of our society at the deepest levels and provoke sociological and philosophical questions that have long preoccupied modern scientists. In 1897 Emile Durkheim published *Le Suicide*, the first sociological study of its kind, arguing that suicide has social causes and was not an innate feature of a person's psychology or a defect in their personality. This was a revolutionary finding that would profoundly shape modern sociology and psychology. Durkheim saw that an individual's level of social connection plays a significant role in their likelihood of attempting suicide by surveying death statistics from France, Prussia (now Germany), and Italy between 1841 and 1872. Those who feel embedded in their community, with strong social ties and a clear sense of belonging, are at a lower risk of suicidal behavior, he found. This sense of integration helps people find meaning in their lives within the broader social framework. Conversely, as people become more isolated or disconnected from society, their vulnerability to suicide increases. The weakening of social bonds and a diminished feeling of being part of a larger collective correlate with a higher propensity for self-harm.

Durkheim identified two types of suicide I believe remain useful for understanding people who take their lives in police custody: anomic and fatalistic suicide.

What Durkheim called anomic suicide is the act of taking one's life as a result of weakened social cohesion, where people feel disconnected from society. This is a death born out of social despair and the instability of a society lacking inclusive values capable of integrating people into economies of care, purpose, meaning, and longevity. The deaths documented throughout this book have made plain the effects of America's evaporating safety net on the mental, physical, and material well-being of everyday people, and how we use law enforcement to resolve the disenfranchisement and social ruin that follow.

I believe the death of twenty-two-year-old Kalief Browder was an anomic suicide. Browder's story drew national attention in 2015 and awakened many Americans to the reality of our predatorial cash bail system. When Kalief was only sixteen years old he was arrested and sent to New York's infamous Rikers Island for allegedly stealing a backpack. Rikers has a long-documented history of human rights violations.[67] While awaiting trial Kalief was routinely beaten by prison guards, forced into fights with other inmates, and placed into solitary confinement for nearly eight hundred days.[68] Countless studies have shown solitary confinement to be a form of psychological torture that exponentially increases the risk of self-injury and suicide.[69] Kalief endured this gauntlet for more than two years before the charges against him were dropped. But the violence and isolation had taken their toll. Kalief became withdrawn, socially isolated, temperamental, and a shell of himself after he was incarcerated. His attempts to integrate into society through school, employment, and friendships were not enough to bring him back from Rikers.[70] Kalief took his life on June 6, 2015. While he may not have died in the custody of police, he never recovered from the psychological terror of being forced to fight for his life in jail while his ties to society were severed in prolonged solitary confinement. Trauma fragments time in the body. A part of Kalief never left Rikers.[71]

If we think across the distance between ourselves and the victims of police violence, suicide becomes much more than another person's death; it becomes a type of self-immolation. Through our need for safety in a nation incapable of taking care of the vulnerable, we use police to punish and eliminate parts of a whole that cannot fit into the collective. This is the definition of losing a part of ourselves. Kalief was a part of all of us.

And what about living under laws that also repress the agency of the collective? When people experience overwhelming social constraints that severely limit their personal freedom and sense of self, they may resort to what Durkheim called fatalistic suicide. This type of suicide is associated with environments where extreme external control creates oppressive living conditions. In these situations, people might choose to end their lives rather than continue to endure.

My lab investigated this problem by gathering data on the alarming number of suicide deaths in jail facilities notorious for repressive and violent conditions in California, Pennsylvania, and Maryland. Between 2009 and 2018 we found 260 reported deaths inside Los Angeles County jails.[72] Violence and the repression of inmates appeared to have a collateral effect on those who allegedly took their own lives. We discovered that suicide was the second leading cause of death over this nine-year period ($n = 46$), with thirty-five out of these forty-six cases occurring before the person stood trial. In 2009, the most lethal year during our study, there were four suicides every six months.[73] We also learned that several suicide deaths showed signs of recent physical violence on the bodies.

For example, a forty-four-year-old white man named Jay McCabe died in 2012 while detained at Century Regional Detention Facility.[74] Although his death was ruled a suicide from hanging, he had recent blunt-force head trauma that the investigator failed to explain or link to his suicide. McCabe died before standing trial. A twenty-two-year-old Black man named Lewis Nyarecha died in 2018 from apparent suicide inside Twin Towers.[75] His autopsy also revealed recent blunt force head trauma and lethal levels of the antipsychotic drug quetiapine in his blood postmortem. Jail deputies claimed the head injury occurred when they accidently dropped him while removing his lifeless body from the top bunk in his cell. Like McCabe, Nyarecha also died before standing trial.

We also found high numbers of suicides in carceral facilities in Pennsylvania and Maryland. We discovered thirty-one deaths inside Dauphin County Prison (DCP) between 2008 and 2022. Suicide was the second leading cause of death inside DCP during this period with eight documented cases. DCP is a midsized jail facility located in Harrisburg, Pennsylvania, that has gained local and national attention for the abuse, negligence, and death of men detained inside, with much of this violence targeting Black men. A report in 2023 initiated by the county found hundreds of use-of-force incidents inside DCP, which included restraining inmates in chairs and subjecting prisoners to physical violence and pepper spray.[76]

Maryland detention centers were equally notorious for violence and use of force against prisoners.[77] We found that suicide was the second leading cause of death ($n = 72$) across all ten facilities. Most troubling was the discovery that suicide was the leading cause of death ($n = 45$) for people who died within the first ten days of jail admission. All forty-five of these deaths happened before trial.[78]

The data gathered by my lab should be accessible to any investigator attempting to make sense of a reported suicide inside jail. Each of the suicides in Los Angeles, Dauphin County, and Maryland appeared fatalistic. They surely took place in an environment designed to extract the life, will, and agency of captives. But the task before medical examiners investigating these cases was limited to identifying the individual mechanism of self-harm, not the context or institutional history where this final act took place. Death investigators appear to be seeking the worst version of a free individual when making a suicide determination: a person who stands independent of society and is solely responsible for what happens throughout the course of their lives.

Situating these deaths within a broader frame changes their meaning; these suicides were not simply the acts of individuals but the product of institutions with histories of violence, neglect, and discrimination. Our defunct criminal justice system is what killed them. The failure to see the social structure of these deaths is a reflection of the moral education we've received from local and state officials who cover for police and insist jails are our only solution—that police violence is necessary, natural, reasonable.

INCONVENIENT VICTIMS

With the fifth and final death classification, "undetermined," we return to the issues I brought up before this odyssey of death and dying. We live in an era where the fates of the living and the dead are determined not by supernatural forces but by human institutions and the values that sustain them. While there remains space for mysteries in our modern world, more often than not they occur because we are asking the wrong questions or because, despite our best efforts using the tools of science and medicine, we simply don't know enough to explain the matter at hand. The questions death investigators ask and the data they decide to leverage or ignore makes the difference between a homicide, accident, suicide, or natural death.

For this reason, I contend that "undetermined" is a classification most out of place for an in-custody death. Jail deaths occur in a highly regulated and surveilled environment; what inmates eat, the water they drink, the air they breathe, when they sleep, and who they visit are all under the control of jail deputies. Deaths during arrest carry a data trail that includes witness statements from police, family, EMTs, physicians, dashcam footage, and bystanders. In-custody deaths, whether in jail or on the streets, occur in data-rich environments, even if that information is withheld or redacted from the public. According to NAME, the undetermined manner of death should be the least used by investigators and reserved for cases with either competing manners of death or where details about what happened are completely lacking.[79]

We should grant coroners and medical examiners the ability to weigh competing physiological mechanisms when studying an in-custody death. When investigators were evaluating the death of Michael Mears they pointed to heart disease, cocaine use, and excited delirium as physiological contributing factors. The medical examiner, however, remained clear that the death was homicide and not another competing classification. Police reported the death an accident, and still the medical examiner decided not to leave the case in limbo by using the "undetermined" classification. The death investigator in Michael's case had a wealth of information available to them during autopsy, leaving no question about the context or events surrounding his death. "Undetermined" was not appropriate for Michael's death; in this instance the investigator was correct.

When my lab looked at this issue throughout Los Angeles County, we found that 24 out of 318 deaths were reported as undetermined between 2008 and 2019—making it one of the least used classifications for this period (figure 5.5). When we compared deaths in jail to deaths during arrest, we found only 12 percent of street deaths and 7.5 percent of carceral deaths were classified under this category. When we looked more carefully at the jail cases, we found several autopsies with documented evidence of either physical violence or recent medical neglect on the part of jail staff.

For example, when eighteen-year-old Jorge Rosales died inside Twin Towers in 2011, his death was labeled undetermined despite an autopsy that recorded a black eye, broken blood vessels in both eyes (scleral hemorrhage), scalp and facial contusions, bruising and abrasions on his arms,

FIGURE 5.5 Demographic data on undetermined deaths in law enforcement custody (during arrest or pursuit and in carceral facilities) in Los Angeles County from 2008 to 2019

IN-CUSTODY UNDETERMINED DEATHS IN LOS ANGELES COUNTY, 2008–2019								
RACE						TOTAL	AGE	
Asian	Black	Hispanic/ Latin American	Middle Eastern	Unknown	White		Average	Mode
–	16	14	–	–	11	41	35	35
GENDER								
Female		Male						
5		36						

Source: UCLA BioCritical Studies Lab, Los Angeles County In-Custody Death Data 2008-2019, https://www.terencekeel.com/the-coroner-report-project

and acute hemorrhagic pancreatitis, an incredibly rare illness for men his age.[80] Records show that Jorge was subject to a use-of-force incident involving police just days before his death. Jorge had yet to stand trial before he died. There was also the death of Markese Braxton in 2018 inside Twin Towers.[81] His death was left undetermined with deep soft tissue hemorrhages on his hands, back, shoulders, and legs. Markese also had blood in the space between his brain and skull.

These cases suggested that death investigators were abusing the undetermined death classification, using it to cover the inhumane conditions inside. The heavily surveilled context of a jail and the data-rich environment of being in police custody make it difficult to justify not knowing what takes place while under the power of the state.

COVERING FOR THE STATE

The many victims of police violence carry our society's failure in and on their bodies. To discern these signs requires thinking beyond the void of neutrality that leaves medical examiners and coroners unwilling to show us the links between the law, its enforcement, and our flesh and bones. This requires new questions about the decision-making of police, alternative data sources about the lethal patterns of law enforcement, a more capacious understanding of "officer-involved," and most importantly medical language that reveals, connects, and clarifies rather than obscures or hedges in favor of the law. The truth about the circumstances leading to a person's death in custody should be based on proper scientific inquiry that examines not just bodies but the legal, political, and structural conditions we authorize over the lives of people taken into custody.

Until we think differently about the consequences of lethal police encounters, we will continue using science to examine the bodies of the dead without paying attention to the counties, cities, streets, and jail cells where they perished—as though their deaths were caused by forces other than society.

CHAPTER 6

THE BODIES WE DON'T SEE

A t least three people will die today because of police. The victims will most likely be Black, Latino, and male. They may also be women, white, teenagers, Indigenous, disabled, Asian, unhoused, Middle Eastern, Republican, mixed-race, Muslim, poor, transgender, nonbinary, and people yet to be convicted of a crime.

If investigators examine their bodies, they are likely to conclude that the death was caused by heart disease, substance abuse, or complications associated with some other preexisting condition. The coroner or medical examiner will avoid clear language binding the actions of police to the bodies of their victims. They will write instead that the dead "became unresponsive," "went into cardiac arrest," or "experienced a seizure." These events will be narrated in detached clinical language as if only biological processes were involved, not the society around and within the victim. Family, friends, and witnesses will be recruited to corroborate this compelling story. Law enforcement will likely be in the room during the autopsy. The medical examiner or coroner will consciously or unconsciously feel pressure to cover for police—the distance between death investigators and the communities they serve will be filled by the weight of the law.

If the death record is released to the public, it will be too thin or vague for families and communities seeking justice and closure. Investigators might also redact the file, place it on security hold, or simply not record the death as police-related.

A handful of local journalists will write stories that only a few will read or remember. Legacy media chasing other headlines will not bother covering these deaths, unless the violence was spectacular or the victim a saint.

If an inquest or criminal trial is held, precedent will ensure the officers involved are cleared of any wrongdoing. State attorneys will lecture us about the reasonableness of lethal violence and neglect, and how both are an unfortunate but necessary part of policing. Our death investigators will agree.

And tomorrow, this will happen again.

Over time our tolerance for police killings will grow, and we will slowly lose the desire to know the difference between justice and violence—only the victim's family and the organizations behind them will resist this regression, but they will not be taken seriously. Death will become an acceptable solution for dealing with people who cannot be integrated into the collective or find themselves on the wrong side of laws that are prejudiced and inhumane. These people will die because of traffic violations, petty theft, loitering, mental illness, opioid addiction, being a military veteran with PTSD, using counterfeit money, or being too poor to pay bail.

Names will pile up in the memories of loved ones and haunt their killers. There will be no national registry, federal database, or memorial for the bodies that police and death investigators hide. More and more people we know, love, work with, live next to, or pass by on freeways, trains, and sidewalks will simply not come home. We won't remember how this all started. We will believe this is how we've always dealt with criminals and threats to our safety. And it will be too late to stop the law from closing in on any of us should we cross it.

Many parts of the world I described are already here. None of the people you've met in these pages believed their lives would end at the hands of police, or that medical examiners and coroners would offer cover for the state. But the perishing of John Horton III, Alesia Thomas, Daniel Pastorek, Glenda Reymer, and so many others happened because death has become an instrument for dealing with people failed many times over by the nation.

Each of the tragedies in this book was set into motion by legal, political, and economic mistakes: relieving death investigators of their ability to shape criminal law with the wisdom of local communities, American courts adopting a colorblind vision of justice ill-prepared to recognize legal and political discrimination, the failure of American physicians and public health scientists to develop a coordinated health reform agenda that addresses the structural causes to diminished life expectancy, the creation of a fragmented death reporting system attenuated by the absence of federal mandates requiring police to release functional data on in-custody deaths, the rise of law-and-order politics that abandoned reform and embraced punishment as the goal of policing, the deindustrialization of the American workforce that left unorganized labor vulnerable to the precarity of life in a nation without a social safety net, and state officials rationalizing the constitutionality of police violence. The use of law enforcement to police these problems away has allowed in-custody deaths to become a crisis that targets people beyond the reach of democracy.

Over the course of writing this book I learned that drawing attention to lives lost to police violence elicits a strange reaction. When I spoke to friends, family, colleagues, and elected officials about how and why people die in custody, I was often met with the response: "How terrible, but I am not surprised." This told me that many of us know law enforcement is capable of unrestrained violence but believe *we* will not become its target. I would then share how every segment of American society can be found in our nation's death ledger and that too often we think about criminal justice from within a binary moral universe: people are either good and law abiding or they are not. This understanding leaves little space for the complexity of human behavior, or for seeing the connections between society and biology that we carry. Worse, it tethers our political imagination to a pessimistic understanding of human nature where trust in each other is thin and mistakes mark us forever.

I believe Alesia Thomas would still be alive if someone other than police had followed her home after leaving her babies at the police station. Daniel Pastorek might still be with us if the courts in Allegheny County had compassion and decided not to prosecute him for minor offenses or if the county had a facility to support people struggling with substance abuse. And certainly, John Horton would still be alive if police had decided not to bring him to jail while in the middle of his health crisis. Each of these decisions to enforce the law indiscriminately was rooted in the cruel belief that we are not entitled to mistakes in this country.

Once the complexity of social life has been reduced to a black-and-white ethical equation, it becomes easy to divide people between the chosen and the condemned. The chosen are law-abiding and committed to the common good derived either from the will of God or an implicit social contract. The condemned are people whose actions, behavior, and ideas are misaligned with the resolve of the collective; these people are threats to private property, social order, economic stability, and our safety. The condemned can be subjected to lethal force without tarnishing the moral integrity of police, the laws they enforce, or the safety created from the forfeiture of their lives.

Our politics reflect the belief that people on the wrong side of the law are not like us. Many Americans support criminalizing illicit drug use despite evidence showing its ineffectiveness as a deterrent or the fact that most users only violate drug-related laws.[1] We believe cash bail is a fair system that keeps dangerous people off the street even though investigations throughout California, New Jersey, New York, and Pennsylvania have demonstrated its predatory nature and that people from low-income communities are more likely than the wealthy to return to court if released.[2] Public health advocates have published countless reports showing that people suffering from mental illness are better served by health institutions rather than jails or prisons, yet we continue to call police when they are in crisis or place them in carceral facilities that make their conditions worse.[3]

Too many people have and will die in custody because of struggles with substance abuse, mental illness, or poverty. But we all know and love someone with prescription drug or substance issues, depression, trauma, or undiagnosed mental illness. And each decade there are more faces at the bottom of the well of structural inequality.[4] Still, we insist our safety depends on police, jails, prisons, and laws that do not work. Why? Because more of us believe there should be consequences for breaking rules—not enough of us believe criminals can be helped with institutions that offer care, shelter, and dignity.

Helen Jones, the mother of John Horton III, whose story I shared with you at the opening of this book, spent over a decade trying to convince elected officials, journalists, news media, local organizations, and practically anyone who would listen that her son was killed by deputies inside the jail and that the medical examiner participated in covering for police. Very few took her seriously because she was Black, her son was supposedly a criminal, and we generally don't believe everyday people carry expertise about how our society works. Other families I spoke with were confronted with the same wall of indifference. And because we inherited a death investigation system insulated from the judgment and insight of community, there are structural barriers that prevent us from listening to the stories that the dead and their families have to share.

But justice is more than a bureaucratic process. It requires us to return to our humanity. If we are going to avoid a future where in-custody deaths are simply how the law operates in America, it will require a new ethical sensibility toward people on the other side of it.

This shift has already taken root among communities impacted by the life-altering violence of police and the failures of our criminal justice system. What is commonly referred to as the "people's justice movement" is a grassroots effort aimed at solving shortcomings in the formal legal system and designing alternative institutions of conflict resolution and community-based accountability. The movement is as complex as its people, encompassing a range of practices and philosophies intended to empower communities, resolve disputes, repair harms, and create justice outside of traditional court systems. It has found success in increasing oversight and accountability for the actions of law enforcement. There are, for example, efforts being made to help local communities resolve disputes through mediation and dialogue. This is what the Red Hook Community Justice Center in Brooklyn has done, creating its own civilian court that resolves minor crimes such as theft and vandalism, while also dealing with housing disputes and juvenile delinquency.

Communities are taking up acts of "restorative justice" designed to repair harms through mediation and community service. The Conflict

Resolution Center of Baltimore County and Common Justice in New York City have gained national attention because of their success at using professionally trained mediators to help people bridge the distance between those on either side of the law and teaching community members to communicate their values and beliefs about justice during disputes with each other. The results have been incredible. For example, since its founding in 2009 the Conflict Resolution Center of Baltimore County has held over 1,500 "Community Conferences" that have helped over 8,000 youth and more than 16,000 families, victims, and school administrators.[5] Common Justice in New York helped introduce the Fair Access to Victim Compensation bill that was signed into law by Governor Kathy Hochul in 2023. The bill removes the requirement that survivors of harm and violence report to police before being eligible to receive support from New York State's victim compensation program, allowing residents to seek services from city- or state-contracted providers rather than law enforcement.

Then there are initiatives under the umbrella of "transformative justice" aimed at uprooting the core legal, political, and economic conditions responsible for violence within communities. This involves exposing bias in policing and sentencing practices, developing alternatives to incarceration, and creating structures of accountability for the actions of law enforcement. Many organizations engaged in transformative justice have adopted participatory decision-making models that bring members of the community into formal judicial processes through civilian oversight committees.

Dignity and Power Now (DPN), founded by Patrisse Cullors in Los Angeles, has been widely recognized as a beacon of transformative justice that has implemented participatory decision-making methods. The organization was set into motion by a performance art piece created by Cullors following a 2011 class action lawsuit by the American Civil Liberties Union (ACLU) against the Los Angeles County Sheriff's Department for prison abuse inside a county jail. Cullors's work, "STAINED: An Intimate Portrayal of State Violence," was inspired by her brother's violent encounter with LASD and showed the lie in the distinction between police brutality inside and outside of carceral spaces. The work became a catalyst for a countywide movement to end mass incarceration, develop alternatives to jail, hold law enforcement accountable, and integrate the power of the people back into the criminal justice system.

Not long after its inception, DPN became the anchor organization for the Coalition to End Sheriff Violence—a local movement that fought and won civilian oversight of LASD. These efforts resulted in the creation of Los Angeles County's first Civilian Oversight Commission (COC) in January 2016. This nine-member commission is appointed by the County Board of Supervisors and requires four panel seats to be held by members of the community. In 2020, the COC earned subpoena power over the sheriff, allowing it to summon LASD to testify and answer questions in public hearings. The COC hosts one of the few spaces in the county where impacted families and communities can speak freely about their encounters with the law. It also conducts investigations into the practices of LASD and prepares reports with recommendations for adoption by the County Board of Supervisors and the sheriff.

Through the leadership of commissioner Sean Kennedy, the COC helped advance the county's first investigation into sheriff deputy gangs inside the ranks of LASD, building on the work of local investigative journalist Cerise Castle. In 2021 Castle published a fifteen-part story on the history of organized deputy gangs, documenting the legacy of groups such as the "Lynwood Vikings," "Regulators," and "Compton Executioners" who have been terrorizing, punishing, and killing people within jail and throughout Los Angeles County since before the end of legal racial segregation.[6] Since 2024 LASD has instituted a policy prohibiting deputies from participating in these gangs, but it remains to be seen if this mandate will have any effect.

Community-driven institutions of justice and accountability are not without their adversaries. Lawmakers and elected officials remain partial to police and have been unwilling to share power with "the people" on matters of criminal justice. Still, the successes of the "people's justice movement" in New York, Los Angeles, and other cities offer a model of self-governance beyond police and the courts.

What might death investigations look like if power was shared, as it once was in our nation's history, between the people and the state?

In 2023, my lab joined efforts to answer this question for the state of Maryland. We worked with several local organizations and Senator Joanne Benson to write a bill aimed at bringing public oversight and accountability for in-custody deaths. Our bill was originally named Maryland Deaths in Custody Transparency, Reporting, and Oversight Act (SB36) and was driven by the vision of community advocate Dr. Carmen Johnson, founder of Helping Ourselves to Transform—an organization dedicated to guiding people recently released from jail and prison to integrate back into their communities. Johnson formed this nonprofit after spending forty-four months at a prison work camp in West Virginia. As the former housing chair of the Maryland State Conference of the NAACP, Johnson was charged with financial fraud shortly after she became a whistleblower who drew attention to predatory foreclosures erasing the generational wealth of Black communities in Maryland during the subprime mortgage collapse of 2008. Johnson proclaims her innocence and now works as an advocate for criminal justice reform, having survived the trauma and indignity of life "behind the wall."

Johnson and I were introduced by civil rights attorney Elizabeth Rossi of Civil Rights Corps, an organization that uses litigation, policy, and narrative to resensitize people to the brutality of the criminal legal system. Word of my lab's work in Los Angeles had reached Rossi and Johnson through DPN, which was advising them on strategies for supporting system-impacted communities in the DC area. Johnson and Rossi were working with a local court watch organization to obtain records from correctional facilities about people who died while in jail. They were being stonewalled by the county and were without the support of local officials involved in Death in Custody Reporting Act (DCRA) for the state of Maryland. Most correctional facilities in Maryland counties released high-level summary data about people who died during the previous year. This data included race, age, gender, and date of death but not names, case numbers, or cause of death. Without comprehensive data it is difficult to follow up with the families of victims, request autopsies, or document death trends over time. My lab had been gathering in-custody death data in Maryland using the flawed but useful data from the Bureau of Justice Statics, which included details missing in the reports released by Maryland correctional facilities. We combined our data-gathering efforts and were able to assemble a comprehensive but terrifying record of in-custody death across the state.

Soon after, my lab joined an alliance with several criminal justice reform advocates operating in the DC, Maryland, and Virginia area. This included the DC-based organization Life After Release, founded by Qiana Johnson—who like Carmen Johnson was previously incarcerated—which works to reform the inhumane conditions of Maryland carceral facilities. We also worked with the organization Zealous, a national advocacy and education initiative that deploys media, technology, and storytelling to change American perceptions of the criminal justice system.

Together we released a report documenting 180 deaths that occurred in ten jails across the state of Maryland between 2008 and 2019 (figure 6.1). Deaths reflected the overall demographics of the state, with Black people in the clear majority ($n = 97$) followed by whites ($n = 78$) (figure 6.2). Most of the deaths were men under the age of forty-four,

FIGURE 6.1 The locations of ten Maryland detention centers featured in our report, plus the total number of deaths in each facility during the study period (2008–19)

DETENTION CENTERS REPRESENTED IN STUDY	NUMBER OF DEATHS DURING STUDY PERIOD (2008–2019)
Baltimore City Central Booking and Intake Center	44
Baltimore City Detention Center	33
Baltimore County Detention Center	27
Charles County Detention Center	7
Frederick County Detention Center	5
Harford County Detention Center	14
Jennifer Road Detention Center	17
Montgomery County Detention Center	11
Prince George's County Detention Center	13
Wicomico County Detention Center	9
Total	180

Source: Carmen Johnson, Terence Keel, Alexander Li, Anna Robinson-Sweet, Elizabeth Rossi, Grace Sosa, and Jonah Walters, "In-Custody Deaths in Ten Maryland Detention Centers, 2008–2019," UCLA, August 2023, https://ucla.app.box.com/s/z5wuokjrcegd2gvrx2hk3f7tbi938k47

FIGURE 6.2 Breakdown of racial demographics of a sample of deaths in ten Maryland detention centers, 2008–19

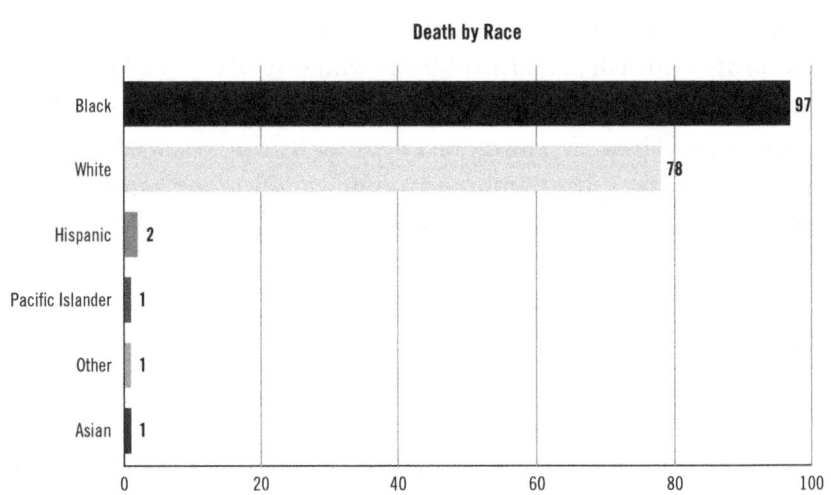

Source: Carmen Johnson, Terence Keel, Alexander Li, Anna Robinson-Sweet, Elizabeth Rossi, Grace Sosa, and Jonah Walters, "In-Custody Deaths in Ten Maryland Detention Centers, 2008–2019," UCLA, August 2023, https://ucla.app.box.com/s/z5wuokjrcegd2gvrx2hk3f7tbi938k47

which was roughly thirty-three years younger than the average life expectancy of the non-jailed population in Maryland (77.3 years) (figure 6.3). Natural death (*n* = 84), suicide (*n* = 45), and death from drugs/alcohol (*n* = 11) were most common in our sample (figure 6.4). Almost half of the people in our study (47.78 percent) died within ten days of their admission to jail, and more people died in the first twenty-four hours than on any other single day in our study (figure 6.5). Also, 85 percent of the people in our study died before they were convicted of a crime. If ever there was a sign that jails end lives, this was it.

From our data we could clearly see that carceral facilities in Maryland were in crisis and new legislation was needed to solve this problem. Johnson led the charge of drafting the Maryland Deaths in Custody Transparency, Reporting, and Oversight Act. At the heart of this bill was a vision of public oversight of deaths that occurred while in custody. We wanted a review board charged with the task of performing a comprehensive administrative and clinical assessment of "every death of an incarcerated individual in the state." Parts of the bill were inspired by

FIGURE 6.3 Average age of all deaths and natural deaths across ten Maryland detention centers compared to average life expectancy in the state

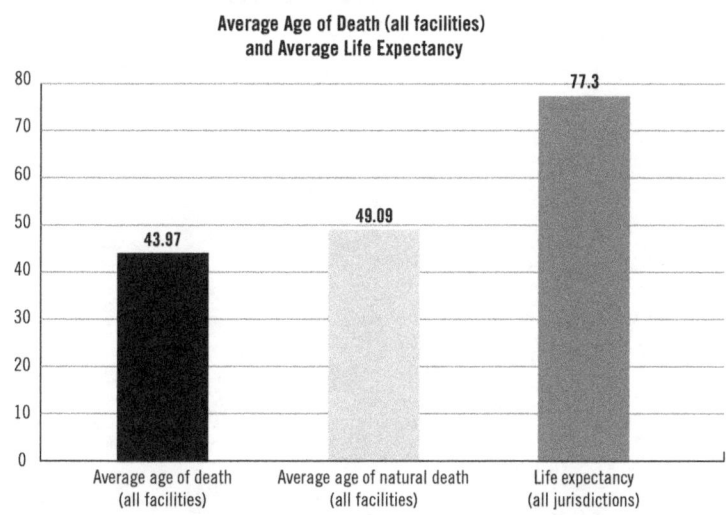

Average Age of Death (all facilities) and Average Life Expectancy

Source: Carmen Johnson, Terence Keel, Alexander Li, Anna Robinson-Sweet, Elizabeth Rossi, Grace Sosa, and Jonah Walters, "In-Custody Deaths in Ten Maryland Detention Centers, 2008–2019," UCLA, August 2023, https://ucla.app.box.com/s/z5wuokjrcegd2gvrx2hk3f7tbi938k47

FIGURE 6.4 Manner of all deaths in ten Maryland detention centers, 2008–19

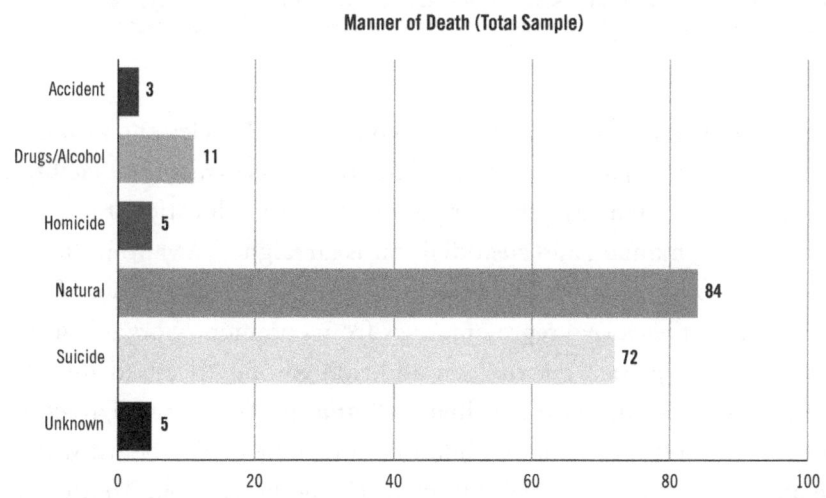

Manner of Death (Total Sample)

Source: Carmen Johnson, Terence Keel, Alexander Li, Anna Robinson-Sweet, Elizabeth Rossi, Grace Sosa, and Jonah Walters, "In-Custody Deaths in Ten Maryland Detention Centers, 2008–2019," UCLA, August 2023, https://ucla.app.box.com/s/z5wuokjrcegd2gvrx2hk3f7tbi938k47

FIGURE 6.5 The number of days each individual in our sample was incarcerated before death

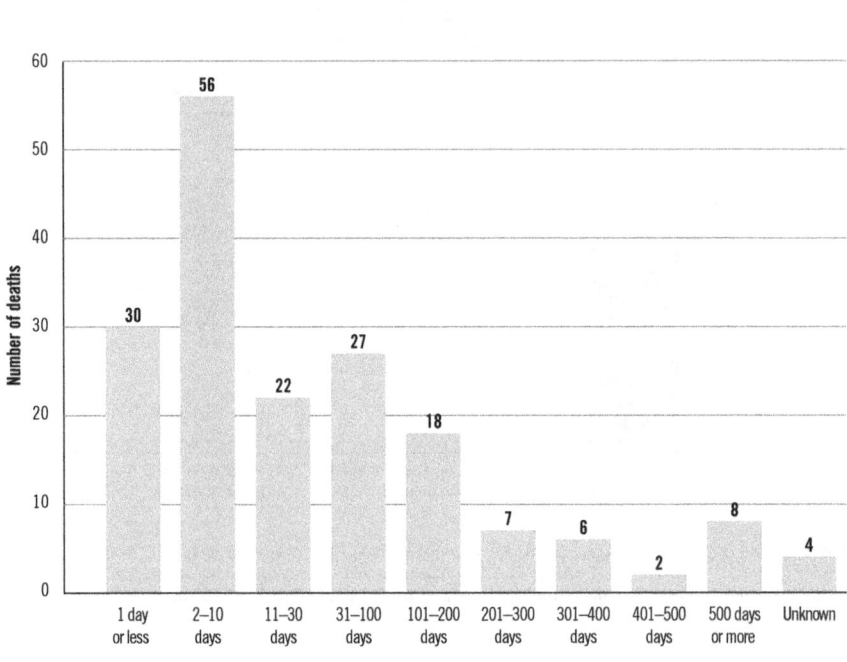

Number of Days Detained Before Death

Source: Carmen Johnson, Terence Keel, Alexander Li, Anna Robinson-Sweet, Elizabeth Rossi, Grace Sosa, and Jonah Walters, "In-Custody Deaths in Ten Maryland Detention Centers, 2008–2019," UCLA, August 2023, https://ucla.app.box.com/s/z5wuokjrcegd2gvrx2hk3f7tbi938k47

the Civilian Oversight Committee (COC) in Los Angeles and also California Bill 2761, passed in 2022, which requires correctional facilities to report within ten days on their public website the location, race, age, gender, date, manner, and custodial status (arraigned, awaiting trial, or convicted) of the victim. The Deaths in Custody Oversight Board was to include "at least two representatives from community organizations that focus on justice reform," in addition to one "licensed forensic pathologist," a "licensed psychiatrist" and an "Executive Director" with the discretion to appoint additional members. The board was to be staffed by the Governor's Office of Crime Prevention, Youth, and Victim Services.

We also wanted a board with structural competence. Our bill included language that required the board to review the living conditions of the facility at the time of death and gather information about "access to windows and outdoor space," availability of "beds, food, clean drinking water, and personal hygiene products," and incident reports of the deceased being a target of threats or violence at any point while inside. With people like Kenneth Adcock and Jorge Rosales in mind, we instructed the board to review the health history of the deceased, how often they sought medical treatment, and if they were given care prior to being in jail. Thinking of John Horton, Sandra Bland, and Kalief Browder, we wanted the board to investigate every reported suicide and conduct interviews with people in jail, family, friends, and jail staff.

At the end of its review, the board was to produce a public report of its findings within thirty days of an individual's death and to publicly release all records gathered during its investigation subject to Maryland's open records laws. The board was also to cooperate and coordinate with the Department of State Police and the Commission on Correctional Standards, which is responsible for ensuring uniformity and equity in the treatment of incarcerated people in Maryland. Finally, we required the board to submit an annual report to the attorney general, the Department of Public Safety and Correctional Services, and any judge presiding over a case related to the incarceration of the deceased. These reports were to summarize the previous year's investigations, flag facilities with troubled reputations, and offer recommendations on how to prevent future deaths and improve the healthcare inside facilities in trouble—the latter being inspired by the high number of natural deaths we found in our study of deaths across the state.

We were proud of our bill and had powerful champions in Senator Benson and House Delegate Gary Simmons. We spent months speaking to delegates in the General Assembly looking to whip up allies and strengthen our bill. Officials saw the vision and more than a few felt the shame of having these deaths under their watch. When the bill was introduced in the Senate, I gave expert testimony that provided context for the deaths inside Maryland jails and detention centers, described the barriers to accessing better data about these cases. I also explained how this act would place the state in line with in-custody death oversight bills passed recently in California (AB 276) and Illinois, with its Reporting of Deaths in Custody Act (HB 3924). Our bill also aligned with the vision of Dr. Roger Mitchell Jr., former chief medical examiner of Washington, DC, and Professor Jay Aronson, who have both called on states to document on death certificates when the loss of life occurred while in custody.[7] More than forty organizations testified in the Senate and House in support of our bill, including the Maryland Office of the Public Defender, Maryland Alliance for Criminal Justice Reform, Maryland Department of Public Safety and Correctional Services, Maryland Department of Health, and National Bar Association. Family members of the deceased and mothers of sons who were still incarcerated gave chilling testimonies urging lawmakers to find their humanity. Our bill was an example of what Ruha Benjamin calls "viral justice."

Confidence in the bill's success swelled after its discussion in the Senate on February 7, 2024. Within days, however, our optimism cooled. We received word that our bill had been dramatically amended by members of the Senate Judicial Committee. Officials had rejected our vision of an alliance between "the people" and the state; they removed our oversight board and replaced it with the Department of State Police, which assumed the role of investigating deaths while in jail, prison, or a detention center. This new version of the bill put police in charge of investigating themselves and required the Department of State Police to post on its website "certain information relating to certain investigation of deaths of incarcerated individuals on its website." What exactly was to be reported and when was left unclear. Most disheartening was the state's commitment to investigating only homicides—one of the least common types of death inside Maryland jails according to my lab's recent report. There were only *five* reported homicides over the eleven-year period of our study. Again, the overwhelming number of deaths inside jail during this time were natural ($n = 84$), suicide ($n = 72$), and related to drugs or alcohol ($n = 11$). This new version of the bill simply refused to measure, study, or acknowledge these other deaths and the systems of discrimination that tally in our bodies while in the custody of the law. Our retitled bill, Correctional Services—Investigation of Suspected Homicide—Reporting, was passed in the Senate and House and signed into law by Governor Wes Moore on May 16, 2024.

Surely any attempt to draft and gather support for a bill proposing public oversight of state institutions will involve political miscalculations, setbacks, and failure. Still, officials could not deny the ethical substance of our bill or the crisis motivating our push for reform. Our vision of justice for the state of Maryland was not fully realized for the same reason public inquests and autopsies written by medical examiners fall short of the people's justice: our criminal justice system trades in the illusion of transparency and accountability but is uncommitted to the substance of democracy or the people behind it. Justice in the hands of the state remains hostage to a binary moral belief system that distorts how we view people on the wrong side of the law and divides us between the chosen and the condemned. We give the state this power because of our intolerance for people who cross the law and a refusal to accept that they would be better served by institutions committed to care, dignity, and repairing the past failures of local and state government.

Instead, we use death like an exacting instrument, erasing the lives of people who cannot be redeemed, saved, or rehabilitated into the collective.

Because of this, someone will die tomorrow inside a jail in the state of Maryland. Their death will be recorded by the medical examiner as natural, suicide, or related to a substance abuse issue. They are likely to die within the first twenty-four hours in a jail but before being convicted of a crime. There will be no third-party or independent investigation. State police will not make a public announcement. Most residents will not hear about this loss until the following year—if at all. We will hide the body from the public record.

And tomorrow, this will happen again.

I wrote this book because, despite everything, I am an optimist.

I believe in-custody deaths will cease when we recognize ourselves in the people lost in handcuffs, on the floors of jail cells, bloody in the streets, and on the stainless-steel dissection tables of the medical examiner. In that moment of self-recognition, they will not be on the wrong side of the law; they will not be condemned, heathen, slave, disabled, unfit, less-than, or a threat to our safety. They will be like any and all of us: a social creature whose life chances are vulnerable to the fears, imagination, and beliefs of the world within and around us.

Until then, these dead will remain bodies we don't see.

ACKNOWLEDGMENTS

I have a great number of people and places to thank for helping make this book possible. Over the course of working on this project I met and befriended many families living in what Christina Sharpe calls "the wake." In their own way they were thriving and had found meaning and purpose through their tragedy. I often told myself if Helen Jones, Khadijah Shabazz, Pulane Lucas, Terry Lovett, Maria Correa, and Ben Capaci could still believe in this nation, given all that had been taken from them, then I could. Their commitment to doing the work of change was inspiring to witness and often the cure I needed for my bouts of pessimism.

I learned from and formed some incredible relationships with organizations standing behind families impacted by police violence. I am fortunate to have worked with Helen Jones and Mark-Anthony Clayton-Johnson at Dignity and Power Now; Carmen Johnson of Helping Ourselves to Transform; Elizabeth Rossi, Natalie Murphy, Susan Li, Madhvi Venkatramen, and Cheryl Bonacci of Civil Rights Corps; Bill Hanes of Court Watch Prince George County; Qiana Johnson of Life After Release; Crystal Maloney, Esul Burton, and Davis Rich of Zealous; Brittany Hailer during her time at the Pittsburgh Institute for Nonprofit Journalism; Joshua Vaughn of PennLive; Paula Shapiro of the American Bar Association; and Delegate Gary Simmons and Senator Joanne Benson of Maryland.

When I first committed to writing a popular book about the victims lost to police violence, it was a far more daunting task than I realized. But there were many who encouraged and inspired me along the way.

Sameer Pandya read some of my earliest and raw attempts to make sense of all this violence and more than a few times reminded me to trust what I know and saw. Eddie Glaude helped think about the contours of the book when it was a germ of an idea. I am grateful to Robin Kelley for his encouragement and for introducing me to Tanya McKinnon. Tanya's enthusiasm was contagious and inspired me in those early moments of writing when you find yourself most vulnerable. Special thanks to Amy Caldwell for her brilliant editorial insights and providing space as I gave form to this book. I found myself returning again and again to Camille Dungy's *Soil: The Story of a Black Mother's Garden* while writing. Her thoughts helped me understand the mothers I was working with who were planting seeds for a better future in this strange land.

There were many colleagues who read advance copies of chapters, imagined and worked through problems together, shared my frustrations, and offered moral support. Thank you to Lauren Brown, Aziza Ahmed, Eram Alam, Ayah Nurridin, Osagie Obasogie, Aaron Panofsky, Jonah Walters, Nikki Jones, Wallace Best, Judith Weisenfeld, Nancy Krieger, Ahmed Ragab, Myrna Perez-Sheldon, and Maggie Woodruff. Grace Sosa, Jade Magaña, and Alex Li were tireless in their support as I was completing the manuscript. Finally, I would like to thank all of the brilliant minds who have been part of the Lab for BioCritical Studies. They played an instrumental role in helping me develop the data and insights shared in this work. But more importantly, their dedication and willingness to see with clear eyes and be part of the change inspired me more than they will ever know. They continue to give me hope that our future is in the right hands.

Early in this process several academic institutions and funding agencies offered time, space, and resources. The UCLA Luskin Center for Public Policy was the first to offer funding support, followed by the Russell Sage Foundation, the Kaiser Family Foundation, and the National Institute of Health–National Library of Medicine. With this seed funding I was able to create the Lab for BioCritical Studies at UCLA, which was then generously supported by Dean Tracy Johnson of the UCLA Division of Life Sciences, Deans Darnell Hunt and Abel Valenzuela of the UCLA Division of Social Sciences, Kelly Lytle-Hernandez and Lorrie Frasure of the UCLA Ralph J. Bunche Center, and Roger Wakimoto of the UCLA Office of Grants and Sponsored Programs. When it was time to start making connections and begin the journey of writing, Safiya Noble and Sarah Roberts at the UCLA Center for Critical Internet Studies offered crucial support. As I began to work on chapters, more than a few institutions provided a venue for sharing my ideas. Thank you to Angela Creager and the History of Science Colloquium at Princeton University, Derek Hicks and the Wake Forest Center for Research, Engagement, and Collaboration in African American Life, and Mary Mitchell and the University of Toronto Centre for Criminology and Sociolegal Studies.

I spent nearly four years witnessing and writing, thinking, and dreaming about violence and death. Rage, depression, and grief had become companions. To deal with them I started boxing and training in Muay Thai. Both changed me more than I could have imagined. The more I trained, the more I understood police violence and the resilience of the people fighting to abolish it. Will, intention, and stamina are at the heart of it all. It is a strange thing to discover inside of you. Law enforcement violence is far from mindless. When police use force, it requires an extraordinary level of presence, purpose, and even vulnerability. The same is true for those working to mend and repair lives broken by state violence. I thank Coach Ed, Coach Jon, and Coach Spencer for teaching me lessons that can only be learned in the deep waters of conflict.

At moments this project took me away from my family. Thank you Yuma, Carter, Jaelen, Sofia, Teresa, and Naima for being patient and loving. Ifé, without you I would not have completed this task. Your love and patience always a gift, you showed me how to clear the trauma of my past to create space to do this work. When I found myself unable to release the grief and horror of these stories, you shouldered the darkness with me. You are a constant source of light and wisdom.

NOTES

CHAPTER 1: LOSING OURSELVES

1. Randy Hanzlick, John Hunsaker, and Gregory Davis, *A Guide for Manner of Death Classification*, National Association of Medical Examiners, February 2002, https://www.charlydmiller.com/LIB03/2002NAMEmannerof death.pdf.

2. Autopsy of John Horton, April 1, 2009, Los Angeles County Medical Examiner, Case Number: 2009-02315.

3. State of California Board of State and Community Corrections, *Title 15 Minimum Standards for Local Detention Facilities: Title 15-Crime Prevention and Corrections*, division 1, chapter 1, subchapter 4, § 1027.5 Safety Checks (January 1, 2023), 26, https://www.bscc.ca.gov/wp-content/uploads/Adult -T15-Effective-1.1.2023-Full-Text.pdf.

4. Autopsy of John Horton.

5. Grant Smith, "Jail Deaths in America: Data and Key Findings of Dying Inside," Reuters, October 16, 2020, https://www.reuters.com/investigates /special-report/usa-jails-graphic/.

6. Jessica Lopez, "Record Number of Deaths in LASD Jails," *University Times* (California State University–Los Angeles), March 22, 2022, https:// csulauniversitytimes.com/record-number-of-deaths-in-lasd-jails/.

7. Debbie L. Sklar, "County to Pay Out $3.25 Million to Settle Wrongful Death Suits," MyNewsLA.com, November 9, 2016, https://mynewsla.com /government/2016/11/09/county-to-pay-out-3-25-million-to-settle-wrongful -death-suits/.

8. For more on how we carry society within our body, see Nancy Krieger, "Embodiment: A Conceptual Glossary for Epidemiology," *Journal of Epidemiology and Community Health* 59, no. 5 (2005): 350–55, doi:10.1136/jech .2004.024562; Hannah Landecker, "Postindustrial Metabolism: Fat Knowledge," *Public Culture* 25, no. 3 (September 2013): 495–522, doi: https://doi.org /10.1215/08992363-2144625; Bessel Van der Kolk, *The Body Keeps the Score: Brain, Mind, and Body in the Healing of Trauma* (New York: Penguin Books, 2015); Resmaa Menakem, *My Grandmother's Hands: Racialized Trauma and the Pathway to Mending Our Hearts and Bodies* (Las Vegas: Central Recovery

Press, 2017); Atif Khan et al., "Environmental Pollution Is Associated with Increased Risk of Psychiatric Disorders in the US and Denmark," *PLoS Biology* 17, no. 8 (2019): e3000353, https://doi.org/10.1371/journal.pbio.3000353; Shane Campbell-Staton et al., "Physiological Costs of Undocumented Human Migration Across the Southern United States Border," *Science* 17, no. 374 (December 2021): 1496–1500, doi: 10.1126/science.abh1924; Hannah Landecker, "How the Social Gets Under the Skin: From the Social as Signal to Society as a Metabolic Milieu," *Köln Z Soziol* 76 (2024): 745–67, https://doi.org/10.1007/s11577-024-00951-5.

9. Ruha Benjamin, *Viral Justice: How We Grow the World We Want* (Princeton, NJ: Princeton University Press, 2023), 19.

10. Ben Quinn, "Iceland's Armed Police Make First Ever Fatal Shooting," *The Guardian*, December 2, 2013, https://www.theguardian.com/world/2013/dec/02/iceland-armed-police-shoot-man-dead-first-time.

11. Erica Bryant, "Government Can't Say How Many People Die in U.S. Jails and Prisons," Vera Institute of Justice, March 16, 2022, https://www.vera.org/news/government-cant-say-how-many-people-die-in-u-s-jails-and-prisons.

12. John Gramlich, "America's Incarceration Rate Falls to Lowest Level Since 1995," Pew Research Center, August 16, 2021, https://www.pewresearch.org/fact-tank/2021/08/16/americas-incarceration-rate-lowest-since-1995/.

13. Wendy Sawyer and Peter Wagner, *Mass Incarceration: The Whole Pie 2023* (Northampton, MA: Prison Policy Initiative, 2023), para. 2, https://www.prisonpolicy.org/reports/pie2023.html.

14. Emily Widra and Tiana Herring, *States of Incarceration: The Global Context 2021* (Northampton, MA: Prison Policy Initiative, 2021), para. 1, https://www.prisonpolicy.org/global/2021.html.

15. Lesley A. Sharp, "Death and Dying in Carceral America: The Prison Hospice as an Inverted Space of Exception," *Medical Anthropology Quarterly* 36, no. 2 (2022): 177–97.

16. Eddie Glaude Jr., *We Are the Leaders We Have Been Looking For* (Cambridge, MA: Harvard University Press, 2024).

CHAPTER 2: ILLIBERAL INVESTIGATORS

1. On this point I disagree with my colleague Stefan Timmermans, who in his study of death investigators in Los Angeles County takes a more apologetic position on the profession. While I recognize that there are medical examiners and coroners who care about the public's vulnerability to police violence and discrimination, the field overall is tilted toward minimizing state accountability, as we will see in this chapter and this book as a whole. Questions about the authority, political stakes, and ethical implications of a medical examiner's work on the suicide of a family member or an infant death are qualitatively different from those involving an in-custody death. The latter reveals how death investigators too often perpetuate an illiberal current in American society that turns against the values of truth, freedom, and equality in service

of racism, sexism, xenophobia, and the politics of exclusion. The profession of forensic medicine is far more politically conservative when evaluating the work it performs within the context of lethal police violence. For Timmermans's assessment, see *Postmortem: How Medical Examiners Explain Suspicious Deaths* (Chicago: University of Chicago Press, 2006). For more on illiberalism in America, see Steven Hahn's *Illiberal America: A History* (New York: W. W. Norton, 2024).

2. Jessica Schladebeck, "Teenage Security Guard Shot and Killed by Los Angeles Police During Shift at Auto Shop," *New York Daily News*, June 19, 2020, https://www.nydailynews.com/2020/06/19/teenage-security-guard-shot -and-killed-by-los-angeles-police-during-shift-at-auto-shop/.

3. Manthan Chheda, "Andres Guardado: Cops Who Killed Teenage Security Guard Destroyed CCTV Cameras, Seized Video Footage," *International Business Times*, June 20, 2020, https://www.ibtimes.sg/andres-guardado-cops -who-killed-teenage-security-guard-destroyed-cctv-cameras-seized-video -footage-47156.

4. CA Govt. § 27491; IL St. CH 55 §5/3-3015.

5. County of Los Angeles Medical Examiner, "Cause and Manner of Death Determined for Andres Guardado Pineda," press release, July 10, 2020, https:// me.lacounty.gov/2020/press-releases/cause-of-death-andres-guardado-pineda/.

6. In a joint study with Nicholas Shapiro's Carceral Ecologies Lab, my lab found that in 2016, roughly 68 percent of the autopsies conducted by the medical examiner for deaths inside Los Angeles County jails were placed on security hold. In 2017 that figure moved to 80 percent, and in 2018, 73 percent of death records involving law enforcement were withheld from the public. Data from this became the basis for the peer-reviewed journal article: Nicholas Shapiro and Terence Keel, "Naturalizing Unnatural Death in Los Angeles County Jails," *Medical Anthropology Quarterly* 38, no. 1 (March 2024): 6–23, https://doi.org/10.1111/maq.12819.

7. Sheriff Alex Villanueva, "Coroner Breaks Protocol by Releasing Autopsy Results—Jeopardizing Investigation," Los Angeles County Sheriff's Department, July 10, 2020, https://sheriff33.lasd.org/coroner-breaks-protocol/.

8. Alicia Victoria Lozano, "Family of Man Killed by Los Angeles Deputy Calls for Outside Investigation," NBC News, June 20, 2020, https://www .nbcnews.com/news/us-news/family-man-killed-los-angeles-deputy-calls -outside-investigation-n1231657.

9. Mark Ridley-Thomas, "Ensuring a Transparent and Independent Investigation into the Shooting Death of Andres Guardado," Los Angeles County Board of Supervisors, September 1, 2020, https://file.lacounty.gov/SDSInter /bos/supdocs/148434.pdf.

10. Los Angeles County Department of Medical Examiner-Coroner, "Inquest in the Death of Andres Guardado Pineda," November 30, 2020.

11. Maxine Waters, "Waters Slams Refusal of LASD Officers Responsible for Andres Guardado's Death to Testify at Coroner's Inquest," press release,

December 1, 2020, https://waters.house.gov/media-center/press-releases/waters
-slams-refusal-lasd-officers-responsible-andres-guardado-s-death.

12. Los Angeles County Department of Medical Examiner-Coroner, "Inquest in the Death of Andres Guardado Pineda."

13. Taylor Romine, "Los Angeles County Sheriff's Deputies Who Shot and Killed 18-Year-Old in 2020 Won't Be Charged, District Attorney Says," CNN.com, April 14, 2023, https://www.cnn.com/2023/04/14/us/andres-guardado-los-angeles-shooting-deputy-no-charges/index.html.

14. This discussion of the coroner's role and its history is drawn from the following sources: Paul F. Mellen, "Coroners' Inquests in Colonial Massachusetts," *Journal of the History of Medicine and Allied Sciences* 40, no. 4 (1985): 462–72; James Mohr, *Doctors and the Law: Medical Jurisprudence in Nineteenth-Century America* (New York: Oxford University Press, 1993); Jeffrey Jentzen, *Death Investigation in America: Coroners, Medical Examiners, and the Pursuit of Medical Certainty* (Cambridge, MA: Harvard University Press, 2009); James N. Adler, "Coroners' Inquests: The Impact of Watts," *UCLA Law Review* 15, no. 1 (1967): 97–117; Randy Hanzlick, "The Conversion of Coroner Systems to Medical Examiner Systems in the United States: A Lull in the Action," *American Journal of Forensic Medicine and Pathology* 28, no. 4 (2007): 208; Roger Mitchell Jr. and Jay Aronson, *Death in Custody: How America Ignores the Truth and What We Can Do About It* (Baltimore: Johns Hopkins University Press, 2023), 200–201.

15. Stephen Berry, *Count the Dead: Coroners, Quants, and the Birth of Death as We Know It* (Chapel Hill: University of North Carolina Press, 2022), 61.

16. Jentzen, *Death Investigation in America*, 11.

17. Jentzen, *Death Investigation in America*, 12.

18. Jentzen, *Death Investigation in America*, 14.

19. Jentzen, *Death Investigation in America*, 11.

20. Mitchell and Aronson, *Death in Custody*, 202.

21. "1790 Federal Census," NA Form 14118 (6–10), National Archives, Washington, DC.

22. "Coroner's Inquest [13 July–2 August 1804]," in *The Papers of Alexander Hamilton*, vol. 26, 1 May 1802–23 October 1804, Additional Documents 1774–1799, Addenda and Errata, ed. Harold C. Syrett (New York: Columbia University Press, 1979), 318–21, https://founders.archives.gov/documents/Hamilton/01-26-02-0001-0270.

23. Jentzen, *Death Investigation in America*, 12.

24. Jentzen, *Death Investigation in America*, 10.

25. My recounting of the Hamburg massacre is drawn from the following sources: US Senate, *Testimony as to the Denial of the Elective Franchise in South Carolina at the Elections of 1875 and 1876 Taken Under the Resolution of the Senate*, vol. 1: *US Congressional Serial Set 44th–2nd Mis. Doc.*

48 (Washington, DC: US Government Printing Office, 1877); "The Hamburg Massacre: A Verdict of Murder Against the Whole Butler Family," *Hartford Daily Courant*, August 2, 1876; "The Hamburg Massacre," *Saturday Review*, August 5, 1876, 169–70; "The Hamburg Massacre: Full List of Persons Charged with the Killing," *San Francisco Chronicle*, August 11, 1876; Berry, *Count the Dead*, 72–74.

26. Renetta DuBose, "The Untold Story of Hamburg, SC," WJBF Channel 6/ ABC News, February 22, 2021, https://www.wjbf.com/top-stories/the-untold -story-of-hamburg-sc/.

27. "The Hamburg Massacre," *San Francisco Chronicle*.

28. At this time in history the Republican Party was aligned with the freedom of Black Americans, especially under the leadership of the Radi- cal Republicans who orchestrated Reconstruction. The Democratic Party, however, was filled with former confederates and segregationists, especially in the South. Party alliances did not change until the New Deal coalition during the presidency of Franklin D. Roosevelt, which began to attract Black voters, pulling them away from the Republican Party and setting the course for the current, although uneasy, alignment between Democrats and Black voters, and between Republicans and whites in the South and along the Rust Belt.

29. "Speech of Senator Benjamin R. Tillman, March 23, 1900," in *Docu- ment Sets for the South in U.S. History*, ed. Richard Purday (Lexington, MA: D. C. Heath, 1991), 147.

30. Barbara Holden-Smith, "Lynching, Federalism, and the Intersec- tion of Race and Gender in the Progressive Era," *Yale Journal of Law and Feminism* 8, no. 1 (1996): 31–78; Eric A. Stewart, Daniel P. Mears, Patricia Y. Warren, Eric P. Baumer, and Ashley N. Arnio, "Lynchings, Racial Threat, and Whites' Punitive Views Towards Blacks," *Criminology* 56, no. 3 (August 2018): 455–80.

31. For more on how the Southern courts undermined abolition and dimin- ished the rights of newly emancipated Blacks, see Giuliana Perrone, *Nothing More Than Freedom: The Failure of Abolition in American Law* (Cambridge: Cambridge University Press, 2023).

32. Baron v. The Mayor and City Council of Baltimore, 32 U.S. (7 Pet.) 243 (1833).

33. Douglas A. Blackmon, *Slavery by Another Name: The Re-Enslavement of Black Americans from the Civil War to World War II* (New York: Anchor Books, 2008); W. E. B. Du Bois, *Black Reconstruction in America, 1860–1880* (New York: Free Press, 1935); James Forman Jr., "Juries and Race in the Nineteenth Century," *Yale Law Journal* 113, no. 4 (2004): 931; Thomas Ward Frampton, "The Jim Crow Jury," *Harvard Civil Rights–Civil Liberties Law Review* 71 (2021): 651.

34. George Rutherglen, "The Thirteenth Amendment in Legal Theory," *Virginia Law Review* 83, no. 3 (1997); Sanford Levinson, "Why *Strauder v.*

West Virginia Is the Most Important Single Source of Insight on the Tensions Contained Within the Equal Protection Clause of the Fourteenth Amendment," *Saint Louis University Law Journal* 62, no. 3 (2018): 683–710, https://scholarship.law.slu.edu/lj/vol62/iss3/9; Kenneth Katkin, "Incorporation of the Criminal Procedure Amendments: The View from the States," *Nebraska Law Review* 84, no. 1 (2005–6): 397–468; Christopher R. Green, "Incorporation, Total Incorporation, and Nothing but Incorporation," *William & Mary Bill of Rights Journal* 24, no. 1 (October 2015): 93–135.

35. Sally Hadden explains how early American law enforcement emerged from slave patrols in *Slave Patrols: Law and Violence in Virginia and the Carolinas* (Cambridge, MA: Harvard University Press, 2003).

36. Walter Allen, *Governor Chamberlain's Administration in South Carolina: A Chapter of Reconstruction in the Southern States* (New York, NY: G. P. Putnam's Sons/Knickerbocker Press, 1888), 313–18.

37. "Speech of Senator Benjamin R. Tillman," 147.

38. Berry, *Count the Dead*, 73; Margaret A. Burnham, *By Hands Now Known: Jim Crow's Legal Executioners* (Cambridge, MA: Belknap Press of Harvard University Press, 2022).

39. For example, see Julie Johnson-McGrath, "Speaking for the Dead: Forensic Pathologists and Criminal Justice in the United States," *Science, Technology, & Human Values* 20, no. 4 (1995): 438–59, http://www.jstor.org/stable/689869; Hanzlick, "The Conversion of Coroner Systems to Medical Examiner Systems in the United States"; Stefan Timmermans, *Postmortem: How Medical Examiners Explain Suspicious Deaths* (Chicago: University of Chicago Press, 2006).

40. Julie Johnson-McGrath makes this argument in "Coroners, Corruption, and the Politics of Death: Forensic Pathology in the United States," in *Legal Medicine in History*, ed. Michael Clark and Catherine Crawford (Cambridge: Cambridge University Press, 1994), 268–89.

41. Richard Simon, "Alpheus Hodges: A Name to Remember for Obscure Reasons," *Los Angeles Times*, March 15, 1993, https://www.latimes.com/archives/la-xpm-1993-03-15-me-461-story.html.

42. Maymie R. Krythe, "First Hotel of Old Los Angeles," *Historical Society of Southern California Quarterly* 33, no. 1 (March 1951): 45.

43. Johnson-McGrath, "Coroners, Corruption, and the Politics of Death," 272; Hanzlick, "The Conversion of Coroner Systems to Medical Examiner Systems in the United States," 280.

44. Jentzen, *Death Investigation in America*, 16; James C. Mohr, *Doctors and the Law: Medical Jurisprudence in Nineteenth-Century America* (Baltimore: Johns Hopkins University Press, 1996), 76–93.

45. Jentzen, *Death Investigation in America*, 18–19.

46. Hanzlick, "The Conversion of Coroner Systems to Medical Examiner Systems in the United States," 280–81.

47. Randy L. Hanzlick, "A Synopsis of the 1928 National Research Council's Bulletin on 'The Coroner and the Medical Examiner,'" *Academic Forensic Pathology* 4, no. 1 (March 2014): 90–93, https://doi.org/10.23907/2014.015.

48. Hanzlick, "The Conversion of Coroner Systems to Medical Examiner Systems in the United States," 280–81.

49. Daniel Byman, "White Supremacy, Terrorism, and the Failure of Reconstruction in the United States," *International Security* 46, no. 1 (2021): 53–103.

50. For more on the history of lynching and the campaign against it, see Ida B. Wells-Barnett, *Crusade for Justice: The Autobiography of Ida B. Wells*, ed. Alfreda Duster (Chicago: University of Chicago Press, 1972); Philp Dray, *At the Hands of Persons Unknown: The Lynching of Black America* (New York: Random House, 2003); Sherrilyn Ifill, *On the Courthouse Lawn: Confronting the Legacy of Lynching in the Twenty-first Century* (Boston: Beacon Press, 2007).

51. "Ordinances of the Town of Seattle," *Seattle Weekly Gazette*, March 4, 1865. See also Alexandra Harmon, *Indians in the Making: Ethnic Relations and Indian Identities Around Puget Sound* (Berkeley: University of California Press, 1998), 95–98; Coll Thrush, *Native Seattle: Histories from the Crossing-Over Place* (Seattle: University of Washington Press, 2007), 84–85.

52. US Congress, *United States Code: Immigration and Nationality, 8 U.S.C. §§ -1401 Suppl. 2 1964*, https://www.loc.gov/item/uscode1964 -016008006/.

53. Elina Shatkin, "The Ugly, Violent Clearing of Chavez Ravine Before It Was Home to the Dodgers," *LAist*, October 17, 2018, https://laist.com/news /la-history/dodger-stadium-chavez-ravine-battle. For more on the larger racial politics of space in postwar Los Angeles, see Gaye Theresa Johnson, "Spatial Entitlement: Race, Displacement, and Sonic Reclamation in Postwar Los Angeles," in *Black and Brown in Los Angeles: Beyond Conflict and Coalition*, ed. Josh Kun and Laura Pulido (Berkeley: University of California Press, 2014), 316–40, http://www.jstor.org/stable/10.1525/j.ctt4cgfx4.17.

54. Fannie Lou Hamer, "Testimony Before the Credential Committee at the Democratic National Convention, Atlantic City, New Jersey, August 22, 1964," in *The Speeches of Fannie Lou Hamer: To Tell It Like It Is*, ed. Maegan Parker Brooks and Davis W. Houck (Jackson: University Press of Mississippi, 2011), 42–45.

55. Michael Crutcher Jr., *Tremé: Race and Place in a New Orleans Neighborhood* (Athens: University of Georgia Press, 2010), 50–65. For a more general discussion of how US freeway systems built in the postwar era undermined nonwhite communities, see Eric Avila, *Folklore of the Freeway: Race and Revolt in the Modernist City* (Minneapolis: University of Minnesota Press, 2014).

56. For an interpretive account of racial violence in America from the Civil War through the twenty-first century, see Dominic J. Capeci Jr., "Forward:

American Race Rioting in Historical Perspective," in *Encyclopedia of American Race Riots*, ed. Walter Rucker Jr. and James Upton (Westport, CT: Greenwood Press, 2007), xviiii–xlii. For discussions of white mob violence, see Stewart Tolnay and E. M. Beck, *A Festival of Violence: An Analysis of Southern Lynchings, 1882–1930* (Champaign: University of Illinois Press, 1995); and Michael Pfeifer, *Lynching Beyond Dixie: American Mob Violence Outside the South* (Champaign: University of Illinois Press, 2013). For a fascinating discussion of legal racial violence, and its legacy within contemporary American law, see Geoff Ward, David Cunningham, Hedwig Lee, and Sarah Gaby, "(Dis)Continuities in Racialized Legal Violence," *Annals of the American Academy of Political and Social Science* 694, no. 1 (2021): 22–31.

57. John H. Lanbein, "Historical Foundations of the Law of Evidence: A View from the Ryder Sources," *Columbia Law Review* 96, no. 5 (June 1996): 1168–1202; Michael J. Klarman, "The Racial Origins of Modern Criminal Procedure," *Michigan Law Review* 99, no. 1 (October 2000): 48–97.

58. Alan Raphael, "Confrontation Clause and Testimonial Evidence: After Two Supreme Court Decisions, Standard Remains Unclear," *Public Interest Law Reporter* 12, no. 1 (Winter 2006): 1–16; Stephen Ashlett, "Crawford's Curious Dictum: Why Testimonial Nonhearsay Implicated the Confrontation Clause," *Tulane Law Review* 82, no. 1 (November 2007): 297–338; Thomas F. Burke III, "The Test Results Said What: The Post-Crawford Admissibility of Hearsay Forensic Evidence," *South Dakota Law Review* 52, no. 1 (2008): 1–36.

59. US Constitution, Amend. VI.

60. Robert A. Miller, "Self-Incrimination in Preliminary Investigations: John Doe Proceedings and Coroners' Inquests," *South Dakota Law Review* 7 (1962): 167–73; "Constitutional Rights at Inquest Proceedings: The Kennedy Challenge," *Catholic University Law Review* 19, no. 2 (1969–70): 227–75.

61. Paul MacMahon, "The Inquest and the Virtues of Soft Adjudication," *Yale Law & Policy Review*, no. 2 (Spring 2015): 275–322.

CHAPTER 3: SOCIETY LIVES IN THE BODY

1. "Obama: Police Acted 'Stupidly' in Gates Case," July 20, 2009, ABC News, https://abcnews.go.com/US/story?id=8148986&page=1.

2. See the Pew Research Center's extensive report and analysis of media coverage of Obama's statements on the Gates arrest: Emily Guskin, Mahvish Khan, and Amy Mitchell, "The Arrest of Henry Louis Gates, Jr.," Pew Research Center, July 26, 2010, https://www.pewresearch.org/journalism/2010/07/26/arrest-henry-louis-gates-jr/.

3. Guskin et al., "The Arrest of Henry Louis Gates, Jr."

4. Deborah Tedford, "Obama Tries to Defuse Gates Controversy," NPR, July 24, 2009, https://www.npr.org/2009/07/24/106987976/obama-tries-to-defuse-gates-controversy.

5. Lyndon B. Johnson, "Speech to the Nation on Civil Disorders," July 27, 1967. Transcript acquired from the University of Virginia, Miller Center, https://millercenter.org/the-presidency/presidential-speeches/july-27-1967 -speech-nation-civil-disorders.

6. Lyndon B. Johnson quoted in Nick Kotz, *Judgment Days: Lyndon Baines Johnson, Martin Luther King Jr., and the Laws That Changed America* (Boston: Mariner Books, 2006), 341.

7. Daniel Schorr, "A New, 'Post-Racial' Political Era in America," *All Things Considered*, NPR, January 28, 2008, https://www.npr.org/2008/01/28 /18489466/a-new-post-racial-political-era-in-america.

8. John McWhorter, "Racism in America Is Over," *Forbes*, December 30, 2008, updated July 13, 2012, https://www.forbes.com/2008/12/30/end-of -racism-oped-cx_jm_1230mcwhorter.html.

9. Jonathan Metzl, *Dying of Whiteness: How the Politics of Racial Resentment Is Killing America's Heartland* (New York: Basic Books, 2019).

10. Cal. Pen. Code § 271.

11. Cal. Pen. Code § 271.5.

12. For more on the effects of the criminal justice system and child protective services on Black American families, see Dorothy Roberts's brilliant work *Torn Apart: How the Child Welfare System Destroys Black Families and How Abolition Can Build a Safer World* (New York: Basic Books, 2022).

13. Autopsy of Alesia Thomas, July 26, 2012, Los Angeles County Medical Examiner, Case Number: 2012-04793.

14. Autopsy of Alesia Thomas.

15. Autopsy of Alesia Thomas. My comments on sickle cell trait in this section draws on the work of Duana Fullwiley, *The Encultured Gene: Sickle Cell Health Politics and Biological Difference in West Africa* (Princeton, NJ: Princeton University Press, 2011).

16. "Media Statement from CDC Director Rochelle P. Walensky, MD, MPH, on Racism and Health," CDC Archive, April 8, 2021, https://archive .cdc.gov/#/details?url=https://www.cdc.gov/media/releases/2021/s0408-racism -health.html.

17. David Chae, Amani Nuru-Jeter, Nancy Adler, Gene Brody, Jue Lin, Elizabeth Blackburn, and Elissa Epel, "Discrimination, Racial Bias, and Telomere Length in African-American Men," *American Journal of Preventive Medicine* 46, no. 2 (February 2014): 103–11, https://doi.org/10.1016/j.amepre .2013.10.020; Chandra Ford, "Graham, Police Violence, and Health Through a Public Health Lens Symposium: Beyond Bad Apples; Exploring the Legal Determinants of Police Violence," *Boston University Law Review* 100, no. 3 (2020): 1093–1110; Chandra Ford and Collins Airhihenbuwa, "Critical Race Theory, Race Equity, and Public Health: Toward Antiracism Praxis," *American Journal of Public Health* 100, no. S1 (April 2010): S30–S35, https://doi .org/10.2105/AJPH.2009.171058; Gilbert Gee and Chandra Ford, "Structural

Racism and Health Inequities: Old Issues, New Directions," *Du Bois Review: Social Science Research on Race* 8, no. 1 (April 2011): 115–32, https://doi.org/10.1017/S1742058X11000130; Jennifer Scott, Denise Danos, Robert Collins, Neal Simonsen, Claudia Leonardi, Richard Scribner, and Denise Herd, "Structural Racism in the Built Environment: Segregation and the Overconcentration of Alcohol Outlets," *Health & Place* 64 (July 2020): 102385, https://doi.org/10.1016/j.healthplace.2020.102385; Ryan Whitacre, Adeola Oni-Orisan, Nadia Gaber, Carlos Martinez, Liza Buchbinder, Denise Herd, and Seth M. Holmes, "COVID-19 and the Political Geography of Racialisation: Ethnographic Cases in San Francisco, Los Angeles and Detroit," *Global Public Health* 16, nos. 8–9 (September 2021): 1396–1410, https://doi.org/10.1080/17441692.2021.1908395.

18. "Media Statement from CDC Director Rochelle P. Walensky."

19. For a comprehensive discussion of the origins of American public health, see Nancy Krieger, *Epidemiology and the People's Health: Theory and Context* (Oxford: Oxford University Press, 2013).

20. Jim Downs, *Sick from Freedom: African-American Illness and Suffering During the Civil War and Reconstruction* (Oxford: Oxford University Press, 2012), 21–25.

21. Downs, *Sick from Freedom*, 62.

22. Downs, *Sick from Freedom*, 60.

23. For more on the eugenics movement in the US and Europe, see Daniel J. Kevles, *In the Name of Eugenics: Genetics and the Uses of Human Heredity* (Cambridge, MA: Harvard University Press, 1998); Stefan Kühl, *The Nazi Connection: Eugenics, American Racism, and German National Socialism* (Oxford: Oxford University Press, 2002); Paul A. Lombardo, *Three Generations, No Imbeciles: Eugenics, the Supreme Court, and Buck v. Bell* (Baltimore: Johns Hopkins University Press, 2010); Alexandra Minna Stern, *Eugenic Nation: Faults and Frontiers of Better Breeding in Modern America* (Berkeley: University of California Press, 2015); Molly Ladd-Taylor, *Fixing the Poor: Eugenic Sterilization and Child Welfare in the Twentieth Century* (Baltimore: Johns Hopkins University Press, 2020); Rebecca M. Kluchin, *Fit to Be Tied: Sterilization and Reproductive Rights in America* (Cambridge: Cambridge University Press, 2021).

24. For more on the history of racism in American science, medicine, and legal thought, see Christopher Willoughby, *Masters of Health: Racial Science and Slavery in U.S. Medical Schools* (Chapel Hill: University of North Carolina Press, 2022); Rana Hogarth, *Medicalizing Blackness: Making Racial Difference in the Atlantic World, 1780–1840* (Chapel Hill: University of North Carolina Press, 2017); Dorothy Roberts, *Fatal Invention: How Science, Politics, and Big Business Re-Create Race in the Twenty-First Century* (New York: New Press, 2011); Harriet Washington, *Medical Apartheid: The Dark History of Medical Experimentation on Black Americans from Colonial*

Times to the Present (New York: Anchor Books, 2008); Audrey Smedley, *Race in North America: Origins and Evolution of a Worldview* (Boulder, CO: Westview Press, 1998); and Thomas Gosett, *Race: The History of an Idea in America* (Oxford: Oxford University Press, 1997).

25. Lee Baker, *From Savage to Negro: Anthropology and the Construction of Race, 1896–1954* (Berkeley: University of California Press, 1998), 79.

26. W. E. B. Du Bois, *The Philadelphia Negro: A Social Study* (Philadelphia: University of Pennsylvania Press, 1899), 163.

27. Amy Fairchild, David Rosner, James Colgrove, Ronald Bayer, and Linda Fried, "The Exodus of Public Health: What History Can Tell Us About the Future," *American Journal of Public Health* 100, no. 1 (January 2010): 54, https://doi.org/10.2105/AJPH.2009.163956.

28. Fairchild et al., "The Exodus of Public Health," 54–63.

29. For more on how the coercive reforms of racial hygiene and eugenics were led by Black Americans, see, for example, Michele Mitchell, *Righteous Propagation: African Americans and the Politics of Racial Destiny After Reconstruction* (Durham: University of North Carolina Press, 2005).

30. For more on the racist contradictions of Progressive Era social science, see Thomas Leonard, *Illiberal Reformers: Race, Eugenics and American Economics in the Progressive Era* (Princeton, NJ: Princeton University Press, 2017).

31. Luca Fiorito, "Progressive-Era Racism and Another 'Blaming the Victim' Narrative: Thomas Nixon Carver's 'Make the Name "Nigger" Honorable' (1905)," *Erasmus Journal for Philosophy and Economics* 17, no. 1 (May 2024): 325–35, https://doi.org/10.23941/ejpe.v17i1.812.

32. Melissa A. Thomasson, "Racial Differences in Health Insurance Coverage and Medical Expenditures in the United States: A Historical Perspective," *Social Science History* 30, no. 4 (Winter 2006): 4.

33. See Mitchell, *Righteous Propagation*. See also my essay "Charles V. Roman and the Spectre of Polygenism in Progressive Era Public Health Research," *Social History of Medicine* 28, no. 4 (November 2015): 742–66, https://doi.org/10.1093/shm/hkv035.

34. For more on the persistence of Progressive Era racism and the eugenics movement into modern medicine, life science, and the social sciences more generally, see Alexandra Stern, *Eugenic Nation: Faults and Frontiers of Better Breeding in Modern America* (Berkeley: University of California Press, 2015), and Michael Yudell, *Race Unmasked: Biology and Race in the Twentieth Century* (New York: Columbia University Press, 2014).

35. Franklin D. Roosevelt, "Address to Advisory Council of the Committee on Economic Security," November 14, 1934, American Presidency Project, https://www.presidency.ucsb.edu/documents/address-advisory-council-the-committee-economic-security.

36. Thomasson, "Racial Differences in Health Insurance Coverage and Medical Expenditures in the United States," 4.

37. Howard Markel, "Give 'Em Health, Harry," *Milbank Quarterly* 93, no. 1 (March 2015): 1–7, https://doi.org/10.1111/1468-0009.12096.

38. Daniel Sledge, *Health Divided: Public Health and Individual Medicine in the Making of the Modern American State* (Lawrence: University Press of Kansas, 2017), 181.

39. Sledge, *Health Divided*, 181.

40. Sledge, *Health Divided*, 188.

41. Harry S. Truman, *Memoirs by Harry S. Truman*, vol. 2: *Years of Trial and Hope* (Garden City, NY: Doubleday, 1956), 23.

42. Thomasson, "Racial Differences in Health Insurance Coverage and Medical Expenditures in the United States," 7.

43. James Feigenbaum, Christopher Muller, and Elizabeth Wrigley-Field, "Regional and Racial Inequality in Infectious Disease Mortality in U.S. Cities, 1900–1948," *Demography* 56, no. 4 (2019): 1371–88, https://doi.org/10.1007/s13524-019-00789-z.

44. W. E. B. Du Bois, *The Negro American Family: A Social Study Made by Atlanta University Under the Patronage of the Trustees of the John F. Slater Fund* (Atlanta: Atlanta University Press, 1908); Stuart Galishoff, "Germs Know No Color Line: Black Health and Public Policy in Atlanta, 1900–1918," *Journal of the History of Medicine* 40, no. 1 (January 1985): 22–41, https://doi.org/10.1093/jhmas/40.1.22; Seema Jayachandran, Adriana Lleras-Muney, and Kimberly Smith, "Modern Medicine and the Twentieth Century Decline in Mortality: Evidence on the Impact of Sulfa Drugs," *American Economic Journal: Applied Economics* 2, no. 2 (April 2010): 118–46, https://doi.org/10.1257/app.2.2.118; Douglas Ewbank, "History of Black Mortality and Health Before 1940," *Milbank Quarterly* 65 (1987): 100–128, https://doi.org/10.2307/3349953.

45. For more on the connections between the rise of the pharmaceutical industry and the retreat of government from tackling systems of inequality that produce unhealthy people, see Joseph Dumit, *Drugs for Life: How Pharmaceutical Companies Define Our Health* (Durham, NC: Duke University Press, 2012), and Dorothy Roberts, *Fatal Invention: How Science, Politics, and Big Business Re-Create Race in the Twenty-First Century* (New York: New Press, 2018).

46. State of California, Department of Industrial Relations, US Census Survey, "Negroes and Mexican Americans in South and East Los Angeles: Changes Between 1960 and 1965 in Population, Employment, Income, and Family Status," November 1965, 9.

47. US Department of Commerce, Bureau of the Census, Special Census Survey of the South and East Los Angeles Areas, November 1965, series P-23, no. 17, March 23, 1966.

48. State of California, "Negroes and Mexican Americans in South and East Los Angeles," 17.

49. *Violence in the City*, 74.

50. For a brilliant discussion of the history of Black rebellion during this period, see Elizabeth Hinton, *America on Fire: The Untold History of Police Violence and Black Rebellion Since the 1960s* (New York: Liveright, 2021).

51. Kathy Williamson, "Watts Brothers Tell Incident That Triggered Riot," *Los Angeles Sentinel*, August 11, 2005.

52. Lauren Berlant, "Slow Death (Sovereignty, Obesity, Lateral Agency)," *Critical Inquiry* 33, no. 4 (2007): 754–80.

53. Burt Folkart, "Marquette Frye, Whose Arrest Ignited the Watts Riots in 1965, Dies at Age 42," *Los Angeles Times*, December 25, 1986.

54. "Shriver's Testimony on Poverty Funds Released: Director Told House Group That Money Sent Here Before Watts Riot Was Not Used," *Los Angeles Times*, October 11, 1965.

55. Lyndon B. Johnson quoted in Kotz, *Judgment Days*, 340–41.

56. Williamson, "Watts Brothers Tell Incident that Triggered Riot."

57. My use of "slow death" here is of course inspired by Orlando Patterson's notion of social death in *Slavery and Social Death: A Comparative Study* (Cambridge, MA: Harvard University Press, 1982), and also the work of environmental scholar Rob Nixon in his book *Slow Violence and the Environmentalism of the Poor* (Cambridge, MA: Harvard University Press, 2013).

58. For a comprehensive account of the rebellions in American cities during the 1960s, see Hinton, *America on Fire*.

59. Metzl, *Dying of Whiteness*, 18.

60. Steven H. Woolf, "Falling Behind: The Growing Gap in Life Expectancy Between the United States and Other Countries, 1933–2021," *American Journal of Public Health* 113 (2023): 970–80, https://doi.org/10.2105/AJPH.2023.307310.

61. Woolf, "Falling Behind."

62. Woolf, "Falling Behind," 976.

63. Elizabeth Arias, Jiaquan Xu, Betzaida Tejada-Vera, and Brigham Bastian, "U.S. State Life Tables, 2019," *National Vital Statistics Reports* 70, no. 18 (2022): 1–17.

64. Arias et al., "U.S. State Life Tables, 2019," 3.

65. Metzl, *Dying of Whiteness*, 191–268.

66. Woolf, "Falling Behind."

67. See Arias et al., "U.S. State Life Tables, 2019," and Woolf, "Falling Behind."

68. Woolf, "Falling Behind," 976.

69. Arias et al., "U.S. State Life Tables, 2019."

70. Lars Kessing, Eleni Vradi, and Per Kragh Andersen, "Life Expectancy in Bipolar Disorder," *Bipolar Disorders* 17, no. 5 (2015): 543–48, https://doi.org/10.1111/bdi.12296.

71. Lars Kessing, Eleni Vradi, Roger McIntyre, and Per Kragh Andersen, "Causes of Decreased Life Expectancy over the Life Span in Bipolar Disorder,"

Journal of Affective Disorders 180 (2015): 142–47, https://doi.org/10.1016/j
.jad.2015.03.027.

72. Sarah DeGue, Katherine Fowler, and Cynthia Calkins, "Deaths Due to
Use of Lethal Force by Law Enforcement: Findings from the National Violent
Death Reporting System, 17 U.S. States, 2009–2012," *American Journal of
Preventive Medicine* 51, no. 5 (2016): S173–S187, https://doi.org/10.1016/j
.amepre.2016.08.027.

73. Ayobami Laniyonu and Phillip Atiba Goff, "Measuring Disparities in
Police Use of Force and Injury Among Persons with Serious Mental Illness,"
BMC Psychiatry 21, no. 1 (October 2021): 500, https://doi.org/10.1186/s12888
-021-03510-w.

74. Sirry Alang, Taylor Rogers, Lillie Williamson, Cherrell Green, and
April Bell, "Police Brutality and Unmet Need for Mental Health Care," *Health
Services Research* 56, no. 6 (2021): 1104–13, https://doi.org/10.1111/1475
-6773.13736.

75. Sarah Turner, Natalie Mota, James Bolton, and Jitender Sareen,
"Self-Medication with Alcohol or Drugs for Mood and Anxiety Disorders: A
Narrative Review of the Epidemiological Literature," *Depression and Anxiety*
35, no. 9 (2018): 851–60, https://doi.org/10.1002/da.22771.

76. People v. O'Callaghan, B265928 (Cal. Ct. App. Mar. 13, 2017).

CHAPTER 4: COLLECTING FRAGMENTS

1. Saidiya Hartman, "Venus in Two Acts," *Small Axe* 12, no. 2 (June
2008): 1–14.

2. My argument in this chapter aligns with Wendy Brown's observations
about the corrosive effects of neoliberalism and its assault on democracy,
equality, and our ability to fashion a coherent view of American society in her
work *In the Ruins of Neoliberalism: The Rise of Antidemocratic Politics in the
West* (New York: Columbia University Press, 2019).

3. Brittany Hailer, "Records Show Allegheny County Medical Examiner Did Not Perform Full Autopsy on Incarcerated Man," *Pennsylvania
Capital-Star*, September 19, 2023, https://penncapital-star.com/civil-rights
-social-justice/records-show-allegheny-county-medical-examiner-did-not
-perform-full-autopsy-on-incarcerated-man/.

4. United Health Foundation, *America's Health Rankings: 2020 Annual
Report*, December 2020, https://www.americashealthrankings.org/learn
/reports/2020-annual-report, 76.

5. Kris Mamula, "Report: Allegheny County Loses 50,000 Jobs in Five
Years," *Pittsburgh Post-Gazette*, April 2, 2023.

6. Allegheny County Department of Human Services, *2020 Point-in-Time
Homelessness Data*, August 2020, https://www.alleghenycountyanalytics
.us/wp-content/uploads/2020/08/20-ACDHS-13-Homeless_PIT2020_Brief
_v3.pdf.

7. Coroner's Act of Pennsylvania, Act of August 9, 1955, P.L. 323, as amended, added by the Act of October 24, 2019, P.L. 931, No. 154 (Act 154), 16 P.S. §§ 1214 and 1231–60.

8. Alexander Hamilton, "First Speech of June 21," June 21, 1788, available at Teaching American History, https://teachingamericanhistory.org/document
/alexander-hamilton-speech/.

9. Kathryn Carter, *Democracy in Darkness: Secrecy and Transparency in the Age of Revolutions* (New Haven, CT: Yale University Press, 2023).

10. "From Thomas Jefferson to James Currie, 28 January 1786," Founders Online, National Archives, https://founders.archives.gov/documents/Jefferson
/01-09-02-0209. Original source: *The Papers of Thomas Jefferson*, vol. 9, 1 November 1785–22 June 1786, ed. Julian P. Boyd (Princeton, NJ: Princeton University Press, 1954), 239–40.

11. Michael Schudson, *The Rise of the Right to Know: Politics and the Culture of Transparency, 1945–1975* (Cambridge, MA: Belknap Press, 2018), 5.

12. Margaret Kwoka, *Saving the Freedom of Information Act* (Cambridge: Cambridge University Press, 2021), 25.

13. Allegheny County v. Hailer, 298 A.3d 476 (Pa. Commw. Ct. 2023).

14. Chester County Office of the Coroner v. T. Keel, et al. (2023), Docket No. AP 2022-2809.

15. Brittany Hailer, online interview by Terence Keel, September 8, 2023, Zoom call.

16. Mike Masterson, "Dying in Custody (Part 1)," *Asbury Park Press*, February 5, 1995.

17. Death in Custody Reporting Act of 2000, Pub. L. No. 106-297, 114 Stat. 1045.

18. Wendy Sawyer and Peter Wagner, "Mass Incarceration: The Whole Pie 2024," press release, Prison Policy Initiative, March 14, 2024, https://www
.prisonpolicy.org/reports/pie2024.html.

19. *Deaths in Custody: Additional Action Needed to Help Ensure Data Collected by DOJ Are Utilized: Hearing Before the Permanent Subcommittee on Investigations of the U.S. Senate Committee on Homeland Security and Governmental Affairs*, 117th Cong. (September 20, 2022) (statement of Gretta L. Goodwin, director, Homeland Security and Justice, US Government Accountability Office), 2, GAO-22-106033, https://www.hsgac.senate.gov
/wp-content/uploads/imo/media/doc/Goodwin%20Testimony.pdf.

20. *Uncounted Deaths in America's Prisons and Jails: How the Department of Justice Failed to Implement the Death in Custody Reporting Act: Hearing Before the Permanent Subcommittee on Investigations of the U.S. Senate Committee on Homeland Security and Governmental Affairs*, 117th Cong. (September 20, 2022) (testimony of Andrea Armstrong, Distinguished Professor of Law, Loyola University New Orleans, College of Law), 8, https://

www.hsgac.senate.gov/wp-content/uploads/imo/media/doc/Armstrong%20
Testimony.pdf.

21. M. Steenkamp et al., "The National Violent Death Reporting System: An
Exciting New Tool for Public Health Surveillance," *Injury Prevention: Journal
of the International Society for Child and Adolescent Injury Prevention* 12
Suppl. 2 (December 2006): ii3–ii5, https://doi.org/10.1136/ip.2006.012518.

22. California Assembly Bill 2761, chaptered September 29, 2022, https://
legiscan.com/CA/text/AB2761/id/2609263.

23. D. Pulane Lucas, "My Son Died in LA County Custody. Months Later,
His Death Hasn't Been Counted," *The Appeal*, September 8, 2023, https://
theappeal.org/los-angeles-in-custody-death-stanley-wilson-jr/.

24. Justin M. Feldman et al., "Quantifying Underreporting of Law-
Enforcement-Related Deaths in United States Vital Statistics and News-Media-
Based Data Sources: A Capture-Recapture Analysis," *PLOS Medicine* 14, no.
10 (October 2017): e1002399, https://doi.org/10.1371/journal.pmed.1002399;
Frank Edwards, Hedwig Lee, and Michael Esposito, "Risk of Being Killed
by Police Use of Force in the United States by Age, Race-Ethnicity, and Sex,"
Proceedings of the National Academy of Sciences 116, no. 34 (August 2019):
16793–98, https://doi.org/10.1073/pnas.1821204116; "Fatal Police Violence
by Race and State in the USA, 1980–2019: A Network Meta-Regression," *The
Lancet* 398, no. 10307 (October 2, 2021): 1239–55, https://doi.org/10.1016
/S0140-6736(21)01609-3.

25. See "Fatal Police Violence by Race and State in the USA"; Feldman et
al., "Quantifying Underreporting of Law-Enforcement-Related Deaths."

26. Julie E. Malphurs and Donna Cohen, "A Newspaper Surveillance
Study of Homicide-Suicide in the United States," *American Journal of Forensic Medicine and Pathology* 23, no. 2 (June 2002): 142–48, https://doi
.org/10.1097/00000433-200206000-00006.

27. Feldman et al., "Quantifying Underreporting of Law-Enforcement-
Related Deaths." Also, in 2021, the GBD 2019 Police Violence US Subna-
tional Collaborators significantly expanded and revised the conclusions of
the Harvard study. See "Fatal Police Violence by Race and State in the USA."
They also used a crowd-sourced data method to develop a rate of underreporting and misclassification to identify discrepancies in death reports sent to the
NVDRS for any given year between 1980 and 2019. They estimated that more
than half (55 percent) of law enforcement–related deaths were improperly
recorded by police.

28. For more on the history and data on capital punishment in America,
see Death Penalty Information Center, "Execution in the U.S. 1608-2002:
The Espy File," https://deathpenaltyinfo.org/executions/executions-overview
/executions-in-the-u-s-1608-2002-the-espy-file, accessed June 27, 2025. My
lab was limited to using the racial classifications reported by law enforcement in the data we sourced. For example, police use "Black" to include

African Americans as well as populations from the Caribbean and recent migrants to the US from Africa. People with Middle Eastern ancestry that are white-presenting can be and often are reported by police as white given the fact that many county intake forms used by law enforcement do not have "Middle Eastern" as a racial category. There are also instances where Middle Eastern people are reported as "unknown." At the moment many police departments do not report people as mixed race, as intake forms do not include mixed race as a distinct category. Instead, they chose "unknown" or assign identity to multiple racial groups. Despite these limitations the demographic data available over this twenty-year period tracks with what is known about racial profiling among law enforcement personnel. For more on racial bias in policing, see Aline Ara Santos Carvalho, Táhcita Medrado Mizael, and Angelo A. S. Sampaio, "Racial Prejudice and Police Stops: A Systematic Review of the Empirical Literature," *Behavior Analysis in Practice* 15, no. 4 (May 2021): 1213–20, https://doi.org/10.1007/s40617-021-00578-4; Phillip Atiba Goff and Kimberly Barsamian Kahn, "Racial Bias in Policing: Why We Know Less Than We Should," *Social Issues and Policy Review* 6, no. 1 (2012): 177–210, https://doi.org/10.1111/j.1751-2409.2011.01039.x.

29. California Office of Traffic Safety, "OTS Crash Rankings Results," OTS Crash Rankings, Los Angeles County, State of California, 2020, https://www.ots.ca.gov/media-and-research/crash-rankings-results/?wpv_view_count=1327&wpv-wpcf-year=2020&wpv-wpcf-city_county=Los+Angeles+County&wpv_filter_submit=Submit.

30. Grant Smith, "Jail Deaths in America: Data and Key Findings of Dying Inside," Reuters, October 16, 2020, https://www.reuters.com/investigates/special-report/usa-jails-graphic/.

31. Los Angeles Sheriff's Department, *Custody Division Population Quarterly Report*, April–June 2022, https://lasd.org/wp-content/uploads/2022/09/Transparency_Custody_Division_Population_2022_Second_Quarter_Report.pdf.

32. Smith, "Jail Deaths in America."

33. Robert Garrova, "Central Jail Closure," *LAist*, January 31, 2024, https://laist.com/brief/news/criminal-justice/activists-frustrated-with-countys-5-year-plan-to-close-uninhabitable-mens-central-jail.

34. Taylor Walker, "A New 5-Year Plan for Closing Men's Central Jail," WitnessLA, February 5, 2024, https://witnessla.com/a-new-5-year-plan-for-closing-mens-central-jail/.

35. My lab released a report in February 2023 examining the thirty-eight deaths that took place inside Los Angeles County jails during this particularly lethal year. See Alexander Li, Grace Sosa, and Terence Keel, *Report: Los Angeles County Jail Deaths 2009: Evaluating the Demographics of 38 Deaths in Los Angeles County Jails*, https://ucla.app.box.com/s/z91kfdg2032pyx93w869gnfyoy3rna3n.

36. Nicholas Shapiro and Terence Keel, "Naturalizing Unnatural Death in Los Angeles County Jails," *Medical Anthropology Quarterly* 38, no. 1 (March 2024): 6–23, https://doi.org/10.1111/maq.12819.

37. Cal. Gov. Code § 6254.

38. CA Ord. 2023-0032 § 4, 2023.

39. The data produced from this report appears in Nicholas Shapiro and Terence Keel, "Naturalizing Unnatural Death in Los Angeles County Jails," *Medical Anthropology Quarterly* 38, no. 1 (March 2024): 6–23, https://doi.org/10.1111/maq.12819.

40. Los Angeles County Anti-Racism, Diversity and Inclusion (ARDI) Initiative, *State of Black Los Angeles County*, official report, September 2023, https://storymaps.arcgis.com/collections/cc7914ce627845448d235549b353f411?item=5.

41. This report became the basis of a peer-reviewed article that was published two years later in the academic journal *Medical Anthropology Quarterly*. See Nicholas Shapiro and Terence Keel, "Naturalizing Unnatural Death in Los Angeles County Jails," *Medical Anthropology Quarterly* 38, no. 1 (March 2024): 6–23, https://doi.org/10.1111/maq.12819.

42. Zoom conversation with Alex Piquero, March 28, 2024.

43. German Lopez, "Police Officers Are Prosecuted for Murder in Less Than 2 Percent of Fatal Shootings," *Vox*, April 2, 2021, https://www.vox.com/21497089/derek-chauvin-george-floyd-trial-police-prosecutions-black-lives-matter.

44. Naomi Murakawa, *The First Civil Right: How Liberals Built Prison America* (Oxford: Oxford University Press, 2014), 2–3.

45. Murakawa, *The First Civil Right*, 3.

46. See Stuart Schrader's discussion of how police power was expanded by the federal government in *Badges Without Borders: How Global Counterinsurgency Transformed Policing in America* (Oakland: University of California Press, 2019), 137–41.

47. Lyndon B. Johnson, "Statement by the President Following the Signing of Law Enforcement Assistance Bills," September 22, 1965, in The American Presidency Project, ed. Gerhard Peters and John T. Woolley, https://www.presidency.ucsb.edu/node/240464.

48. Schrader, *Badges Without Borders*, 139.

49. Murakawa, *The First Civil Right*, 3.

50. For a brilliant discussion of America's use of law enforcement and carceral systems to manage social, economic, and political crisis, see Ruth Wilson Gilmore, *Golden Gulag: Prisons, Surplus, Crisis, and Opposition in Globalizing California* (Berkeley: University of California Press, 2007); Michelle Alexander, *The New Jim Crow: Mass Incarceration in the Age of Colorblindness* (New York: New Press, 2010); Kelly Lytle Hernandez, *City of Inmates: Conquest, Rebellion, and the Rise of Human Caging in Los Angeles,*

1771–1965 (Chapel Hill: University of North Carolina Press, 2017); Sarah Haley, *No Mercy Here: Gender, Punishment, and the Making of Jim Crow Modernity* (Chapel Hill: University of North Carolina Press, 2019); Alex Vitale, *The End of Policing* (New York: Verso, 2021); Orisanmi Burton, *Tip of the Spear: Black Radicalism, Prison Repression, and the Long Attica Revolt* (Berkeley: University of California Press, 2023).

51. William Bennett, John Dilulio, and John P. Walters, *Body Count: Moral Poverty and How to Win America's War Against Crime and Drugs* (New York: Simon & Schuster, 1996). See also John Dilulio, "The Coming of the Super-Predators," *Washington Examiner*, November 27, 1995, https://www .washingtonexaminer.com/magazine/1558817/the-coming-of-the-super-predators/.

52. Dilulio, "The Coming of the Super-Predators."

53. Jesse Byrnes, "Clinton Regrets Using Term 'Superpredator' in 1996 Crime Speech," *The Hill*, February 24, 2016, https://thehill.com/blogs/blog -briefing-room/news/270811-clinton-i-shouldnt-have-used-the-superpredator -remark/.

54. Kate Sullivan, "Bernie Sanders: 'Not Happy' I Voted for 'Terrible' 1994 Crime Bill," CNN, July 28, 2019, https://www.cnn.com/2019/07/28/politics /bernie-sanders-not-happy-terrible-1994-crime-bill/index.html.

55. Charles Bell, "The Hidden Side of Zero Tolerance Policies: The African American Perspective," *Sociology Compass* 9, no. 1 (January 2015): 14–22, https://doi.org/10.1111/soc4.12230.

56. Steven D. Levitt, "Understanding Why Crime Fell in the 1990s: Four Factors That Explain the Decline and Six That Do Not," *Journal of Economic Perspectives* 18, no. 1 (March 2004): 163–90, https://doi.org/10.1257 /089533004773563485.

CHAPTER 5: PERISHING

1. Bradford Bouley, *Pious Postmortems: Anatomy, Sanctity, and the Catholic Church in Early Modern Europe* (Philadelphia: University of Pennsylvania Press, 2017), 1.

2. Bouley, *Pious Postmortems*, 75–76.

3. Bouley, *Pious Postmortems*, 1.

4. "The State vs. The Dead Body of Roster," Spartanburg County, Coroner's Inquisition, July 27, 1844, South Carolina Department of Archives and History; accessed through CSI: Dixie, https://csidixie.org/inquests/2950.

5. "The State vs. The Dead Body of Dick," Union County, Coroner's Inquisition, March 19, 1837, South Carolina Department of Archives and History; accessed through CSI: Dixie, https://csidixie.org/inquests/3238.

6. Randy Hanzlick, John Hunsaker, and Gregory Davis, *A Guide for Manner of Death Classification*, National Association of Medical Examiners, February 2002, https://www.charlydmiller.com/LIB03/2002NAMEmanner ofdeath.pdf, 5.

7. Hanzlick et al., *A Guide for Manner of Death Classification*, 7.

8. Autopsy of Kenneth Wayne Adcock, November 29, 2014, Los Angeles County Medical Examiner, Case Report, Case Number: 2014-08065.

9. Autopsy of Kenneth Wayne Adcock.

10. Consolidated Fire Protection District of Los Angeles County, *Request for Approval of the Agreement for Services with the California Department of Corrections and Rehabilitation*, official report to the Board of Supervisors, August 16, 2011, https://file.lacounty.gov/SDSInter/bos/bc/164169_BoardLetter-CDCR.Aug162011.wAttachments.pdf; Consolidated Fire Protection District of Los Angeles County, *Approval to Renew Agreement for California Department of Corrections and Rehabilitation Services*, official report to the Board of Supervisors, December 5, 2023, https://file.lacounty.gov/SDSInter/bos/supdocs/186119.pdf.

11. Francine Uenuma, "The History of California's Inmate Firefighter Program," *Smithsonian*, September 1, 2022, https://www.smithsonianmag.com/history/the-history-of-californias-inmate-firefighter-program-180980662/.

12. Ted Goldberg, "Rare Honors This Weekend for Inmate Firefighters Killed on the Job," KQED, October 6, 2018, https://www.kqed.org/news/11686212/rare-honors-this-weekend-for-inmate-firefighters-killed-on-the-job; Abby Vesoulis, "Inmates Fighting California Wildfires More Likely to Be Hurt," *Time*, November 16, 2018, https://time.com/5457637/inmate-firefighters-injuries-death/; "Mourning the Loss of Fallen Inmate Wildland Firefighter Shawna Lynn Jones," National Park Service, March 1, 2016, https://www.nps.gov/samo/learn/news/mourning-the-loss-of-fallen-inmate-wildland-firefighter-shawna-lynn-jones.htm; Ted Goldberg, "Report Details Dramatic Moments Before Inmate Firefighter Suffered Fatal Injuries," July 17, 2017, KQED, https://www.kqed.org/news/11572823/report-details-dramatic-moments-before-inmate-firefighter-suffered-fatal-injuries; Associated Press, "Inmate Firefighter Dies After Collapsing in Training Hike," April 22, 2018, KQED, https://www.kqed.org/news/11664047/inmate-firefighter-dies-after-collapsing-in-training-hike.

13. Uenuma, "The History of California's Inmate Firefighter Program."

14. Erin Hatton, ed., *Labor and Punishment: Work In and Out of Prison* (Oakland: University of California Press, 2021); Andrew Ross, Tommasso Bardelli, and Aiyuba Thomas, *Abolition Labor: The Fight to End Prison Slavery* (New York: OR Books, 2013).

15. Four years after Adcock's death, thirty-three-year-old Anthony Colacino died from heart failure in 2018 after collapsing on a training hike at Sierra Conservation Center prison just outside of San Francisco. See Associated Press, "Inmate Firefighter Dies After Collapsing in Training Hike."

16. Keri Blakinger, "Why Was 2023 Such a Deadly Year in Los Angeles County Jails? It Depends on Whom You Ask," *Los Angeles Times*, March 26, 2024, https://www.latimes.com/california/story/2024-03-26/why-was-2023-such-a-deadly-year-in-los-angeles-county-jails.

17. According to Hanzlick et al., "When death involves a combination of natural processes and external factors such as injury or poisoning, preference is given to the non-natural manner of death." See *Guide for Manner of Death Classification*, 6.

18. Osagie Obasogie and Zachary Newman, "The Endogenous Fourth Amendment: An Empirical Assessment of How Police Understandings of Excessive Force Become Constitutional Law," *Cornell Law Review* 104, no. 5 (2019): 1281–1335.

19. Autopsy of Glenda Reymer, June 22, 2001, Los Angeles County Medical Examiner, Case Report, Case Number: 2001-04527.

20. Autopsy of Glenda Reymer, June 22, 2001, Los Angeles County Medical Examiner, Forensic Consultant's Report, Case Number: 2001-04527.

21. Aljoscha Dreisoerner, Nina Junker, Wolff Schlotz, Julia Heimrich, Svenja Bloemeke, Beate Ditzen, and Rolf van Dick, "Self-Soothing Touch and Being Hugged Reduce Cortisol Responses to Stress: A Randomized Controlled Trial on Stress, Physical Touch, and Social Identity," *Comprehensive Psychoneuroendocrinology* 8 (November 2021): 100091, https://doi.org/10.1016/j.cpnec.2021.100091; Ruth Gallop, "Failure of the Capacity for Self-Soothing in Women Who Have a History of Abuse and Self-Harm," *Journal of the American Psychiatric Nurses Association* 8, no. 1 (February 2002): 20–26, https://doi.org/10.1067/mpn.2002.122425.

22. Long Beach Police Department, Incident Report #010049876, June 22, 2001.

23. Kurt Streeter, "Woman Killed in Standoff with Long Beach Police," *Los Angeles Times*, June 24, 2001, https://www.latimes.com/archives/la-xpm-2001-jun-24-me-14221-story.html.

24. Autopsy of Glenda Reymer, Forensic Consultant's Report, Case Number: 2001-04527.

25. Autopsy of Glenda Reymer, June 22, 2001, Los Angeles County Medical Examiner, Investigator's Narrative, Case Number: 2001-04527.

26. Los Angeles County District Attorney's Office, Memorandum Regarding Fatal Shooting of Glenda Reymer, memorandum to Chief Jerome E. Lance, Long Beach Police Department, March 18, 2002, J.S.I.D. File # 01-0533, L.B.P.D. File # 0100-49876 / CC# 01-04527.

27. Cal. Penal Code § 835 (2023).

28. Cal. Penal Code § 417 (a)(1) (2023).

29. Los Angeles County District Attorney's Office, Memorandum Regarding Fatal Shooting of Glenda Reymer.

30. "Jacksonville Maker of 'Less-Lethal' Ammunition Settles Lawsuit," News 4 Jax, August 11, 2004, https://www.news4jax.com/news/2004/08/11/jacksonville-maker-of-less-lethal-ammunition-settles-lawsuit/.

31. Autopsy of Michael Mears, December 26, 2014, Los Angeles County Medical Examiner, Investigator's Narrative, Case Number: 2014-08828.

32. Autopsy of Michael Mears, Investigator's Narrative, Case Number: 2014-08828.

33. Autopsy of Michael Mears, December 26, 2014, Los Angeles County Medical Examiner, Anatomical Summary, Case Number: 2014-08828.

34. Los Angeles County District Attorney's Office, In-Custody Death of Michael Mears, memorandum to Commander Timothy Nordquist, Force Investigation Division, Los Angeles Police Department, Justice System Integrity Division, July 28, 2020, https://da.lacounty.gov/sites/default/files/pdf/JSID -ICD-07-28-2020-Mears.pdf, 3.

35. Autopsy of Michael Mears, Anatomical Summary, Case Number: 2014-08828.

36. Etienne Blais and David Brisebois, "Improving Police Responses to Suicide-Related Emergencies: New Evidence on the Effectiveness of Co-Response Police–Mental Health Programs," *Suicide and Life-Threatening Behavior* 51, no. 6 (2021): 1095–1105, https://doi.org/10.1111/sltb.12792; Stephen Puntis, Devon Perfect, Abirami Kirubarajan, Sorcha Bolton, Fay Davies, Aimee Hayes, Eli Harriss, and Andrew Molodynski, "A Systematic Review of Co-Responder Models of Police Mental Health 'Street' Triage," *BMC Psychiatry* 18, no. 1 (August 2018): 256, https://doi.org/10.1186/s12888-018-1836-2; Henry Steadman, Martha Deane, Randy Borum, and Joseph Morrissey, "Comparing Outcomes of Major Models of Police Responses to Mental Health Emergencies," *Psychiatric Services* 51, no. 5 (May 2000): 645–49, https://doi.org/10.1176/appi.ps.51.5.645.

37. Osagie Obasogie, "Excited Delirium and Police Use of Force," *Virginia Law Review* 107, no. 8 (December 2021): 1545–1620.

38. Obasogie, "Excited Delirium and Police Use of Force"; Brianna da Silva Bhatia, Michele Heisler, Joanna Naples-Mitchell, Altaf Saadi, and Julia Sherwin, *"Excited Delirium" and Deaths in Police Custody*, Physicians for Human Rights, 2022; Rachel Kincaid, "'Excited Delirium' Training Encourages Law Enforcement Violence," *Tulane Law Review*, Forthcoming (2024).

39. Martin Kaste, "California Bans 'Excited Delirium' Term as a Cause of Death," NPR, October 15, 2023, https://www.npr.org/2023/10/15/1206041620 /california-bans-excited-delirium-term-as-a-cause-of-death.

40. Abi Dymond, *Electric-Shock Weapons, Tasers, and Policing: Myths and Realities* (Abingdon: Routledge, 2022).

41. Terence Keel and Jonah Walters, "Oleoresin Capsicum: The Racial-Political History of a Ubiquitous Chemical Munition," *Isis* 114, no. 4 (December 2023): 687–709, https://doi.org/10.1086/727679.

42. Los Angeles County District Attorney's Office, Memorandum Regarding Fatal Shooting of Glenda Reymer, 4.

43. Keel and Walters, "Oleoresin Capsicum," 698.

44. Maria Sole Campinoti, "Officers Involved in Tasing Man Who Caught Fire and Later Died Won't Be Criminally Charged, New York Attorney General's Office Says," CNN.com, October 14, 2023, https://www.cnn. com/2023/10/14/us/new-york-jason-jones-taser-arrest-catskill/index.html.

45. Samuel Stratton, Christopher Rogers, and Karen Green, "Sudden Death in Individuals in Hobble Restraints During Paramedic Transport," *Annals of Emergency Medicine* 25, no. 5 (May 1995): 710–12, https://doi.org/10.1016 /S0196-0644(95)70187-7; Gary Vilke, "Restraint Physiology: A Review of the Literature," *Journal of Forensic and Legal Medicine* 75 (October 2020): 102056, https://doi.org/10.1016/j.jflm.2020.102056.

46. Jeeyoung Jun et al., "Adverse Events of Conscious Sedation Using Midazolam for Gastrointestinal Endoscopy," *Anesthesia and Pain Medicine* 14, no. 4 (October 2019): 401–6, https://doi.org/10.17085/apm.2019.14.4.401; Sarah Park et al., "Persistent Paradoxical Reaction to Midazolam Despite General Anesthesia with Dexmedetomidine," *Case Reports in Anesthesiology* (2024): 4152422, https://doi.org/10.1155/2024/4152422.

47. Autopsy of Michael Mears, Investigator's Narrative, Case Number: 2014-08828.

48. Autopsy of Michael Mears, Case Number: 2014-08828.

49. Paolo Spirito, Francesco Chiarella, Lorenzo Carratino, Massimo Zoni Berisso, Paolo Bellotti, and Carlo Vecchio, "Clinical Course and Prognosis of Hypertrophic Cardiomyopathy in an Outpatient Population," *New England Journal of Medicine* 320, no. 12 (March 1989), https://www.nejm.org/doi /full/10.1056/NEJM198903233201201; George Makavos, Chris Kairis, Maria-Eirini Tselegkidi, Theodoros Karamitsos, Angelos Rigopoulos, Michel Noutsias, and Ignatios Ikonomidis, "Hypertrophic Cardiomyopathy: An Updated Review on Diagnosis, Prognosis, and Treatment," *Heart Failure Reviews* 24, no. 4 (July 2019): 439–59, https://doi.org/10.1007/s10741-019-09775-4; William McKenna, John Deanfield, Azhar Faruqui, Diane England, Celia Oakley, and John Goodwin, "Prognosis in Hypertrophic Cardiomyopathy: Role of Age and Clinical, Electrocardiographic and Hemodynamic Features," *American Journal of Cardiology* 47, no. 3 (March 1981): 532–38, https://doi.org/10.1016 /0002-9149(81)90535-X.

50. Graham v. Connor, 490 U.S. 386 (1989).

51. Hill v. Miracle, 853 F. 3d 306 (6th Cir. 2017).

52. Los Angeles County District Attorney's Office, In-Custody Death of Michael Mears, memorandum to Commander Timothy Nordquist, Force Investigation Division, Los Angeles Police Department, Justice System Integrity Division, July 28, 2020, https://da.lacounty.gov/sites/default/files/pdf/JSID -ICD-07-28-2020-Mears.pdf, 7.

53. Hanzlick et al., *A Guide for Manner of Death Classification*, 6.

54. Autopsy of Justin Ames, August 27, 2008, San Bernardino County Coroner, Case Number: 2008-06199.

55. Vehicle-related cases were included in these figures for accidental death; UCLA BioCritical Studies Lab, Los Angeles County In-Custody Death Data, 2008–2019.

56. Autopsy of Eric Poland, April 4, 2000, Los Angeles County Medical Examiner, Case Number: 2008-06199.

57. Autopsy of Terelle Thomas, December 17, 2019, Dauphin County Coroner's Office Autopsy Number: ADC19-131; Case Number: J-2019-12-0905.

58. Autopsy of Edward Contreras, October 12, 2019, Los Angeles County Medical Examiner, Case Number: 2019-07692; Autopsy of Gracie Contreras, October 12, 2019, Los Angeles County Medical Examiner, Case Number: 2019-07690.

59. David Brown, *Emergency Vehicle Operations—Eluding and Pursuing*, Chicago Police Department, 2020, https://directives.chicagopolice.org/#directive/public/6607.

60. Samantha Melamed, "DA Diverting Drug Cases for Treatment—The Aim Is to Not Jail People for Being Addicted, but Put Them in Touch with Help to Get Clean," *Philadelphia Inquirer*, November 30, 2020, https://www.inquirer.com/news/philadelphia-district-attorney-larry-krasner-drug-diversion-decriminalization-criminal-justice-reform-20191203.html; "Baltimore's No-Prosecution Policy for Low-Level Drug Possession and Prostitution Finds Almost No Rearrests for Serious Offenses," Johns Hopkins Bloomberg School of Public Health, October 19, 2021, https://publichealth.jhu.edu/2021/baltimores-no-prosecution-policy-for-low-level-drug-possession-and-prostitution-finds-almost-no-rearrests-for-serious-offenses.

61. This is one of many conclusions that Alex Vitale leaves us to grapple with in *The End of Policing* (New York: Verso, 2017).

62. Matthew Garnett and Sally Curtin, *Suicide Mortality in the United States, 2001–2021*, NCHS Data Brief No. 464, 2023, https://www.cdc.gov/nchs/products/databriefs/db464.htm; Gonzalo Martínez-Alés, Tammy Jiang, Katherine Keyes, and Jaimie Gradus, "The Recent Rise of Suicide Mortality in the United States," *Annual Review of Public Health* 43 (April 2022): 99–116, https://doi.org/10.1146/annurev-publhealth-051920-123206.

63. "Public Trust in Government: 1958–2024," Pew Research Center, June 24, 2024, https://www.pewresearch.org/politics/2024/06/24/public-trust-in-government-1958-2024/.

64. Rachel Minkin, "About Half of Americans Say Public K-12 Education Is Going in the Wrong Direction," Pew Research Center, April 4, 2024, https://www.pewresearch.org/short-reads/2024/04/04/about-half-of-americans-say-public-k-12-education-is-going-in-the-wrong-direction/.

65. Brian Kennedy et al., "Americans' Trust in Scientists, Other Groups Declines," Pew Research Center, February 15, 2022, https://www.pewresearch.org/science/2022/02/15/americans-trust-in-scientists-other-groups-declines/.

66. "Majority of Public Favors Giving Civilians the Power to Sue Police Officers for Misconduct," Pew Research Center, July 9, 2020, https://www.pewresearch.org/politics/2020/07/09/majority-of-public-favors-giving-civilians-the-power-to-sue-police-officers-for-misconduct/.

67. Eleventh Report of the Nunez Independent Monitor, Civil Rights Litigation Clearinghouse, 2021, https://clearinghouse.net/doc/112327/; Status Report

by the Nunez Independent Monitor, NYC Government, 2024, https://www.nyc
.gov/assets/doc/downloads/Nunez/2024-04-18%20--%20Monitor's%20Report
.pdf; Erica Bryant, "[It's] a Torture Chamber: Stories from Rikers Island," Vera
Institute of Justice, February 2022, https://www.vera.org/its-a-torture-chamber;
Gregory Morril, Jullian Harris-Calvin, and Tess Cohen, *The Human Rights Crisis at Rikers Island: A Call to Action For All Justice System Stakeholders*, New
York City Bar Association, 2022, https://www.nycbar.org/reports/the-human
-rights-crisis-at-rikers-island-a-call-to-action-for-all-justice-system-stakeholders/.

68. Matt Keyser, "He Spent 1,100 Days in Rikers Island a Legally Innocent
Man. His Story Changed New York's Bail Laws," Arnold Ventures, August 10,
2022, https://www.arnoldventures.org/stories/he-spent-1-100-days-in-rikers
-island-a-legally-innocent-man-his-story-changed-new-yorks-bail-laws.

69. Kayla James and Elena Vanko, *The Impacts of Solitary Confinement*,
Vera Institute of Justice, 2021, https://www.vera.org/publications/the-impacts
-of-solitary-confinement; Craig Haney, "The Psychological Effects of Solitary
Confinement: A Systematic Critique," *Crime and Justice* 47 (January 2018):
365–416, https://doi.org/10.1086/696041.

70. Keyser, "He Spent 1,100 Days in Rikers Island."

71. Justice healing advocate Ifé Mora helped me see this connection
between trauma, time, and the body. See Ifé Mora, "Healing Trauma and
Chronic Stress with Somatics," *Soulivity*, September 30, 2024, https://soulivity
.com/health/healing-trauma-and-chronic-stress-with-somatics.

72. See Nicholas Shapiro and Terence Keel, "Naturalizing Unnatural Death
in Los Angeles County Jails," *Medical Anthropology Quarterly* 38, no. 1
(March 2024): 6–23, https://doi.org/10.1111/maq.12819; Alexander Li, Grace
Sosa, and Terence Keel, *Report: Los Angeles County Jail Deaths 2009: Evaluating the Demographics of 38 Deaths in Los Angeles County Jails*, February
28, 2023, https://ucla.app.box.com/s/z91kfdg2032pyx93w869gnfyoy3rna3n.

73. Li et al., *Report: Los Angeles County Jail Deaths 2009*.

74. Autopsy of Jay McCabe, March 19, 2012, Los Angeles County Medical
Examiner, Case Number: 2012-01913.

75. Autopsy of Lewis Nyarecha, June 6, 2018, Los Angeles County Medical
Examiner, Case Number: 2018-04306.

76. Jonah Walters, Grace Sosa, and Terence Keel, *Deaths in Dauphin
County Prison (Harrisburg, PA), 2008–2022*, June 2024, https://app.box.com
/s/g4risq22x718xskdj3oizzu2h4ue7zqm.

77. *Report of the Task Force to Study Prison Violence in Maryland*, Maryland Department of Public Safety and Correctional Services, 2009, https://
www.ojp.gov/ncjrs/virtual-library/abstracts/report-task-force-study-prison
-violence-maryland; "25 Jail Officers in Baltimore Charged with Using Excessive Force at State Facilities," CBS News, December 3, 2019, https://www
.cbsnews.com/news/baltimore-jail-charges-25-jail-officers-baltimore-maryland
-charged-with-using-excessive-force-2019-12-03/.

78. The refusal of law enforcement to publicly release information about the length of time in jail before death prevented my lab from examining the leading cause of death for people recently admitted into Los Angeles County and Dauphin County jails.

79. Hanzlick et al., *A Guide for Manner of Death Classification*.

80. Autopsy of Jorge Rosales, October 10, 2011, Los Angeles County Medical Examiner, Case Number: 2011-06521.

81. Autopsy of Markese Braxton, June 8, 2018, Los Angeles County Medical Examiner, Case Number: 2018-04322.

CHAPTER 6: THE BODIES WE DON'T SEE

1. Hakique N. Virani and Rebecca J. Haines-Saah, "Drug Decriminalization: A Matter of Justice and Equity, Not Just Health," *American Journal of Preventive Medicine* 58, no. 1 (January 2020): 161–64, https://doi.org/10.1016/j.amepre.2019.08.012; Philip Leger et al., "Policy Brief: CSAM in Support of the Decriminalization of Drug Use and Possession for Personal Use," *Canadian Journal of Addiction* 12 (March 2021): 13–15, https://doi.org/10.1097/CXA.0000000000000101; Thomas Kerr, Will Small, and Evan Wood, "The Public Health and Social Impacts of Drug Market Enforcement: A Review of the Evidence," *International Journal of Drug Policy* 16, no. 4 (August 2005): 210–20, https://doi.org/10.1016/j.drugpo.2005.04.005.

2. Charis Kubrin and Eric Stewart, "Predicting Who Reoffends: The Neglected Role of Neighborhood Context in Recidivism Studies," *Criminology* 44, no. 1 (February 2006): 165–97, https://doi.org/10.1111/j.1745-9125.2006.00046.x; Denis Yukhnenko, Nigel Blackwood, and Seena Fazel, "Risk Factors for Recidivism in Individuals Receiving Community Sentences: A Systematic Review and Meta-Analysis," *CNS Spectrums* 25, no. 2 (April 2020): 252–63, https://doi.org/10.1017/S1092852919001056; Muhammad Sardar, "Give Me Liberty or Give Me . . . Alternatives? Ending Cash Bail and Its Impact on Pretrial Incarceration," *Brooklyn Law Review* 84, no. 4 (June 2019): 1421–58.

3. Coleman v. Brown, 952 F. Supp. 2d 901 (E.D. Cal. 2013); Dominic A. Sisti, Andrea G. Segal, and Ezekiel J. Emanuel, "Improving Long-Term Psychiatric Care: Bring Back the Asylum," *JAMA* 313, no. 3 (January 2015): 243–44, https://doi.org/10.1001/jama.2014.16088; Stephen Allison, Tarun Bastiampillai, and Doris A. Fuller, "Mass Incarceration and Severe Mental Illness in the USA," *The Lancet* 390, no. 10089 (July 2017): 25, https://doi.org/10.1016/S0140-6736(17)31479-4.

4. Derrick Bell, *Faces at the Bottom of the Well: The Permanence of Racism* (New York: Basic Books, 1992).

5. PR Newswire, "Maryland Senators Back CRCBC's New Initiative to Tackle School Violence," Yahoo Finance, October 8, 2024, https://finance.yahoo.com/news/maryland-senators-back-crcbcs-initiative-123100670.html.

6. Cerise Castle, "A Tradition of Violence: The History of Deputy Gangs in the Los Angeles County Sheriff's Department," KnockLA, 2021, https://knock-la.com/tradition-of-violence-lasd-gang-history/.

7. Our ability to draft a bill that drew upon on local activism and legislative changes happening around the nation was an example of what Ruha Benjamin has called "viral justice," which, she explains, "invites us to witness how an idea or action that sprouts in one place may be adopted, adapted, and diffused elsewhere." See Ruha Benjamin, *Viral Justice: How We Grow the World We Want* (Princeton, NJ: Princeton University Press, 2022), 19. See also Roger Mitchell Jr. and Jay Aronson, *Death in Custody: How America Ignores the Truth and What We Can Do About It* (Baltimore: Johns Hopkins University Press, 2023).

INDEX

01 14